HEALTH CARE IN TRANSITION

THE HEALTH CARE FRAUD AND ABUSE CONTROL PROGRAM

ISSUES, ASSESSMENTS AND EFFECTIVENESS

HEALTH CARE IN TRANSITION

Additional books in this series can be found on Nova's website
under the Series tab.

Additional e-books in this series can be found on Nova's website
under the e-book tab.

HEALTH CARE IN TRANSITION

THE HEALTH CARE FRAUD AND ABUSE CONTROL PROGRAM

ISSUES, ASSESSMENTS AND EFFECTIVENESS

CURTIS WOOD
EDITOR

nova publishers
New York

Library of Congress Cataloging-in-Publication Data

ISBN: 978-1-63463-693-3

Published by Nova Science Publishers, Inc. † New York

CONTENTS

PREFACE

In fiscal year 2012, the Department of Health and Human Services (HHS), HHS Office of Inspector General (HHS-OIG), and the Department of Justice (DOJ) obligated approximately $583.6 million to fund Health Care Fraud and Abuse Control (HCFAC) program activities. This book describes how HHS and DOJ obligated funds for the HCFAC program; examines how HHS and DOJ assess HCFAC activities and whether key program outputs have changed over time; and examines what is known about the effectiveness of the HCFAC program in reducing health care fraud and abuse.

Chapter 1 – GAO has designated Medicare and Medicaid as high-risk programs partly because their size, scope, and complexity make them vulnerable to fraud. Congress established the HCFAC program and provided funding to HHS and DOJ to help reduce fraud and abuse in Medicare and Medicaid.

GAO was asked to examine how HHS and DOJ are using funds to achieve the goals of the HCFAC program, and to examine performance assessments and other metrics that HHS and DOJ use to determine the program's effectiveness. This report (1) describes how HHS and DOJ obligated funds for the HCFAC program, (2) examines how HHS and DOJ assess HCFAC activities and whether key program outputs have changed over time, and (3) examines what is known about the effectiveness of the HCFAC program in reducing health care fraud and abuse.

To describe how HHS and DOJ obligated funds, GAO obtained financial information from HHS and DOJ for fiscal year 2012. To examine how HHS and DOJ assess HCFAC activities and whether key outputs have changed over time, GAO reviewed agency reports and documents, and interviewed agency officials. To examine what is known about the effectiveness of the HCFAC program, GAO conducted a literature review and interviewed experts.

In comments on a draft of this report, HHS noted examples of CMS's efforts to reduce health care fraud, though these examples were not included in the HCFAC return-on-investment calculation. Additionally, HHS and DOJ provided technical comments, which GAO incorporated as appropriate.

Chapter 2 – The Health Insurance Portability and Accountability Act of 1996 (HIPAA) established a national Health Care Fraud and Abuse Control Program (HCFAC or the Program) under the joint direction of the Attorney General and the Secretary of the Department of Health and Human Services (HHS)[1], acting through the Inspector General, designed to coordinate Federal, state and local law enforcement activities with respect to health care fraud and abuse. In its seventeenth year of operation, the Program's continued success confirms the soundness of a collaborative approach to identify and prosecute the most egregious instances of health care fraud, to prevent future fraud and abuse, and to protect program beneficiaries.

In: The Health Care Fraud and Abuse Control Program
Editor: Curtis Wood
ISBN: 978-1-63463-693-3

Chapter 1

HEALTH CARE FRAUD AND ABUSE CONTROL PROGRAM: INDICATORS PROVIDE INFORMATION ON PROGRAM ACCOMPLISHMENTS, BUT ASSESSING PROGRAM EFFECTIVENESS IS DIFFICULT*

United States Government Accountability Office

WHY GAO DID THIS STUDY

GAO has designated Medicare and Medicaid as high-risk programs partly because their size, scope, and complexity make them vulnerable to fraud. Congress established the HCFAC program and provided funding to HHS and DOJ to help reduce fraud and abuse in Medicare and Medicaid.

GAO was asked to examine how HHS and DOJ are using funds to achieve the goals of the HCFAC program, and to examine performance assessments and other metrics that HHS and DOJ use to determine the program's effectiveness. This report (1) describes how HHS and DOJ obligated funds for the HCFAC program, (2) examines how HHS and DOJ assess HCFAC activities and whether key program outputs have changed over time, and (3) examines what is known about the effectiveness of the HCFAC program in reducing health care fraud and abuse.

To describe how HHS and DOJ obligated funds, GAO obtained financial information from HHS and DOJ for fiscal year 2012. To examine how HHS and DOJ assess HCFAC activities and whether key outputs have changed over time, GAO reviewed agency reports and documents, and interviewed agency officials. To examine what is known about the effectiveness of the HCFAC program, GAO conducted a literature review and interviewed experts.

In comments on a draft of this report, HHS noted examples of CMS's efforts to reduce health care fraud, though these examples were not included in the HCFAC return-on-

---

* This is an edited, reformatted and augmented version of a United States Government Accountability Office publication, No. GAO-13-746, dated September 2013.

investment calculation. Additionally, HHS and DOJ provided technical comments, which GAO incorporated as appropriate.

WHAT GAO FOUND

In fiscal year 2012, the Department of Health and Human Services (HHS), HHS Office of Inspector General (HHS-OIG), and the Department of Justice (DOJ) obligated approximately $583.6 million to fund Health Care Fraud and Abuse Control (HCFAC) program activities. About 78 percent of obligated funds were from mandatory HCFAC appropriations (budgetary resources provided in laws other than appropriation acts), 11 percent of obligated funds were from discretionary HCFAC appropriations (budgetary resources provided in appropriation acts), and 12 percent were obligated funds from other appropriations that HHS, HHS-OIG, and DOJ used to support HCFAC activities. HCFAC funds were obligated to support a variety of activities, including interagency Medicare Fraud Strike Force Teams—which provide additional investigative and prosecutorial resources in geographic areas with high rates of health care fraud—located in 9 cities nationwide.

HHS, HHS-OIG, and DOJ use several indicators to assess HCFAC activities, as well as to inform decision-makers about how to allocate resources and prioritize those activities. For example, in addition to other indicators, the United States Attorneys' Offices use indicators related to criminal prosecutions, including the number of defendants charged and the number of convictions. Additionally, many of the indicators that HHS, HHS-OIG, and DOJ use—such as the dollar amount recovered as a result of fraud cases—reflect the collective work of multiple agencies since these agencies work many health care fraud cases jointly. Outputs from some key indicators have changed in recent years. For example, according to the fiscal year 2012 HCFAC report, the return-on-investment—the amount of money returned to the government as a result of HCFAC activities compared with the funding appropriated to conduct those activities—has increased from $4.90 returned for every $1.00 invested for fiscal years 2006- 2008 to $7.90 returned for every $1.00 invested for fiscal years 2010-2012.

Several factors contribute to a lack of information about the effectiveness of HCFAC activities in reducing health care fraud and abuse. The indicators agencies use to track HCFAC activities provide information on the outputs or accomplishments of HCFAC activities, not on the effectiveness of the activities in actually reducing fraud and abuse. For several reasons, assessing the impact of the program is challenging. For example, it is difficult to isolate the effect that HCFAC activities, as opposed to other efforts such as changes to the Medicare provider enrollment process, may have in reducing health care fraud and abuse. It is also difficult to estimate a health care fraud baseline—a measure of the extent of fraud—that is needed to be able to track whether the amount of fraud has changed over time as a result of HCFAC or other efforts. HHS has a project under way to establish a baseline of probable fraud in home health care, and will determine whether this approach to estimating a baseline of fraud should be expanded to other areas of health care. Results from this project and other studies could provide HHS and DOJ with additional information regarding which activities are the most effective in reducing health care fraud and abuse, and could potentially inform agency decisions about how best to allocate limited resources.

ABBREVIATIONS

ACL	Administration for Community Living
ASPE	Office of the Assistant Secretary for Planning and Evaluation
ASPA	Office of the Assistant Secretary for Public Affairs
CMS	Centers for Medicare & Medicaid Services
CHIP	Children's Health Insurance Program
HHS	Department of Health and Human Services
HHS-OIG	Department of Health and Human Services' Office of Inspector General
DOJ	Department of Justice
EOUSA	Executive Office for United States Attorneys
FBI	Federal Bureau of Investigation
FDA	Food and Drug Administration
HCFAC	Health Care Fraud and Abuse Control
HEAT	Health Care Fraud Prevention and Enforcement Action Team
HIPAA	Health Insurance Portability and Accountability Act of 1996
JMD	Justice Management Division
OAS	Office of Audit Services
OCIG	Office of Counsel to the Inspector General
OEI	Office of Evaluation and Inspections
OGC	Office of General Counsel
OI	Office of Investigations
OMP	Office of Management and Policy
SMP	Senior Medicare Patrol
Strike Force	Medicare Fraud Strike Force
USAOs	U.S. Attorneys' Offices

* * *

September 30, 2013

The Honorable Thomas R. Carper
Chairman
The Honorable Tom Coburn, M.D.
Ranking Member
Committee on Homeland Security and Governmental Affairs
United States Senate

The Honorable Orrin G. Hatch
Ranking Member
Committee on Finance United States Senate

The Honorable Charles E. Grassley
Ranking Member

Committee on the Judiciary
United States Senate

The Honorable Claire McCaskill
Chairman
Subcommittee on Financial and Contracting Oversight
Committee on Homeland Security and Governmental Affairs
United States Senate

GAO has designated Medicare and Medicaid as high-risk programs because their size, scope, and complexity make them particularly vulnerable to fraud and abuse.[1] According to the Department of Health and Human Services' Office of Inspector General (HHS-OIG), common health care fraud schemes include providers or suppliers billing for services or supplies not provided or not medically necessary, purposely billing for a higher level of service than that provided, and paying kickbacks to providers for referring beneficiaries for specific services or to certain entities. To help reduce fraud and abuse in health care programs, including Medicare and Medicaid, Congress established the Health Care Fraud and Abuse Control (HCFAC) program as a part of the Health Insurance Portability and Accountability Act of 1996 (HIPAA).[2] The departments of Health and Human Services (HHS) and Justice (DOJ) jointly administer the HCFAC program and, in fiscal year 2012, received over $486 million in HCFAC appropriations. Several components within HHS and DOJ receive appropriations to carry out HCFAC activities, including the Centers for Medicare & Medicaid Services (CMS)—the agency within HHS that administers Medicare, Medicaid, and the Children's Health Insurance Program (CHIP)[3]—the HHS-OIG, and DOJ's components—the Civil, Civil Rights, Criminal, and Justice Management divisions, the U.S. Attorneys' Offices (USAOs), and the Federal Bureau of Investigation (FBI).[4,5]

By statute, HHS and DOJ are required to issue a joint report annually to Congress on the amounts appropriated through the HCFAC program, and the amounts recovered as a result of HCFAC activities. In fiscal year 2012, HHS and DOJ reported having won or negotiated over $3 billion in health care judgments and settlements through the activities of the HCFAC program. The agencies also reported obtaining additional administrative penalties in health care fraud cases and proceedings as a result of these activities. In fiscal year 2012, about $4.2 billion was collected, a portion of which was deposited into the Medicare Trust Funds as a result of health care judgments and settlements and administrative penalties (including those that occurred before fiscal year 2012). We have previously reported that although there have been convictions involving multimillion dollar schemes that defrauded the Medicare program, there are no reliable estimates of the amount of fraud in the Medicare program or for the health care industry as a whole.[6] Additionally, although HHS and DOJ work to reduce health care fraud and abuse through the HCFAC program, concerns have been raised about whether the HCFAC program has been effective in reducing health care fraud and abuse.

Given these concerns, you asked us to examine how HHS and DOJ have used their appropriations to achieve the goals of the HCFAC program, and to examine performance assessments and other metrics HHS and DOJ use to determine the HCFAC program's performance and effectiveness. This report (1) describes how HHS and DOJ obligated funds for the HCFAC program; (2) examines how HHS and DOJ assess HCFAC activities and whether key program outputs have changed over time; and (3) examines what is known about the effectiveness of the HCFAC program in reducing health care fraud and abuse.

For our review, we included agencies within HHS (including HHS-OIG) and DOJ that received mandatory and discretionary HCFAC funding in fiscal year 2012 whose activities are described in the annual HCFAC report,[7] and whose funding is included in the annual report's return-oninvestment calculation (which compares the amount of monetary results to the federal government, such as funds returned to the Medicare Trust Funds as a result of HCFAC activities, with the funding appropriated to conduct those activities).[8,9] For CMS, we only included the HCFAC funding that was included in the HCFAC return-on-investment calculation.[10] We excluded all of the remaining HCFAC funding that CMS receives because it is not included in the HCFAC return-on-investment calculation and generally supports program integrity activities in Medicare Parts C and D, which are similar to the activities conducted under the Medicare Integrity Program.[11]

To describe how HHS and DOJ obligated funds for the HCFAC program, we obtained information about how the agencies obligated their HCFAC appropriations for fiscal year 2012, by expenditure category (such as personnel).[12,13] We received this information from the HHS, HHS-OIG, and DOJ components that received HCFAC funding.[14] Additionally, we obtained information on obligations of other appropriations that HHS, HHS-OIG, and DOJ components used to support HCFAC activities.[15] Additionally, we interviewed officials at HHS and DOJ components, and reviewed agency documents to examine the process by which HHS and DOJ have obligated HCFAC funds. We reviewed the data for any errors and followed up with agency officials for clarification when necessary. On the basis of these activities, we determined that these data were sufficiently reliable for the purpose of our report.

To examine how HHS and DOJ assess HCFAC activities, and whether key program outputs have changed over time, we interviewed officials from HHS, HHS-OIG, and DOJ to obtain information on indicators reported by their agencies. We asked these officials about indicators listed in the HCFAC report, as well as other indicators that HHS, HHSOIG, and DOJ components use to assess HCFAC activities. We also collected information from agency officials about how they use the indicators and other data analyses to determine how to target HCFAC resources and prioritize activities. We reviewed agency documents, including the fiscal year 2012 HCFAC report, agency annual and semiannual reports, strategic plans, performance plans, congressional budget justifications, and other reports to obtain information on HCFAC activities that HHS, HHS-OIG, and DOJ components conducted. We reviewed the return-on-investment calculation outlined in the HCFAC report to determine what funding and amounts recovered are included, as well as the method used to calculate the return-on-investment. 16 To examine whether key program outputs have changed from fiscal year 2008 to 2012, we reviewed current and past HCFAC reports. We selected outputs from the annual HCFAC report to review, which the agencies consider to be key program outputs. For this analysis, we also took account of other funding (i.e., funds that agencies used to support HCFAC activities that were not specifically appropriated for the HCFAC program). We also interviewed agency officials regarding other factors that may have contributed to changes in program outputs in specific years.

To examine what is known about the effectiveness of the HCFAC program in reducing health care fraud and abuse, we conducted a review of relevant literature to identify measures used to assess the effectiveness of law enforcement programs, challenges associated with evaluating law enforcement programs, and the issues related to establishing a baseline estimate of the type and extent of fraud needed to measure progress over time. We included in our search both health care fraud enforcement programs specifically and law enforcement programs in general. We conducted literature searches in 44 online databases with health care and/or law enforcement content containing peer-reviewed publications and government reports to identify studies published from January 2003 through March 2013 using health care fraud, law enforcement, and performance measurement search terms. We conducted a preliminary review of abstracts for over 300 articles and selected 49 articles for closer review based on the following criteria: the article (1) identified performance indicators to assess the effectiveness of enforcement programs in general or health care fraud enforcement programs specifically; (2) discussed establishing a health care fraud baseline; or (3) identified challenges in evaluating law enforcement programs. Additionally, we interviewed HHS and DOJ officials to obtain information on the effectiveness of HCFAC activities and to determine the status of efforts by a CMS contractor to establish a health care fraud baseline. We also interviewed experts on health care fraud to discuss strengths and limitations of measuring the effectiveness of health care fraud enforcement programs, such as the HCFAC program.[17]

We conducted this performance audit from September 2012 to September 2013 in accordance with generally accepted government auditing standards. Those standards require that we plan and perform the audit to obtain sufficient, appropriate evidence to provide a reasonable basis for our findings and conclusions based on our audit objectives. We believe that the evidence obtained provides a reasonable basis for our findings and conclusions based on our audit objectives.

BACKGROUND

Health Care Fraud and Abuse Control Program

The HCFAC program was established under HIPAA to (1) coordinate federal, state, and local law enforcement efforts to control fraud and abuse associated with health plans; (2) conduct investigations, audits, evaluations, and inspections of delivery and payment for health care in the United States; (3) facilitate the enforcement of federal health care fraud and abuse laws; (4) provide guidance to the health care industry in the form of advisory opinions, safe harbor notices, and special fraud alerts; and (5) establish a national database of adverse actions against health care providers.[18] HIPAA requires that HHS and DOJ issue a joint annual report to Congress that outlines the amounts returned to the Medicare Trust Funds for the previous fiscal year under various categories, such as amounts of criminal fines and civil monetary penalties—penalties for certain activities, such as knowingly presenting a Medicare claim that is not medically necessary. Additionally, HHS and DOJ are required to report the amounts deposited into and expended from the Medicare Trust Funds to conduct HCFAC activities during the previous fiscal year and the justification for those expenditures. In addition to the mandatory appropriations provided under HIPAA, which Congress increased in 2010, DOJ and HHS-OIG have received discretionary funding through annual appropriations for the HCFAC program since fiscal year 2009.[19]

The annual HCFAC report includes a summary of the key HCFAC activities that the agencies and their components carried out and provides information on the outputs or outcomes of those activities. For example, the report includes information on the amount of money returned to the Medicare Trust Funds as a result of HCFAC activities. Additionally, the report includes sections that describe the activities each agency and component that received HCFAC funding conducted. These sections provide information on the outputs of each component's activities. For example, DOJ's USAO section highlights the number of new criminal investigations initiated and the number of civil matters pending.

HCFAC Appropriations

HHS and DOJ receive funding from several appropriations to conduct their HCFAC program activities. Figure 1 describes HCFAC appropriations to HHS, HHS-OIG, and DOJ. Mandatory funds are appropriated by HIPAA from the Medicare Trust Funds, and are available until expended, meaning that the funds can be spent in other years.[20] A large portion of these funds are appropriated to HHS-OIG; the law appropriates the remainder to both HHS and DOJ, which must determine together how to allocate the funds—referred to as the wedge—between the agencies.

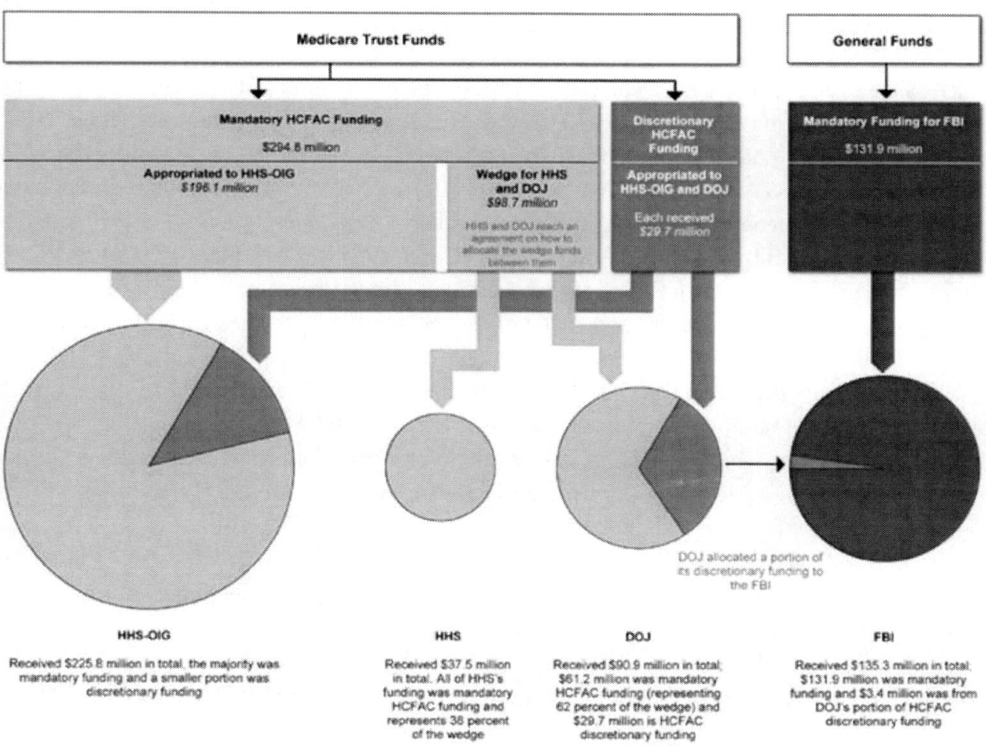

Source: GAO analysis of fiscal year 2012 annual HCFAC report and other agency documents.

Note: In fiscal year 2012, total appropriations to the Department of Health and Human Services (HHS), HHS's Office of Inspector General (HHS OIG), and the Department of Justice (DOJ) for HCFAC activities amounted to $486.1 million.

This includes the $131.9 million in mandatory appropriations that the Federal Bureau of Investigation (FBI) received to conduct health care fraud and abuse activities and the portion of the DOJ discretionary funding that it allocated to the FBI ($3.4 million).

Figure 1. Appropriations for the Health Care Fraud and Abuse Control (HCFAC) Program for Fiscal Year 2012, By Agency.

In each fiscal year, beginning with fiscal year 2009, Congress appropriated discretionary funding to DOJ and HHS-OIG to finance activities conducted under the HCFAC program. In addition, Congress also appropriated discretionary funds to CMS for program integrity activities it conducts in Medicare and Medicaid, which was outside the scope of our review.[21] Although the FBI is a component of DOJ and was allocated a portion of DOJ's discretionary HCFAC funding (about $3.4 million), the FBI also received mandatory funding under HIPAA to conduct health care fraud and abuse activities. This mandatory funding was appropriated from the general fund of the U.S. Treasury.

In addition to the HCFAC mandatory and discretionary funding that HHS, DOJ, and its components receive, the agencies use funding from other appropriations to support HCFAC activities. For example, HHS's Office of General Counsel (OGC) uses appropriations from HHS's General Departmental Management appropriation to support its HCFAC activities.

Activities Conducted under the HCFAC Program

HHS and DOJ components conduct a variety of activities under the HCFAC program using mandatory and discretionary HCFAC funding. Among other activities, HHS components identify and investigate fraud through programs, including the Administration for Community Living's (ACL) Senior Medicare Patrol programs, which are designed to educate and train Medicare beneficiaries to identify fraud. HHS's OGC supports a variety of program integrity work, including assisting DOJ on False Claims Act cases.[22] HHS's Food and Drug Administration (FDA) conducts the Pharmaceutical Fraud Program, which is designed to detect pharmaceutical, biologics, and medical device fraud. CMS uses a portion of HHS's HCFAC funding to improve its financial oversight of the Medicaid program and CHIP, and for a pilot project related to fraud in community mental health centers. CMS also uses its portion of HCFAC funding to support its efforts related to the Medicare Fraud Strike Force (Strike Force) teams, which consist of investigators and prosecutors who use advanced data analysis techniques to identify, investigate, and prosecute potentially fraudulent billing patterns in geographic areas with high rates of health care fraud.

HHS-OIG conducts a variety of activities to identify and reduce fraud, waste, and abuse. For example, HHS-OIG assesses civil monetary penalties and imposes other administrative penalties—such as excluding individuals and entities from participating in federal health care programs—against individuals and entities for certain types of conduct. Each of HHS-OIG's components receives HCFAC funding for the work it conducts. Among other activities:

- The Office of Investigations (OI) coordinates and conducts investigations of allegations of fraud, waste, and abuse in Medicare and Medicaid.

- The Office of Evaluation and Inspections (OEI) conducts national evaluations on issues related to preventing fraud, waste, and abuse, and promoting economy, efficiency, and effectiveness of HHS programs.
- The Office of Audit Services (OAS) conducts independent audits of HHS programs, grantees, and contractors.
- The Office of Counsel to the Inspector General (OCIG) exercises the authority to impose civil and administrative penalties related to health care fraud, as well as issue advisory opinions.
- The Office of Management and Policy (OMP) provides management, guidance, and resources in support of the other HHS-OIG components.

DOJ's components have the primary role in enforcing U.S. laws related to health care fraud and abuse, including both criminal and civil matters. For example:

- The Criminal Division prosecutes criminal health care fraud and leads the Strike Force teams.
- The Civil Division represents the U.S. in civil fraud matters, such as False Claims Act cases and has the authority to bring criminal charges under the Federal Food, Drug, and Cosmetic Act.
- The USAOs litigate or prosecute civil and criminal health care fraud cases in their 94 districts throughout the country and are part of the Strike Force teams.
- The Civil Rights Division enforces several laws related to cases of abuse, substandard care, or needless institutionalization of certain individuals.
- The Justice Management Division (JMD) provides financial oversight of the DOJ components.
- The FBI serves as an investigative agency with jurisdiction in both federal and private health insurance programs, and participates in task forces and undercover operations to investigate health care fraud.

Although the agencies and components conduct certain activities without assistance from other agencies and components, HHS, CMS, HHS-OIG, and DOJ—including the FBI—frequently collaborate to investigate and prosecute fraud in federal health care programs. For example, HHS-OIG, FBI, and DOJ investigators and prosecutors comprise Strike Force teams. Table 2 in appendix I provides further detail on these activities.

AGENCIES OBLIGATED $583.6 MILLION FOR HCFAC ACTIVITIES IN FISCAL YEAR 2012; MOST OBLIGATIONS WERE FOR PERSONNEL

In fiscal year 2012, HHS, HHS-OIG, and DOJ obligated approximately $583.6 million to fund HCFAC activities. About 78 percent of obligated funds were from mandatory HCFAC appropriations, 11 percent of obligated funds were from discretionary HCFAC appropriations, and 12 percent of obligated funds were from other appropriations.[23] Most of the obligations for HCFAC activities were for personnel costs; some agencies reported obligating funds for services under contract and supplies. Additionally, HHS-OIG and DOJ obligated over 8 percent of their HCFAC funds to support Strike Force teams located in 9 cities nationwide.

HHS, HHS-OIG, and DOJ Obligated $583.6 Million in Fiscal Year 2012; 12 Percent of Obligated Funds Came from Other Appropriations

In fiscal year 2012, HHS, HHS-OIG, and DOJ reported $583.6 million in obligations for HCFAC activities.[24] This total includes obligations of mandatory (about 78 percent) and discretionary (about 11 percent) HCFAC appropriations and other appropriations not specific to the HCFAC program (about 12 percent).[25] HCFAC mandatory funds are available until expended, while discretionary HCFAC funds are available for 2 fiscal years. Other appropriations that agencies use for HCFAC activities vary in how long they are available. Because agencies reported in fiscal year 2012 obligating funds that were carried over from prior fiscal years, and because agencies obligated funds from other appropriations not specific to the HCFAC program, the obligations the agencies reported for HCFAC activities in fiscal year 2012—$583.6 million—exceed the HCFAC funds appropriated to the agencies for that year. For example, HHS, HHS-OIG, and DOJ were appropriated $486.1 million in HCFAC mandatory and discretionary funding for fiscal year 2012. However, for fiscal year 2012, these agencies reported HCFAC obligations of $583.6 million, including over $67 million in obligations of other appropriations, as well as obligations of funds appropriated in prior fiscal years. In fiscal year 2012, DOJ incurred about 48 percent of the agencies' total HCFAC obligations (about $280.3 million), 26 while HHS-OIG incurred about 44 percent ($258.8 million), and HHS incurred the remaining 8 percent ($44.4 million). See figure 2 for the distribution of HCFAC obligations by appropriations type—HCFAC mandatory, HCFAC discretionary, and other appropriations—by HHS, HHS-OIG, and DOJ's components for fiscal year 2012. See table 3 in appendix II for the distribution of HCFAC obligations by appropriations type—HCFAC mandatory, HCFAC discretionary, and other appropriations—for HHS, HHS-OIG, and DOJ's components for fiscal years 2008 through 2012.

Mandatory HCFAC Funding

A portion of the mandatory HCFAC appropriation that supports HHS and DOJ's HCFAC activities—or wedge funds—is allocated to each agency. According to a HHS official, in fiscal year 2010, the departments reached a standing agreement for the following allocations: approximately 38 percent for HHS and 62 percent for DOJ. 27 Prior to fiscal year 2010, HHS and DOJ negotiated each year how to divide the wedge funds between the two agencies, which a HHS official described as time-consuming. HHS distributes its wedge funds to HHS components based on their annual funding requests that the Secretary approves. In fiscal year 2012, HHS distributed mandatory funding to ACL for the Senior Medicare Patrol programs, OGC to support program integrity work of its clients, FDA to support the Pharmaceutical Fraud Program, and CMS to support Medicaid and CHIP financial specialists and a pilot project related to fraud in community mental health center providers in Texas, Florida, and Louisiana.[28] According to a DOJ official, DOJ distributes mandatory HCFAC funds—its portion of wedge funds—to its components to carry out their HCFAC activities, and the distribution of such funds has not varied much since the inception of the program. Separately, HHS-OIG receives a mandatory appropriation for its HCFAC activities. This appropriation is

HHS-OIG's primary source of funding for Medicare and Medicaid fraud investigations, as well as for audits, evaluations, and inspections it conducts related to the Medicare and Medicaid programs.

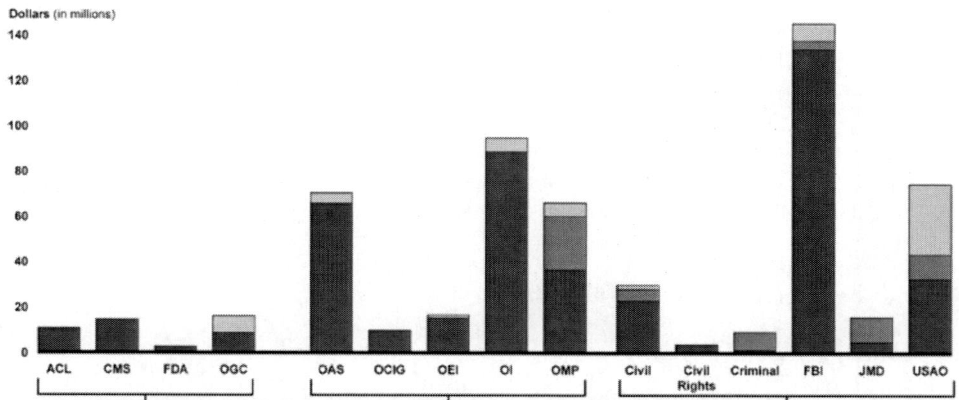

	Department of Health and Human Services (HHS)[a]				HHS-Office of Inspector General (HHS-OIG)[a,d]					Department of Justice (DOJ)[a]					
	ACL	CMS[b]	FDA	OGC[c]	OAS	OCIG	OEI	OI	OMP	Civil	Civil Rights	Criminal[e]	FBI	JMD[f]	USAO
Total	10.6	14.9	2.8	16.2	70.5	10.5	16.6	95.0	66.2	29.9	5.2	9.3	145.7	15.8	74.6
Agency total	$44.4				$258.8					$280.3					

Source: GAO analysis of HCFAC obligations that HHS, HHS-OIG, and DOJ reported for their components in fiscal year 2012.

Notes: Agency total HCFAC obligations may not equal the sum of HCFAC obligations for the agency's components due to rounding.

[a]The Department of Health and Human Services' (HHS) components that received HCFAC funding in fiscal year 2012 were: Administration for Community Living (ACL), Centers for Medicare & Medicaid Services (CMS), Food and Drug Administration (FDA), and Office of General Counsel (OGC). HHS's Office of Inspector General's (HHS-OIG) components that received HCFAC funding in fiscal year 2012 were: Office of Audit Services (OAS), Office of Counsel to the Inspector General (OCIG), Office of Evaluation and Inspections (OEI), Office of Investigations (OI), and Office of Management and Policy (OMP). The Department of Justice's (DOJ) components that received HCFAC funding were: DOJ's Civil Division, Civil Rights Division, Criminal Division, the 94 U.S. Attorneys' Offices (USAO), the Justice Management Division (JMD), and the Federal Bureau of Investigation (FBI).

[b]For fiscal year 2012, CMS reported amounts in HCFAC mandatory appropriations, about $1.6 million, that the agency reserved to fund HCFAC activities in future years. These funds were allocated to CMS in fiscal year 2012, but were not obligated.

[c]HHS's OGC reported estimated obligations of other appropriations, which included reimbursements for attorney services provided to OGC clients within HHS, that supported HCFAC activities.

[d]HHS-OIG's reported obligations also include any funding the agency received as reimbursement for the costs of conducting investigations and audits and other activities when such costs are ordered by a court, voluntarily agreed to by the payor, or otherwise authorized under 42 U.S.C. §1320a-7c(b).

[e]DOJ's Criminal Division stated that it uses some of its annual appropriation for health care fraud activities. However, Division officials indicated that the Division infrequently funds HCFAC activities with other appropriations and, as a result, the Division does not track its use of these appropriations for HCFAC activities.

[f] For fiscal year 2012, DOJ reported allocations of HCFAC mandatory and discretionary appropriations that the department reserved for future use to fund HCFAC activities, about $4.7 million in mandatory HCFAC appropriations and about $10.8 million in discretionary HCFAC appropriations. These funds were allocated to JMD, but were not obligated. We have included these HCFAC allocations under the JMD, in addition to the $208,676 in mandatory HCFAC obligations JMD reported. However, in the return-on-investment included in the fiscal year 2012 annual HCFAC report, only a portion of these allocations (about $13.2 million) were included in the calculation. JMD may use these funds for unanticipated HCFAC costs.

Figure 2. Fiscal Year 2012 Health Care Fraud and Abuse Control (HCFAC) Obligations (in Millions), by Agency Component and Type of Appropriations.

Discretionary HCFAC Funding

In fiscal year 2012, DOJ and HHS-OIG obligated discretionary HCFAC appropriations. According to the information each agency reported to us, each DOJ component received a share of DOJ's discretionary HCFAC appropriation for their HCFAC activities. A DOJ official told us that DOJ components generally received the same amount of funding from the agency's discretionary HCFAC appropriation for their HCFAC activities in fiscal year 2012 as they had in prior fiscal years. Additionally, the official indicated that a large portion of DOJ's HCFAC discretionary appropriation supports the Strike Force teams because DOJ believes that these teams reduce fraud. One component in HHS-OIG—OMP—received discretionary HCFAC appropriations. 29 OMP officials told us that most obligations of these funds are for overhead expenses for the HHS-OIG components that are handled by OMP (such as rent and utilities).

Other Appropriations Supporting HCFAC Activities

HHS, HHS-OIG, and DOJ components obligated over $67 million in funds from other appropriations in addition to the mandatory and discretionary HCFAC appropriations they obligated for HCFAC activities in fiscal year 2012. Within HHS, one component—OGC—used other appropriations to supplement its HCFAC funding. 30 To carry out its HCFAC activities, OGC obligated funds from the annual HHS General Department Management appropriation, which accounted for almost half of its overall obligations for HCFAC activities in fiscal year 2012. ACL, CMS, and FDA did not use other appropriations to support their HCFAC activities.

Each of HHS-OIG's components obligated funds from other appropriations to support HCFAC activities in fiscal year 2012. From other appropriations, HHS-OIG obligated about $18.9 million of these appropriations for HCFAC activities in fiscal year 2012, which represented about 7 percent of its overall HCFAC obligations. HHS-OIG reported that the other appropriations used to support HCFAC activities included funds appropriated specifically to support HHS-OIG's Medicare and Medicaid program integrity work. For example, in fiscal year 2012, each HHS-OIG component reported obligating funds appropriated in section 6034 of the Deficit Reduction Act (which, among other things, established the Medicaid Integrity Program and provided HHS-OIG with increased funding for Medicaid fraud and abuse control activities) to conduct HCFAC activities.[31]

Most of DOJ's components also used funding from other appropriations to support HCFAC activities, specifically the USAOs, the FBI, the Civil Division, and the Civil Rights Division.[32] The USAOs obligated the most funding from other appropriations among all of the DOJ components, about $31.1 million in fiscal year 2012. This accounted for 42 percent of the USAOs' overall obligations for HCFAC activities in fiscal year 2012. Officials from the USAOs reported obligating funds from DOJ's annual appropriations and the DOJ's "Three Percent" funds to support HCFAC activities.[33] According to USAO officials, a portion of the USAOs' annual appropriation is used to fund attorneys, paralegals, auditors and investigators, and litigation support for resource intensive health care fraud cases. Officials from the Civil Division told us that they also used "Three Percent" funds to continue the division's health care fraud litigation work, such as to investigate qui tam cases alleging false claims and to prepare cases for trial.[34] The Civil Rights Division reported using DOJ's Salaries and Expenses, General Legal Activities appropriation to fund the rent for office space used by personnel, and the FBI reported using its annual appropriation to cover personnel expenses for investigators working health care fraud cases beyond those covered by HCFAC funds.

Most HCFAC Obligations Were for Personnel in Fiscal Year 2012

HHS, HHS-OIG, and DOJ reported that most of their HCFAC obligations were for personnel costs in fiscal year 2012, with some exceptions based on the type of HCFAC activities each component performs (see table 3 of appendix II for HCFAC obligations for fiscal years 2008 through 2012 for HHS, HHS-OIG, and DOJ's components).[35] A large portion of most HHS components' HCFAC obligations were for personnel costs. The same was true for HHS-OIG and DOJ. Each agency relied on personnel to conduct HCFAC activities—HHS-OIG employed investigators to examine potential fraud cases and DOJ employed investigators, attorneys, and other support personnel to investigate and prosecute fraud cases. Additionally, HHS-OIG employed auditors and evaluators to study issues related to the Medicare and Medicaid programs, including issues related to fraud in these programs, as well as a variety of other issues.

HHS, HHS-OIG, and DOJ components also reported that their next largest amount of HCFAC obligations was for contractual services and supplies. Components reported using these contractual services and supplies for transportation, rent, supplies, or other contractual services— such as for litigation consultants (for example, medical experts) and litigation support (for example, paralegals to review case documentation), among other things. Obligations for personnel and contracted services and supplies generally accounted for almost all of a component's HCFAC obligations. Specifically, for HHS's components, obligations for personnel costs represented the largest portion of FDA's, CMS's, and OGC's obligations for HCFAC activities for fiscal year 2012. In contrast, most of ACL's obligations in fiscal year 2012 were for expanding grants to the Senior Medicare Patrol programs.

Each of HHS-OIG's components, with the exception of OMP, reported obligations for personnel costs as their largest HCFAC obligations for fiscal year 2012, devoting 87 percent or more of their obligations to personnel in fiscal year 2012. For OMP, over 70 percent of its obligations were devoted to rent, communication, utilities, equipment, printing, and other contractual services. OMP officials told us that certain overhead expenses incurred by the

HHS-OIG components—for example, rent payments—are handled by OMP. About half or more of DOJ components' obligations for HCFAC activities were for personnel costs. In fiscal year 2012, the USAOs, Civil Division, Criminal Division, Civil Rights Division, and FBI reported that obligations for personnel costs ranged from 47 percent (Civil Division) to 84 percent (USAOs) of their obligations. For example, for the Civil Division, obligations for contractual services and supplies represented 53 percent of its HCFAC obligations; and officials told us that they use contracted services for litigation consultants (such as medical experts to review medical records or to prepare exhibits to be used at trial) and for litigation support (such as paralegals to review case documentation).

Over $47 Million in Obligations in Fiscal Year 2012 Supported Strike Force Teams in Nine Cities

In fiscal year 2012, HHS-OIG and DOJ obligated over $47 million in HCFAC funds to support Strike Force teams. This represented about 8.1 percent of the $583.6 million in obligations for HCFAC activities. DOJ officials told us that Strike Force teams are an important and valuable tool for identifying potential health care fraud schemes. (See table 1 for the HCFAC obligations by Strike Force location for fiscal year 2012, and see appendix II, table 4 for information on HCFAC obligations devoted to Strike Force teams for fiscal years 2008-2012.)

In fiscal year 2012, DOJ and HHS-OIG obligated over $12.9 million for the Strike Force team in Miami, which represented over 27 percent of funding for all Strike Force teams. The first Strike Force team was officially launched in Miami in fiscal year 2007, based in part on an HHS-OIG evaluation that found aberrant claims patterns for infusion therapy for Medicare beneficiaries with HIV/AIDs that differentiated South Florida Medicare providers and beneficiaries from the rest of the country.[36] Additionally, obligations for Miami's Strike Force team were more than twice as much as in Detroit, the team with the second highest obligations for fiscal year 2012 ($5.1 million).

Based on the obligations reported for fiscal year 2012, HHS-OIG's Office of Investigations accounted for 45 percent of the total obligations used for Strike Force teams. The FBI incurred 25 percent, DOJ's Criminal Division incurred 17 percent, and the USAOs incurred 13 percent of obligations for the Strike Force teams. HHS-OIG's Office of Investigations and the FBI's agents conduct investigations and gather evidence, such as through surveillance for Strike Force cases, while DOJ's Criminal Division and the USAOs' attorneys are the primary prosecutors of Strike Force cases. Additionally, although not reflected in the table above, CMS obligated approximately $350,656 in discretionary HCFAC appropriations to support Strike Force Teams. CMS's HCFAC obligations were not associated with any one individual Strike Force city.

Since fiscal year 2010, the USAOs have used some of their HCFAC discretionary appropriation for three Special Focus teams—in San Francisco, Boston, and Philadelphia. These Special Focus teams are similar to the Strike Force teams, but handle pharmaceutical civil cases rather than criminal cases. Approximately $2.8 million of the USAOs' HCFAC obligations in fiscal year 2012 were for these Special Focus teams. This amount was in addition to the HCFAC obligations they used for the Strike Force teams.

Table 1. Total Health Care Fraud and Abuse Control (HCFAC) Obligations by Agency Component and Strike Force Location, Fiscal Year 2012

Strike Force Location & Fiscal Year Launched	Department of Health and Human Services' Office of Inspector General (HHS-OIG)[a]	Department of Justice's (DOJ) Criminal Division	U.S. Attorneys' Offices (USAOs)	Federal Bureau of Investigation (FBI)	Total, by city
Miami, FL Launched FY 2007	$6,276,735	$1,570,190	$1,404,500	$3,711,474	$12,962,899
Detroit, MI Launched FY 2009	$2,483,564	$913,940	$623,000	$1,078,020	$5,098,524
Dallas, TX Launched FY 2011	$3,013,496	$480,834	$458,000	$1,075,460	$5,027,790
Los Angeles, CA Launched FY 2008	$2,360,294	$431,460	$428,000	$1,596,209	$4,815,963
Brooklyn, NY Launched FY 2010	$2,005,588	$855,329	$553,000	$978,934	$4,392,851
Baton Rouge, LA Launched FY 2010	$1,612,787	$943,497	$386,000	$496,083	$3,438,367
Chicago, IL Launched FY 2011	$1,270,269	–	$715,000	$1,394,940	$3,380,209
Houston, TX Launched FY 2009	$783,021	$738,069	$424,000	$621,018	$2,566,108
Tampa, FL Launched FY 2010	$1,341,201	$94.901	$578,000	$535,100	$2,549,202
Headquarters Support of Strike Forces	$187,840	$2,055,643	$485,000	$323,330	$3,051,813
Total	$21,334,795	$8,083,863	$6,054,500	$11,810,568	$47,283,726

Source: GAO analysis of HCFAC obligations reported to GAO by HHS-OIG's Office of Investigations and DOJ's Criminal Division, USAOs, and FBI for fiscal year 2012.

Notes: CMS also obligated $350,656 of its discretionary HCFAC appropriations for headquarters' support of the Strike Force teams. However, these obligations were not associated with any one of the nine Strike Force cities and this amount is not reflected in the table above.

[a]HHS-OIG reported estimated HCFAC obligations to support the Strike Force teams including obligations of non-HCFAC appropriations. In fiscal year 2012, these other appropriations consisted of funds appropriated to HHS-OIG under section 6034 of the Deficit Reduction Act that remained available for obligation in fiscal year 2012. Deficit Reduction Act, Pub. L. No. 109-171, § 6034(c), 120 Stat. 4, 77 (Feb. 8, 2006).

AGENCIES USE SEVERAL INDICATORS TO ASSESS HCFAC ACTIVITIES, AND SOME KEY OUTPUTS CHANGED OVER TIME

HHS, HHS-OIG, and DOJ use several indicators to assess HCFAC activities as well as to inform decision-makers about how to allocate resources. These indicators include those listed in the annual HCFAC report as well as others outlined in agency reports. For example, FDA assesses the work of its Pharmaceutical Fraud Program by tracking the number of criminal investigations opened and the outcomes of criminal convictions obtained, among other indicators. Additionally, many of the indicators that HHS, HHS-OIG, and DOJ use reflect the collective work of multiple agencies since they work many health care fraud cases jointly. Outputs from some of these key indicators have changed in recent fiscal years. For example, the return-on-investment has increased from $4.90 returned for every $1.00 invested for fiscal years 2006-2008 to $7.90 returned for every $1.00 invested for fiscal years 2010-2012.

HHS, HHS-OIG, and DOJ Use Several Indicators to Assess HCFAC Activities and Inform Decisions about Resource Allocation and Prioritization of Activities

HHS, HHS-OIG, and DOJ officials reported using several indicators to assess HCFAC activities and that those indicators serve multiple purposes. Several indicators are included in the annual HCFAC report, while other indicators are reported in agency documents or used internally. Additionally, some indicators are collective—in that they reflect the work of multiple agencies—and other indicators outline the activities conducted by a particular agency or component. Appendix III, tables 5 through 8, provides detailed information on indicators used to assess the activities conducted using HCFAC funding, including those outlined in the HCFAC report, as well as other indicators the agencies use, by agency and component.

HHS Indicators

Each HHS component conducts unique activities related to health care fraud and abuse. As a result of these different types of activities, the indicators that each HHS component uses to highlight the accomplishments of its HCFAC activities vary.

FDA uses indicators associated with its Pharmaceutical Fraud program— which focuses on detecting, prosecuting, and preventing pharmaceutical, biologic, and medical device fraud—including the number of criminal investigations opened during a fiscal year and the outcomes of criminal convictions obtained (such as amount of jail time, probation, or amount of restitution). FDA officials told us that the indicators they use are outlined in the annual HCFAC report. For example, FDA reported in the fiscal year 2012 HCFAC report that it had opened 42 criminal investigations since the inception of the Pharmaceutical Fraud Program, and 17 investigations during fiscal year 2012.

ACL primarily uses indicators that track information related to the Senior Medicare Patrol (SMP) programs—which train senior volunteers to inform fellow beneficiaries on how to detect and prevent fraud, waste, and abuse in the Medicare program—such as indicators related to beneficiary education and training, outreach activities, and events the SMP programs conduct, and cases that were referred for investigation. For instance, ACL tracks the number of group education sessions the SMPs conduct and the estimated number of beneficiaries who attended the sessions. Many of the indicators ACL uses are outlined in an annual HHS-OIG report on the SMP programs, as well as the annual HCFAC report.[37] According to ACL officials, ACL has hired a contractor to assess the adequacy of the current indicators used by ACL and to determine if the indicators are appropriate for evaluating the performance of the SMPs.

HHS's OGC uses several indicators to assess the HCFAC activities it conducts. These indicators include amounts of recoveries for matters on which OGC has assisted—such as False Claims Act matters and civil monetary penalties—and the number of physician self-referral disclosures in which OGC advised.[38] As with the other HHS agencies, OGC's indicators are outlined in the annual HCFAC report.

CMS officials told us that CMS uses a variety of indicators to assess the HCFAC activities included in our review. For the Medicaid and CHIP financial management project, CMS tracks information related to the amount of the federal share of Medicaid funds that were recovered as a result of the project's monitoring and financial management reviews of Medicaid expenditures. For the community mental health centers study, CMS officials told us that they do not have indicators since the project is relatively new. For CMS's efforts associated with the Strike Force teams, officials told us that one indicator they use is the drop in number of claims for particular services, which they believe coincides with the efforts of the Strike Force teams to investigate and prosecute fraud. For example, according to information that CMS provided to us, payments for home health services dropped by nearly one-half from 2008 to 2011 in Miami-Dade County, which officials believe was, in part, due to the Strike Force team's efforts focused on reducing fraud in home health care.

HHS-OIG Indicators

HHS-OIG uses a variety of indicators to assess the work it conducts using HCFAC funds. Some of these indicators reflect the collective work of HHS-OIG's components and some are unique to the activities conducted by a particular component. For example, HHS-OIG tracks the health care savings attributable to HHS-OIG investigations, audits, and evaluations. This indicator includes work from nearly all HHS-OIG components, including the Office of Investigations, the Office of Audit Services, and the Office of Evaluation and Inspections. Among many other indicators, HHSOIG's Office of Counsel to the Inspector General tracks the number of corporate integrity agreements monitored for compliance, which is specific to the work of that office.[39] HHS-OIG officials told us that the indicators they use to assess HCFAC activities are reported in the annual HCFAC report and in other HHS-OIG reports (such as its semi-annual reports to Congress).

DOJ Indicators

DOJ uses several indicators to assess the work it conducts with HCFAC funding. The indicators it uses relate to the activities that each DOJ component conducts to enforce health care fraud and abuse laws. For example, the USAOs use indicators related to criminal prosecutions, including the number of defendants charged and the number of convictions. In addition to those measures, the USAOs also track information related to civil matters, such as the number of pending civil investigations.

In addition to the indicators listed in the annual HCFAC report, officials from DOJ's components told us that they use other indicators to assess the work they conduct related to health care fraud and abuse. Officials told us that these indicators are tracked at the departmental level and aggregate the work of multiple DOJ components. For example, DOJ tracks the percentage of criminal and civil cases resolved favorably. These indicators include health care fraud cases, as well as other cases that DOJ components handle.

Indicators Inform Decisions about Resource Allocation and Prioritization of Activities

Officials from HHS, HHS-OIG, and DOJ told us that they use indicators to inform decision-makers about how to allocate resources. For example, officials from DOJ's Civil Rights Division told us that they use indicators to help determine what resources they need to handle their current caseload. The Civil Rights Division considers the number of cases the division is currently working along with the number of remedial agreements with facilities that the division needs to monitor in the upcoming year when developing requests for funding. Additionally, officials from FDA told us that they review the preceding year's number of investigations and the costs associated with those investigations, when requesting annual funding.

Additionally, HHS, HHS-OIG, and DOJ officials indicated that they use data to inform their decisions about which activities to prioritize, including what cases or studies to undertake, as well as where to locate specific resources. For example, officials from HHS-OIG told us that they use Medicare claims data to identify which service areas to target for investigations, audits, or evaluations, as well as which geographic regions to focus their efforts. Officials said that they continually review whether HHS-OIG staff are located in the most appropriate geographic areas and have relocated staff to areas to enhance the efficiency of HHS-OIG resources. HHS-OIG officials also told us that the agency uses several indicators for internal management purposes. Additionally, officials from DOJ's Criminal Division told us that one factor they consider when deciding how to prioritize cases is to review data analyses to focus on cases with large amounts of alleged fraudulent billing.

Some Key Outputs that Reflect Work of Multiple Agencies Have Changed in Recent Years

Since HHS-OIG and DOJ's components work many health care fraud cases jointly, many of the indicators included in the annual HCFAC report highlight the work of both HHS-OIG and DOJ, as well as various components within each agency. For example, the report includes information on the results of HCFAC activities, such as the dollar amount recovered as a result of fraud cases, which HHS-OIG and DOJ officials say reflects the investigative work done by HHS-OIG and FBI, as well as the work of DOJ's components in prosecuting the cases. Additionally, the report presents several indicators related to the work of the Strike Force teams, such as the number of indictments and complaints involving charges that were filed, the outcomes of the cases, and the total amount of alleged billing to Medicare as a result of these Strike Force cases.

The return-on-investment is another indicator that reflects the work of multiple agencies and has changed in recent years. We have recognized that agencies can use a return-on-investment as a valuable tool for assessing a program's activities and for determining how best to target resources.[40] The return-on-investment is included in the annual HCFAC report and compares the amount of funds that were returned to the Medicare Trust Funds, such as restitution and compensatory damages awarded, with the amount of appropriations for HCFAC activities. Specifically:

- The total returns—the numerator—includes deposits to the Medicare Trust Funds. The calculation includes amounts that were deposited into the Medicare Trust Funds rather than amounts that were ordered or negotiated in health care fraud and abuse cases, but not yet transferred to the Medicare Trust Funds. Officials reported that although there may be large amounts of restitution ordered or agreed upon in health care fraud cases, the amounts actually returned to the Medicare Trust Funds may be lower.[41,42] By including only those funds that have been returned to the Medicare Trust Funds, the return-on-investment is not artificially inflated.

- The total investment—the denominator—includes mandatory and discretionary HCFAC funds that were appropriated to HHS, HHS-OIG, and DOJ (including the FBI's mandatory funds devoted to health care fraud and abuse reduction activities) and does not include funding from other appropriations. DOJ officials told us that the HCFAC funding that CMS receives through HHS's wedge fund is included in the return-on-investment calculation, and a small portion of HCFAC discretionary funds that CMS uses to support the Strike Force teams.[43]
- Return-on-investment is calculated using a 3-year moving average. To account for differences in the amounts returned to the Medicare Trust Funds between years, the return-on-investment is calculated using a 3-year average. For example, a case may have been investigated in fiscal year 2010 but not settled until fiscal year 2012, and thus the funds received from that case would not be deposited until 2012. Similarly, although agencies may carry over HCFAC appropriations into future fiscal years, the amount of appropriations included in the calculation is also based on a 3-year average with carry over amounts included in the year in which they were appropriated.[44]

According to the annual HCFAC report, the return-on-investment for fiscal years 2010-2012 was $7.90 returned to the Medicare Trust Funds for every $1.00 of HCFAC funds appropriated for HCFAC activities. The return-on-investment increased steadily from fiscal year 2008 to 2012. In fiscal years 2006-2008, the return-on-investment was $4.90 to $1.00, and in fiscal years 2010-2012, the return-on-investment was the highest at $7.90 to $1.00. See figure 3 for additional information on the return-oninvestment for fiscal years 2008-2012.

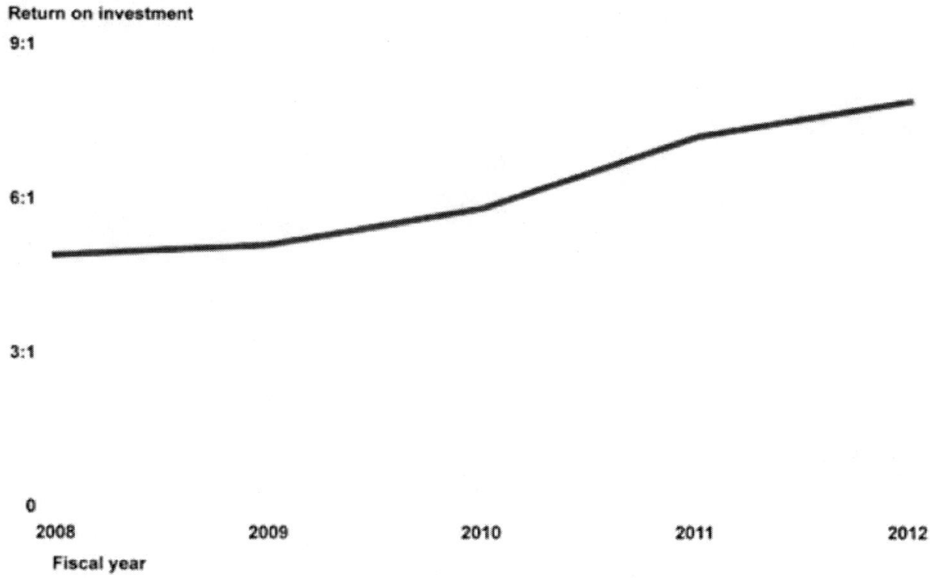

Source: GAO analysis of information provided by DOJ for fiscal years 2008-2012.

Note: The return-on-investment is based on amounts recovered from HCFAC activities and deposited into the Medicare Trust Funds and amounts appropriated to Department of Health and Human Services (HHS), HHS Office of Inspector General, and the Department of Justice (DOJ) to conduct HCFAC activities. The information about the return-on-investment was obtained from DOJ.

The return-on-investment is calculated using a 3-year moving average and, as a result, the calculation for each fiscal year incorporates amounts that were deposited into the Medicare Trust Funds and appropriations from that fiscal year and the two prior fiscal years. For example, the return-oninvestment for fiscal year 2008 is calculated using the amounts from fiscal years 2006, 2007, and 2008. Additionally, because many fraud cases can take years to investigate and prosecute, the amounts deposited into the Medicare Trust Funds may have been the result of prior year's HCFAC activities.

Figure 3. Health Care Fraud and Abuse Control (HCFAC) Program Return-on-Investment, Fiscal Years 2008 through 2012.

A review of other key outputs listed in the annual HCFAC reports from 2008 through 2012 that reflect accomplishments or outputs of activities conducted by multiple agencies using HCFAC funding shows some key outputs have generally increased and some have remained stable. During the same time period, HCFAC obligations and funding from other appropriations used to support HCFAC activities increased about 38 percent. See figure 4 for data on selected key outputs for fiscal years 2008 to 2012, and see appendix IV, table 9 for additional detailed information on the key outputs for fiscal years 2008 to 2012.

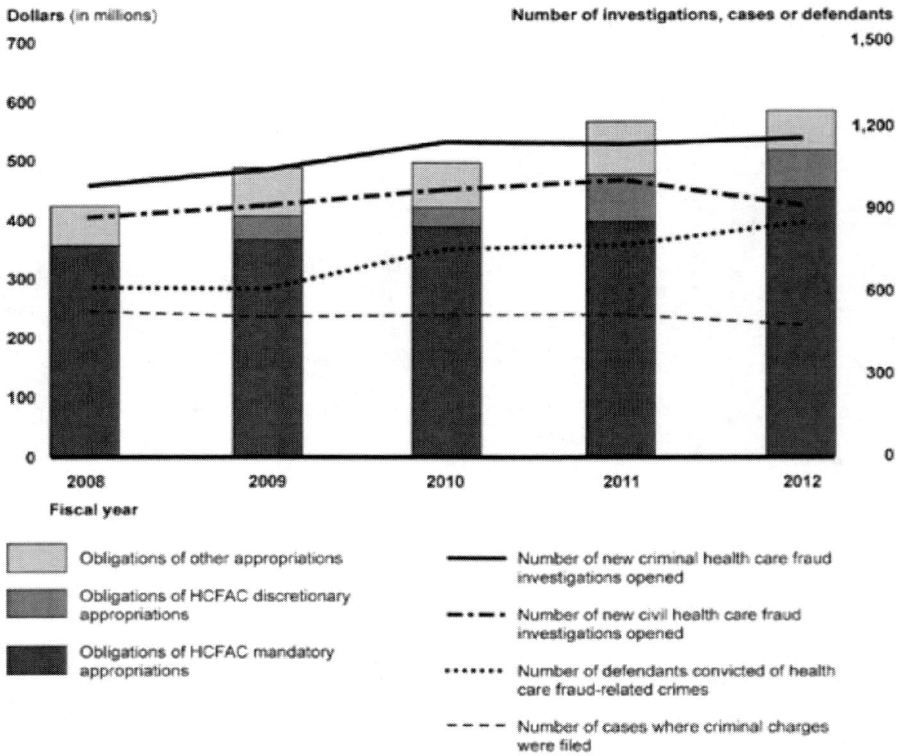

Source: GAO analysis of annual HCFAC reports for fiscal years 2008-2012 and obligations for HCFAC activities reported to GAO by HHS, HHS Office of Inspector General, and Department of Justice.

Note: Since many fraud cases can take years to investigate and prosecute, the number of investigations, cases, and defendants reported in the figure above may have been the result of a prior year's HCFAC activities.

The obligations information included in the figure above reports obligations for HCFAC activities that Department of Justice, Department of Health and Human Services (HHS), and HHS Office of Inspector General reported to GAO for a single fiscal year.

Figure 4. Selected Key Program Outputs and Total Obligations for Health Care Fraud and Abuse Control (HCFAC) Program Activities, Fiscal Years 2008 through 2012.

One key output that has increased since fiscal year 2008 is the number of defendants convicted of health care fraud. For example, the number of defendants convicted of health care fraud generally increased from around 588 in fiscal year 2008 to 826 in fiscal year 2012 (a 40 percent increase).

Some key outputs did not change between fiscal years 2008 and 2012. While funding has increased since 2008, there has not been a consistent pattern of increasing outputs. For example, the number of new criminal health care fraud investigations opened increased from fiscal year 2008 (957 investigations) to fiscal year 2012 (1,131 investigations). Additionally, the number of new civil health care fraud investigations opened did not vary much between 2008 (843 cases) and 2012 (885 cases).

HHS-OIG and DOJ officials indicated that there are a number of factors that might contribute to these trends. DOJ officials told us that the complexity of fraud cases has increased in recent years and requires more substantial resources to investigate and prosecute than other, less-complex cases. Officials stated that this limits the amount of resources they are able to commit to other cases. HHS-OIG and DOJ officials also cited other factors, including external factors (such as an increase in the number of defendants opting to go to trial) and significant changes to federal health care programs (such as the implementation of the Medicare Part D prescription drug program), which might influence these trends.

Nonetheless, HHS-OIG and DOJ officials indicated that they consider the increase since 2008 in some of the key outputs to be significant. For example, HHS-OIG officials noted that there was an increase of 42 civil fraud investigations from 2008 to 2012, and they consider the increase to be of significance given the complexity of fraud schemes and the resources needed to handle these civil cases. Additionally, DOJ officials told us that they consider increases to the number of new criminal fraud investigations opened (an increase of 18 percent) to be significant. DOJ officials also indicated that several key outputs related to the Strike Force teams have increased since 2008. See appendix IV for detailed information on key outputs related to HCFAC activities, including the Strike Force teams.

SEVERAL FACTORS CONTRIBUTE TO LACK OF INFORMATION ABOUT THE EFFECTIVENESS OF HCFAC ACTIVITIES

The indicators used by agencies to track the outputs of HCFAC activities provide information on the accomplishments of HCFAC activities, not on the effectiveness of the activities in reducing health care fraud and abuse. HHS, HHS-OIG, and DOJ officials reported that they consider the indicators to be the outputs or accomplishments of the HCFAC activities they conduct and in that sense they provide a composite picture of the achievements of the HCFAC program. However, difficulty in establishing a causal link between HCFAC activities and output indicators, difficulty in determining the deterrent effect HCFAC activities may have on potential health care fraud and abuse, limited research on the effectiveness of health care fraud interventions, and the lack of a health care fraud baseline hinder a broader understanding of the effectiveness of the HCFAC program in reducing health care fraud and abuse.

Indicators Agencies Use to Assess HCFAC Activities Provide Information on Accomplishments, but Not Effectiveness

The indicators that HHS, HHS-OIG, and DOJ use to track HCFAC activities offer insights on the accomplishments and outputs of HCFAC activities, but they do not measure the effectiveness of the HCFAC program in reducing health care fraud and abuse. HHS, HHS-OIG, and DOJ officials reported that they consider the indicators they use to be the accomplishments or outputs of the HCFAC activities they conduct. For example, the key program outputs discussed earlier in this report reflect accomplishments of activities agencies conduct using HCFAC funding. Officials from HHS, HHS-OIG, and DOJ told us that these indicators can be used to provide insights on program activities or the number of actions a component has been able to accomplish in a specific time frame (e.g., the number of defendants convicted in a fiscal year). However, several HHS and DOJ agency officials told us that they do not consider these indicators to be measures of the performance or the effectiveness of the HCFAC program in reducing health care fraud. The return-oninvestment is an example of an indicator that describes program results but does not measure program effectiveness. We found that the returnon-investment provides information on the accomplishments of HCFAC activities in relationship to the amount of funds appropriated for these activities, but does not provide information on the extent to which the HCFAC program reduces health care fraud.

Additionally, most of the indicators used to track HCFAC activities do not have targets or goals associated with them. Although standard practices for internal controls indicate that ongoing performance monitoring should include comparison of performance indicator data against planned targets, our previous work has recognized that establishing measures and setting specific targets in the law enforcement area can be challenging.[45] Officials from HHS, HHS-OIG, and DOJ told us that they intentionally do not set performance targets for indicators such as the number of health care fraud investigations or prosecutions undertaken because such targets could cause the public to perceive law enforcement as engaging in "bounty hunting" or pursuing arbitrary targets merely to meet particular goals.[46] The officials believe that it is important that agencies carry out law enforcement actions that are based on merit and avoid the appearance that they strive to achieve certain numerical quotas.

Several Factors Make Assessing the Effectiveness of the HCFAC Program Challenging

HHS, HHS-OIG, and DOJ officials, as well as literature we reviewed, indicate that there are several factors that make assessing the effectiveness of the HCFAC program in reducing health care fraud and abuse challenging.

Establishing a Causal Link

It is difficult to establish if the HCFAC program has a direct relationship to changes in the amount of health care fraud and abuse. HHS, HHS-OIG, and DOJ officials told us that HCFAC activities—as well as other efforts by federal agencies and others, including non-government entities—may have helped reduce health care fraud; however, the effect that any of these actions may have had on health care fraud and abuse is difficult to isolate. For example, HHS-OIG officials stated that compliance training and guidance provided by the HHS-OIG to health care organization directors—an activity conducted with HCFAC funding—may have had an effect on health care fraud but that it is difficult to isolate how much of an effect the activity has had. However, according to HHS-OIG officials, a rise in the number of provider compliance programs established by hospital organizations in response to shareholder interest in improving compliance with federal and state health care program requirements may also contribute to reductions in health care fraud. Moreover, many efforts within CMS aim to reduce health care fraud and abuse, in addition to those identified as HCFAC activities, and it is difficult to know which CMS program or activity has had an effect on the incidence of fraud. For example, CMS has implemented a number of initiatives to prevent health care fraud and abuse that are not funded with HCFAC funds. One such effort is a change to the provider enrollment process, which is designed to better ensure that only legitimate providers and suppliers are allowed to bill Medicare. However, it is difficult to isolate the effect that either HCFAC activities or broader CMS efforts may have had in reducing health care fraud and abuse.

Measuring Deterrence

Another factor that limits understanding of the effectiveness of the HCFAC program in reducing health care fraud and abuse is the difficulty in quantifying the HCFAC program's effect in deterring health care fraud and abuse. DOJ officials provided anecdotal evidence that HCFAC activities help to deter would-be offenders. For example, a Justice Management Division official asserted that DOJ prosecutions that result in doctors being sentenced to prison for health care fraud and abuse deter other doctors who are contemplating committing fraud. Other DOJ officials reported that cooperating witnesses in health care fraud investigations have told officials of instances where a provider committing potentially fraudulent acts had ceased operations because of the pressure brought on by Strike Force prosecutions. DOJ officials stated that they could recall about a dozen examples of specific individuals who have said they were deterred from committing fraud or ceased a fraudulent operation because they saw another individual get caught. However, these examples are anecdotal and DOJ and HHS-OIG officials stated that it is difficult to know how much health care fraud is deterred as a result of HCFAC activities.

limited Research

Research on the effectiveness of health care fraud and abuse interventions, and on ways to measure the effectiveness of health care fraud and abuse interventions has been limited. We found that none of the 49 articles we selected to review for this study evaluated the effectiveness of the HCFAC program specifically, and few studies examined the effectiveness of health care fraud and abuse interventions in general. A recent review of literature conducted by experts in the field found similar results.[47]

Establishing a Health Care Fraud Baseline

Another challenge that limits the ability to determine whether HCFAC activities are effective in reducing health care fraud and abuse is the lack of a baseline for the amount of health care fraud that exists at any point in time. Having such a baseline could provide information on the amount of health care fraud and how much it has changed in a given year or over time. We have previously reported that there currently is no reliable baseline estimate of the amount of health care fraud in the United States.[48] Several experts told us or have written about the importance of establishing a baseline in assessing the effectiveness of law enforcement programs. A baseline estimate could provide an understanding of the extent of fraud and, with additional information on program activities, could help to inform decision-making related to allocation of resources to combat health care fraud.

HHS and CMS have taken steps to try to establish a health care fraud baseline because, according to the fiscal year 2012 HCFAC report, they appreciate that a baseline would allow the agencies to evaluate the success of fraud prevention activities. HHS officials stated that the Assistant Secretary for Planning and Evaluation initiated work to establish a baseline measurement, and that work was subsequently transferred to CMS's Center for Program Integrity.

According to the fiscal year 2012 HCFAC report, the project is designed to measure probable fraud in home health care agencies and will pilot test a measurement approach and calculate an estimate of probable fraud for specific home health care services. CMS and its contractor will collect information from home health care agencies, the referring physicians, and Medicare beneficiaries selected in a national random sample of home health care claims. The pilot will rely on the information collected along with a summary of the service history of the home health care agency, the referring provider, and the beneficiary to estimate the percentage of total payments that are associated with probable fraud, and the percentage of all claims that are associated with probable fraud for Medicare fee-for-service home health care. CMS reports that after completion of the pilot, it will determine whether the measurement approach should be expanded to other areas of health care. Officials from the Center for Program Integrity stated that as of May 2013, they were beginning the data collection phase of the fraud baseline measurement pilot, which they expect will last two years.

Some HCFAC-funded agencies have attempted to determine the effect of HCFAC activities on specific types of fraud in certain locations. DOJ officials provided examples of reductions in billings for certain services in specific locations and told us that they believe these reductions are associated with the work of the Strike Force teams. For example, DOJ officials reported assessing the amount of home health care billings in certain Strike Force cities before the Strike Force began operations and then again after the Strike Force had begun operations.[49]

Since the amount of home health care billing was measured before and after the Strike Force was implemented, HHS, HHS-OIG, and DOJ officials are able to estimate some effect that the Strike Force team had on the amount of billing in that area. For example, in a May 14, 2013 press conference, the Attorney General noted that after the Detroit Strike Force began investigating cases of potential group-psychotherapy fraud, claims for this type of treatment in Detroit dropped by more than 70 percent since January 2011.[50]

Concluding Observations

Making progress in preventing and reducing health care fraud and abuse is an essential yet challenging task. HHS and DOJ use a number of indicators to assess the activities they conduct to reduce health care fraud and abuse. However, the indicators do not provide information about the effectiveness of the program, and little is known about whether and how well the HCFAC program reduces health care fraud. While positive results on the program's return-on-investment can be seen as an indication of program success, the return-on-investment does not indicate the extent to which the program is reducing fraud. For example, the increasing returns from the fraud that is being investigated and prosecuted may indicate that HCFAC programming is effective in detecting or deterring potentially fraudulent schemes or indicate that there is simply an increase in potentially fraudulent activity. CMS's recent efforts to establish a home health care fraud baseline is a good first step to understanding the extent of the problem and, if implemented as planned, could provide policymakers with information on how much fraud exists and in coming years, how potentially fraudulent activity has increased or decreased over time. However, CMS has not yet determined whether the methodology used to establish a baseline of probable fraud in home health care could be used to assess the amount of fraud in other health care services. Additionally, even with a baseline estimate of the total amount of probable fraud, there will likely be continuing challenges in understanding the effectiveness of the HCFAC program, such as isolating the program's ability to reduce or prevent fraud and abuse. Despite these inherent challenges, if a health care fraud baseline is established more broadly, it may become feasible to study how individual HCFAC activities, and possibly the program as a whole, affects changes in health care fraud. Results from these studies could provide HHS and DOJ with additional information regarding which activities are the most effective in reducing health care fraud and abuse, and could potentially inform agency decisions about how best to allocate limited resources.

Agency Comments

GAO provided a draft of the report to HHS and DOJ. In its written comments, HHS discussed its program integrity efforts to reduce fraud, waste, and abuse. HHS also provided examples of CMS's efforts to reduce fraud, waste, and abuse in Medicare. The examples provided were not included in our review because they were not included in the funding used to calculate the return-on-investment for the HCFAC program. While not commenting specifically on our report, DOJ sent us examples of reductions in Medicare billings for specific services (such as durable medical equipment, home health services, and community mental health center services) in certain Strike Force cities. In their comments, DOJ officials stated that based on their examples, the Strike Force efforts have had a lasting effect on savings to Medicare payments. In addition, HHS and DOJ provided technical comments, which we have incorporated as appropriate.

Kathleen M. King
Director, Health Care

Eileen R. Larence
Director, Homeland Security and Justice

Appendix I: Health Care Fraud and Abuse Control (HCFAC) Program Activities Conducted by Agencies in Fiscal Year 2012

The activities listed in table 2 below represent only activities that are supported with HCFAC funds (as reported in agency documents or interviews with agency officials). The table does not include other activities conducted by the agencies that are not related to health care fraud and abuse control.

Table 2. Agencies, Components, and Health Care Fraud and Abuse Control (HCFAC) Program Activities

Agency	Components	HCFAC Activities
Department of Health and Human Services (HHS)	Office of General Counsel (OGC)	Supports program integrity work of its clients (such as the Centers for Medicare & Medicaid Services) through a variety of activities. Among other activities, OGC works to recover payments by Medicare that are the primary responsibility of other payers under the Medicare Secondary Payer provisions, which preclude Medicare payment for services and items that certain other health insurance or coverage is primarily responsible for paying; to protect Medicare funds when providers seek bankruptcy protections; and to defend CMS and its contractors in cases seeking damages for the alleged wrongful denial of claims and other actions. In addition, OGC assists CMS in implementing provisions of the Patient Protection and Affordable Care Act; and provides legal advice to CMS regarding the development and imposition of Civil Monetary Penalties and defends CMS in administrative appeals and judicial litigation resulting fromthese cases. OGC also participates in the Health Care Fraud Prevention and Enforcement Action Team (HEAT) initiative; and assists the Department of Justice (DOJ)with cases filed under the False Claims Act.
	Administration for Community Living (ACL)	Provides infrastructure, technical assistance, and program support for the Senior Medicare Patrol (SMP) programs. Additionally, in fiscal year 2012, ACL used HCFAC funding to expand SMP programs and funded two technical assistance grantees.

Agency	Components	HCFAC Activities
	Centers for Medicare & Medicaid Services (CMS)	Supports, among many other program integrity activities, the Medicaid and Children's Health Insurance Program (CHIP) financial oversight project, which conducts a variety of financial oversight activities, including monitoring of Medicaid expenditures and financial management reviews of Medicaid. Project activities include reviews of proposed Medicaid state plan methodologies and associated financing sources, to ensure their compliance with federal requirements. Additionally, CMS conducts a pilot project designed to use predictive modeling and data analytics to detect fraud and abuse in community mental health centers in Florida, Texas, and Louisiana. The pilot is related to funding received by community mental health centers for partial hospitalization services, where CMS has seen high levels of fraud and abuse and will identify high risk providers, conduct targeted site visits, and apply appropriate corrective actions, such as revocations, suspensions, and referrals to law enforcement. Finally, CMS uses some of its HCFAC appropriations for its contributions to the Strike Force teams—which are comprised of staff from federal, state, and local investigation agencies, designed to combat Medicare fraud by using technology, such as data analysis techniques—located in nine cities nationwide.
	Food and Drug Administration (FDA)	Conducts Pharmaceutical Fraud Program to detect, investigate, prosecute, and prevent pharmaceutical, biologic, and medical device fraud.
Department of Health and Human Services' Office of Inspector General (HHS-OIG)	Office of Audit Services (OAS)	Conducts independent audits of HHS programs, grantees, and contractors. These audits review CMS operations and external entities that play a role in providing Medicare and Medicaid services, including Medicare contractors, state Medicaid agencies, and providers of healthcare services. These audits review program performance, identify opportunities for reducing costs, assess compliance with federal laws and HHS regulations, recommend recovery of improper payments, and identify vulnerabilities in systems controls and operations. OAS also responds to health care-related complaints received by the OIG Hotline; reviews proposed regulations and laws relating to Medicare and Medicaid; and responds to congressional requests.
	Office of Evaluation and Inspections (OEI)	Conducts national evaluations to provide HHS, Congress, and the public with information on issues related to preventing fraud, waste, and abuse; and promoting economy, efficiency, and effectiveness of HHS programs. OEI reports also include recommendations for improving HHS program operations.

Table 2. (Continued)

Agency	Components	HCFAC Activities
		OEI issues referrals (both internally and externally) to identify specific entities—such as providers and suppliers—that merit further study or investigation.
	Office of Investigations (OI)	Coordinates and conducts investigations of allegations of fraud, waste, and abuse in HHS programs, including Medicare, Medicaid, and CHIP. OI is also responsible for excluding certain individuals and entities, such as physicians and pharmaceutical or device manufacturers, from participating in federal health care programs for certain types of conduct. OI investigators also play an active role in the Strike Force teams. OI also oversees the operations of the OIG Hotline, which receives complaints of fraud, waste, abuse, and mismanagement related to all HHS programs, and serves as the primary point of contact to report fraud.
	Office of Counsel to the Inspector General (OCIG)	Exercises the authority to impose civil and administrative penalties related to health care fraud, including civil monetary penalties. OCIG also litigates appeals of exclusions, and assists on civil False Claims Act cases and settlements. Additionally, OCIG operates the voluntary disclosure program for providers—a program whereby providers can voluntarily report their fraudulent conduct affecting Medicare, Medicaid, and other federal health care programs; monitors compliance with Corporate Integrity Agreements; and provides industry guidance, such as through advisory opinions, fraud alerts, and public outreach/training. According to OCIG officials, OCIG also provides legal support for HHS-OIG's evaluations and audits and legal clearance on issuance of all HHS-OIG subpoenasand uses of electronic surveillance by OI.
	Office of Management and Policy (OMP)	Provides management, guidance, and resources in support of HHS-OIG's other components, including budget formulation and execution, human capital planning, information technology solutions, and administrative services (such as space management, travel, and policies).
Department of Justice (DOJ)	Criminal Division	Initiates and coordinates health care fraud prosecutions and supports the United States Attorney's Offices (USAO) with legal and investigative guidance and training and attorneys to prosecute violations of criminal health care fraud. DOJ's Criminal Division plays an active role in the Strike Force teams, as well as provides legal guidance, such as through annual health care fraud training conferences and review of qui tam, or whistleblower,

Agency	Components	HCFAC Activities
		lawsuits under the False Claims Act to assess whether the defendants in such lawsuits have engaged in criminal activity. DOJ's Criminal Division also supports investigations and prosecutions of fraud and abuse targeting private sector health plans sponsored by employers and/or unions, as well as investigations and prosecutions of health care frauds perpetrated by domestic and international organized crime groups.
	Civil Division	Investigates and resolves matters against a wide array of health care providers and suppliers, often in response to qui tam, or whistleblower, lawsuits filed under the False Claims Act. For example, the Civil Division represents the U.S. government in civil matters, such as cases alleging that a pharmaceutical manufacturer has illegally marketed a prescription drug for an unapproved use and cases alleging that a provider improperly billed Medicare. The Elder Justice and Nursing Home Initiative, within the CivilDivision, coordinates and supports law enforcement efforts to combat elder abuse, neglect, and financial exploitation, by hosting quarterly conference calls with DOJ attorneys to discuss issues or developments in connection with nursing home or failure ofcare cases. DOJ's Civil Division also has the authority to bring criminal charges against pharmaceutical and medical device manufacturers under the Federal Food, Drug, and Cosmetic Act.
	Civil Rights Division	Investigates cases of abuse and grossly substandard care in Medicare and Medicaid-funded long-term care facilities. The Civil Rights Division is the DOJ component responsible for enforcement of the Civil Rights of Institutionalized Persons Act, which authorizes investigation of conditions of confinement at state and local residential institutions (including facilities for persons with developmental disabilities or mental illness, and nursing homes) and initiates civil actions to remedy practices in violation of an individual's rights. The Civil Rights Division also has primary enforcement authority for the Americans with Disabilities Act and investigates allegations of discrimination by publicentities against individuals with disabilities, including discrimination in the form of needless institutionalization of persons who require health care services.
	U.S. Attorney's Offices	Prosecute both civil and criminal health care fraud cases in their districts—94 USAOs throughout the country—that involve a wide variety of health care fraud matters, includingfalse billings by providers; kickbacks to induce referrals of Medicare or Medicaid patients; and failure of care allegations against nursing homes.

Table 2. (Continued)

Agency	Components	HCFAC Activities
		The USAOs often partner with the Criminal and Civil divisions to prosecute health care fraud cases. The USAOs and support personnel in the nine cities where Strike Force teams are located participate in those teams.
	Federal Bureau of Investigation (FBI)	Serves as the primary investigative agency of health care fraud, with jurisdiction to investigate fraud under both federal health care programs and private health insurance plans. The FBI investigates health care fraud through coordinated initiatives with federal, state, and local agencies. Additionally, the FBI participates in task forces and undercover operations to pursue investigations for health care fraud and participates in the Strike Force teams. The FBI also provides training and guidance on health care investigative matters—such as innovative methods of employing advanced investigative techniques—to health care investigators and analysts.

Source: Information from fiscal year 2012 annual HCFAC report, in agency reports, on agency websites, and from interviews with agency officials.

Appendix II: Health Care Fraud and Abuse Control (HCFAC) Program Obligations for Fiscal Years 2008 through 2012

Table 3 summarizes the HCFAC obligations for the Department of Health and Human Services (HHS), including the HHS Office of Inspector General, and Department of Justice components for fiscal years 2008 through 2012 by type of appropriations. An obligation is a definite commitment that creates a legal liability of the government for payment of goods and services ordered or received. The table includes obligations of mandatory HCFAC appropriations, discretionary HCFAC appropriations, and other appropriations used to support HCFAC activities. Mandatory HCFAC appropriations refer to the HCFAC budgetary resources controlled by a law, principally the Health Insurance Portability and Accountability Act of 1996, rather than appropriations acts. Discretionary HCFAC appropriations refer to budgetary resources provided in annual appropriation acts, other than those that fund mandatory programs. Congress appropriated mandatory funding for HCFAC activities beginning in fiscal year 1997, and appropriated discretionary funding for HCFAC activities beginning in fiscal year 2009. Other appropriations include funding from other appropriations not specific to the HCFAC program that the agencies used, in addition to the HCFAC funds, to carry out activities related to health care fraud and abuse. In addition, the table shows the percentage of HCFAC obligations for personnel services and contracted services and supplies.

Table 3. Obligations For Health Care Fraud and Abuse Control (HCFAC) Program Activities, Fiscal Years 2008-2012, By Agency and Component and Type of Appropriations

	Fiscal Year 2008	Fiscal Year 2009	Fiscal Year 2010	Fiscal Year 2011	Fiscal Year 2012
Department of Health and Human Services (HHS)[a]					
Administration for Community Living					
Obligations of Mandatory HCFAC Appropriations	$2,972,070	$3,180,221	$3,364,520	$3,702,737	$10,631,727
Obligations of Discretionary HCFAC Appropriations	N/A	$0	$0	$0	$0
Obligations of Other Appropriations	$0	$0	$0	$0	$0
Total HCFAC Obligations	$2,972,070	$3,180,221	$3,364,520	$3,702,737	$10,631,727
Percentage for Personnel	30%	29%	27%	24%	11%
Percentage for Contracted Services/Supplies	15%	22%	39%	27%	10%
Centers for Medicare & Medicaid Services					
Obligations of Mandatory HCFAC Appropriations	b	b	b	b	$14,530,000
Obligations of Discretionary HCFAC Appropriations	N/A	b	b	b	$350,656
Obligations of Other Appropriations	b	b	b	b	$0
Total HCFAC Obligations	b	b	b	b	$14,880,656
Percentage for Personnel	b	b	b	b	73%
Percentage for Contracted Services/Supplies	b	b	b	b	16%
Food and Drug Administration					
Obligations of Mandatory HCFAC Appropriations	$0	$0	$699,691	$1,988,451	$2,768,273
Obligations of Discretionary HCFAC Appropriations	N/A	$0	$0	$0	$0
Obligations of Other Appropriations	$0	$0	$0	$0	$0
Total HCFAC Obligations	$0	$0	$699,691	$1,988,451	$2,768,273
Percentage for Personnel	—	—	88%	100%	63%
Percentage for Contracted Services/Supplies	—	—	1%	0%	35%
Office of General Counsel					
Obligations of Mandatory HCFAC Appropriations	$5,745,975	$5,712,705	$8,711,228	$8,873,169	$8,854,695
Obligations of Discretionary HCFAC Appropriations	N/A	$0	$0	$0	$0
Obligations of Other Appropriations[c]	$8,080,155	$9,113,745	$6,553,380	$6,680,831	$7,295,487
Total HCFAC Obligations	$13,826,130	$14,826,450	$15,264,608	$15,554,000	$16,150,182
Percentage for Personnel	74%	85%	86%	84%	84%
Percentage for Contracted Services/Supplies	26%	15%	14%	14%	16%

Table 3. (Continued)

	Fiscal Year 2008	Fiscal Year 2009	Fiscal Year 2010	Fiscal Year 2011	Fiscal Year 2012
Department of Health and Human Services' Office of Inspector General (HHS-OIG)[d]					
Office of Audit Services					
Obligations of Mandatory HCFAC Appropriations	$53,638,586	$45,534,873	$55,134,402	$52,261,218	$65,804,004
Obligations of Discretionary HCFAC Appropriations	N/A	$14,314,348	$34,004	$0	$0
Obligations of Other Appropriations	$9,866,186	$6,904,396	$16,859,544	$24,863,597	$4,671,102
Total HCFAC Obligations	$63,504,772	$66,753,617	$72,027,950	$77,124,815	$70,475,106
Percentage for Personnel	91%	90%	91%	91%	92%
Percentage for Contracted Services/Supplies	9%	10%	9%	9%	8%
Office of Evaluation and Inspections					
Obligations of Mandatory HCFAC Appropriations	$11,373,838	$10,344,700	$14,919,144	$15,860,518	$15,410,246
Obligations of Discretionary HCFAC Appropriations	N/A	$0	$0	$0	$0
Obligations of Other Appropriations	$3,136,893	$5,365,036	$1,821,373	$1,297,694	$1,196,973
Total HCFAC Obligations	$14,510,732	$15,709,735	$16,740,517	$17,158,212	$16,607,219
Percentage for Personnel	88%	87%	90%	90%	92%
Percentage for Contracted Services/Supplies	11%	13%	10%	10%	8%
Office of Investigations					
Obligations of Mandatory HCFAC Appropriations	$59,181,222	$68,339,359	$71,854,447	$70,876,633	$88,675,409
Obligations of Discretionary HCFAC Appropriations	N/A	$4,600,019	$0	$19,103,354	$0
Obligations of Other Appropriations	$10,345,534	$5,038,277	$8,242,560	$6,961,168	$6,343,658
Total HCFAC Obligations	$69,526,755	$77,977,656	$80,097,007	$96,941,156	$95,019,067
Percentage for Personnel	89%	87%	84%	82%	87%
Percentage for Contracted Services/Supplies	10%	10%	12%	14%	11%
Office of Counsel to the Inspector General					
Obligations of Mandatory HCFAC Appropriations	$7,363,903	$9,342,140	$8,699,671	$9,879,173	$9,822,896
Obligations of Discretionary HCFAC Appropriations	N/A	$0	$0	$0	$0
Obligations of Other Appropriations	$1,023,655	$511,664	$1,008,637	$741,009	$702,226
Total HCFAC Obligations	$8,387,557	$9,853,804	$9,708,308	$10,620,183	$10,525,122
Percentage for Personnel	96%	96%	95%	94%	97%
Percentage for Contracted Services/Supplies	4%	4%	5%	6%	3%

	Fiscal Year 2008	Fiscal Year 2009	Fiscal Year 2010	Fiscal Year 2011	Fiscal Year 2012
Office of Management and Policy					
Obligations of Mandatory HCFAC Appropriations	$44,335,892	$43,945,152	$37,639,506	$46,779,355	$36,421,764
Obligations of Discretionary HCFAC Appropriations	N/A	$29,927	$18,393,657	$17,113,762	$23,817,566
Obligations of Other Appropriations	$6,493,865	$13,754,488	$6,318,229	$4,782,107	$5,958,176
Total HCFAC Obligations	$50,829,757	$57,729,567	$62,351,393	$68,675,224	$66,197,506
Percentage for Personnel	21%	20%	20%	22%	25%
Percentage for Contracted Services/Supplies	71%	67%	60%	68%	70%
Department of Justice (DOJ)					
Civil Division					
Obligations of Mandatory HCFAC Appropriations	$15,396,015	$16,041,913	$19,874,046	$19,735,915	$22,977,000
Obligations of Discretionary HCFAC Appropriations	N/A	$8,236,767	$2,783,651	$6,405,988	$4,991,000
Obligations of Other Appropriations	$1,636,524	$4,059,000	$2,246,099	$10,211,184	$1,948,000
Total HCFAC Obligations	$17,032,539	$28,337,680	$24,903,796	$36,353,087	$29,916,000
Percentage for Personnel	56%	39%	47%	40%	47%
Percentage for Contracted Services/Supplies	44%	61%	52%	60%	53%
Civil Rights Division					
Obligations of Mandatory HCFAC Appropriations	$2,375,999	$2,476,000	$2,376,000	$3,432,688	$3,823,868
Obligations of Discretionary HCFAC Appropriations	N/A	$0	$1,769,255	$1,942,057	$892,606
Obligations of Other Appropriations	$629,995	$1,016,944	$373,283	$468,911	$453,209
Total HCFAC Obligations	$3,005,995	$3,492,944	$4,518,538	$5,843,656	$5,169,683
Percentage for Personnel	59%	70%	67%	67%	68%
Percentage for Contracted Services/Supplies	41%	30%	32%	32%	32%
Criminal Division					
Obligations of Mandatory HCFAC Appropriations	$3,080,000	$948,746	$1,541,998	$1,482,273	$1,212,507
Obligations of Discretionary HCFAC Appropriations	N/A	$2,881,619	$3,389,957	$5,286,118	$8,083,863
Obligations of Other Appropriations[e]	$0	$0	$0	$0	$0
Total HCFAC Obligations	$3,080,000	$3,830,365	$4,931,955	$6,768,390	$9,296,370
Percentage for Personnel	50%	47%	56%	65%	52%
Percentage for Contracted Services/Supplies	33%	28%	38%	35%	47%
Federal Bureau of Investigation					
Obligations of Mandatory HCFAC Appropriations	$118,085,122	$126,953,586	$129,171,234	$125,166,278	$134,381,774
Obligations of Discretionary HCFAC Appropriations	N/A	$0	$0	$5,902,130	$3,806,330

Table 3. (Continued)

	Fiscal Year 2008	Fiscal Year 2009	Fiscal Year 2010	Fiscal Year 2011	Fiscal Year 2012
Obligations of Other Appropriations	$0	$0	$0	$3,570,676	$7,473,799
Total HCFAC Obligations	$118,085,122	$126,953,586	$129,171,234	$134,639,084	$145,661,903
Percentage for Personnel	78%	78%	80%	82%	81%
Percentage for Contracted Services/Supplies	22%	20%	18%	16%	17%
Justice Management Division [f]					
Obligations of Mandatory HCFAC Appropriations	$0	$0	$157,621	$5,416,098	$4,951,367
Obligations of Discretionary HCFAC Appropriations	N/A	$0	$0	$7,266,1530	$10,799,404
Obligations of Other Appropriations	$0	$0	$0	$0	$0
Total HCFAC Obligations	$0	$0	$157,621	$12,682,251	$15,750,771
Percentage for Personnel	—	—	100%	3.3%	3.75%
Percentage for Contracted Services/Supplies	—	—	0%	0%	0.46%
U.S. Attorney's Offices					
Obligations of Mandatory HCFAC Appropriations	$31,421,769	$33,255,655	$32,893,926	$29,723,423	$32,659,037
Obligations of Discretionary HCFAC Appropriations	N/A	$9,023,000	$6,227,568	$15,338,747	$10,760,057
Obligations of Other Appropriations	$26,061,218	$35,035,966	$31,652,106	$31,896,207	$31,122,465
Total HCFAC Obligations	$57,482,987	$77,314,620	$70,773,600	$76,958,377	$74,541,560
Percentage for Personnel	84%	78%	83%	83%	84%
Percentage for Contracted Services/Supplies	15%	20%	16%	17%	16%

Legend: N/A=Not Applicable; $0 means no funds obligated in that fiscal year for the type of appropriation; and "—" means no percentage in that fiscal year for the type of appropriation.

Source: GAO analysis of HCFAC obligations reported to GAO by HHS, HHS-OIG, and DOJ.

Notes:

[a]Two HHS components, the Office of the Assistant Secretary for Planning and Evaluation (ASPE) and the Office of the Assistant Secretary for Public Affairs (ASPA), had HCFAC obligations for fiscal year 2011 only—$45,000 for ASPE and $690,894 for ASPA. These amounts are not reflected in the table.

[b]We chose to report on the activities that CMS conducted in fiscal year 2012 because those activities were included in that year's HCFAC return-on-investment calculation. In total for fiscal year 2012, CMS reported about $14.9 million in HCFAC appropriations, about $1.6 million of which was allocated in fiscal year 2012 but not obligated, which CMS reserved to fund HCFAC activities in future years. We did not request fiscal years 2008 through 2011 HCFAC obligations from CMS because the agency conducted activities other than those that were funded with HHS's mandatory HCFAC appropriations in fiscal year 2012. For example, in fiscal year 2010, CMS used its HCFAC mandatory appropriations for the One Program Integrity database, a centralized web-based portal that enables users, such as law enforcement, to access claims, provider, and beneficiary data from a centralized source.

[c]HHS's OGC reported estimated obligations of other appropriations, which included reimbursements for attorney services provided to OGC clients within HHS, that supported HCFAC activities.

[d]HHS-OIG's reported obligations also include any obligations of funds the agency received as reimbursement for the costs of conducting investigations and audits and other activities when such costs are ordered by a court, voluntarily agreed to by the payor, or otherwise authorized under 42 U.S.C. §1320a-7c(b).

[e]DOJ's Criminal Division stated that it uses some other appropriations for health care fraud activities. However, officials indicated that the division infrequently funds HCFAC activities with other appropriations and, as a result, the division does not track the amount of other appropriations used specifically for the HCFAC program.

[f] For fiscal years 2011 and 2012, DOJ reported amounts in HCFAC mandatory and discretionary appropriations that the department reserved for future use to fund HCFAC activities. In fiscal year 2011, DOJ reported about $5.2 million in mandatory HCFAC appropriations and about $7.3 million in discretionary HCFAC appropriations; in fiscal year 2012, DOJ reported about $4.7 million in mandatory HCFAC appropriations and about $10.8 million in discretionary appropriations. These funds were allocated to the Justice Management Division, but were not obligated. We have included these HCFAC funds under the Justice Management Division, in addition to the $180,494 (in fiscal year 2011) and $208,676 (in fiscal year 2012) in mandatory HCFAC obligations the division reported.

Table 4 summarizes HCFAC obligations for Strike Force teams for fiscal years 2008 through 2012 by the geographic location of the Strike Force teams. Strike Force teams consist of investigators and prosecutors who use data analysis techniques to identify, investigate, and prosecute potentially fraudulent activities in geographic areas with high rates of fraud.

Table 4. Total Health Care Fraud and Abuse Control (HCFAC) Program Obligations by Strike Force Location and Fiscal Year, 2008 through 2012

			Fiscal Year		
Strike Force Location & Fiscal Year Launched	**2008**	**2009**	**2010**	**2011**	**2012**
Miami, FL Launched FY 2007	$5,335,321	$7,504,704	$8,344,504	$10,020,003	$12,962,899
Detroit, MI Launched FY 2009	$524,578[a]	$2,687,385	$3,963,202	$4,930,594	$5,098,524
Dallas, TX Launched FY 2011	$6,838 a	$28,247	$40,070[a]	$3,696,685	$5,027,790
Los Angeles, CA Launched FY 2008	$4,197,914	$4,488,269	$4,861,523	$6,487,639	$4,815,963
Brooklyn, NY Launched FY 2010	$43,782[a]	$308,666[a]	$4,785,975	$4,915,032	$4,392,851
Baton Rouge, LA Launched FY 2010	$71,757[a]	$253,915[a]	$1,806,066	$3,422,416	$3,438,367
Chicago, IL Launched in FY 2011	$39,334[a]	$145,841[a]	$434,390[a]	$2,954,041	$3,380,209
Houston, TX Launched in FY 2009	—	$2,611,054	$2,801,064	$3,038,569	$2,566,108
Tampa, FL Launched FY 2010	$251,702[a]	$566,604[a]	$1,450,824	$2,613,618	$2,549,202

Table 4. (Continued)

			Fiscal Year		
Strike Force Location & Fiscal Year Launched	**2008**	**2009**	**2010**	**2011**	**2012**
Headquarters Support of Strike Forces	—	—	$1,618,348	$5,985,725	$3,051,813
Total HCFAC Obligations	**$10,471,226**	**$18,594,685**	**$30,105,966**	**$48,064,322**	**$47,283,726**

Source: GAO analysis of HCFAC obligations reported to GAO by the Department of Health and Human Services' Office of Inspector General's (HHS-OIG) Office of Investigations and the Department of Justice's Criminal Division, the U.S. Attorneys' Offices, and the Federal Bureau of Investigation for fiscal years 2008 through 2012.

Notes: CMS also obligated $350,656 of its discretionary HCFAC appropriations for headquarters' support of the Strike Force teams. However, these obligations were not associated with any one of the nine Strike Force cities and the this amount is not reflected in the table above.

[a]HHS-OIG reported obligations for the Strike Forces in these cities prior to their official launch, because HHS-OIG investigators worked to gather evidence on cases in those cities.

APPENDIX III: INDICATORS USED BY AGENCIES TO ASSESS HEALTH CARE FRAUD AND ABUSE CONTROL (HCFAC) PROGRAM ACTIVITIES

Table 5. Collective Indicators Reported in the Annual Health Care Fraud and Abuse Control (HCFAC) Program Report, and Outcomes/Outputs for Associated Indicator, for Fiscal Year 2012

	Indicators reported in HCFAC report by agencies to assess activities	**Outcomes/outputs of indicators for Fiscal Year 2012**
Collective indicators, in which multiple agencies contribute (including Department of Health and Human Services' Office of Inspector General (HHS-OIG) and Department of Justice (DOJ))	Amount won or negotiated through health care fraud judgments and settlements	Over $3.0 billion in judgments and settlements
	Amount deposited with the Department of Treasury and the Center for Medicare &Medicaid Services, transferred to other Federal agencies, or paid to private persons (result of fiscal year's HCFAC efforts as well as efforts from previous fiscal years)	Approximately $4.2 billion deposited

	Indicators reported in HCFAC report by agencies to assess activities	Outcomes/outputs of indicators for Fiscal Year 2012
	Number of new criminal health care fraud investigations opened	1,131 new criminal investigations involving 2,148 potential defendants
	Number of cases where criminal charges were filed	452 cases involving 892 defendants
	Number of defendants convicted of health care fraud-related crimes	826 defendants convicted
	Number of new civil health care fraud investigations opened	885 new civil investigations opened
	Number of individuals and entities excluded from participation in federal health care programs by HHS-OIG	3,131 individuals and entities excluded
	Return-on-investment	$7.90 returned for every $1.00 expended for fiscal years 2010-2012
Indicators related to the Strike Force Teams located in 9 cities nationwide	Number of indictments, informations (an accusation of a criminal offense made by a public officer rather than a grand jury), and complaints involving charges filed against number of defendants	117 indictments, informations, and complaints filed against 278 defendants
	Amount of alleged billing to Medicare from defendants	Over $1.5 billion in alleged collective billings to Medicare
	Number of defendants that pled guilty	251 guilty pleas negotiated
	Number of defendants convicted in jury trials	Guilty verdicts obtained for 29 defendantsin 13 jury trials
	Number of individuals that were sentenced to imprisonment and amount of average term	201 defendants sentenced with average prison term of 48 months

Legend:

I indicates that measure is included in Fiscal Year 2012 annual HCFAC report

indicates that measure is included in Department of Health and Human Services' Office of Inspector General (HHS-OIG) July 2013 report on Senior Medicare Patrol programs.

Source: Agency reports, including fiscal year 2012 annual HCFAC report, and interviews with HHS officials.

[a]Unless otherwise noted, the information on outcomes/output for each measure is for fiscal year 2012.

[b]For the outcomes and outputs for indicators associated with ACL's Senior Medicare Patrol program, we used the most currently available data, which was calendar year 2012 data obtained from the July 2013 HHS-OIG report on the Senior Medicare Patrol program. The outcomes and output for these indicators is also included in the fiscal year 2012 HCFAC report; however, the outcomes and output is calendar year 2011 data.

[c]In HHS-OIG's July 2013 report on Senior Medicare Patrol program, this indicator for Medicare and Medicaid funds recovered attributable to the programs was expanded to account for both expected and actual funds recovered. However, in the fiscal year 2012 report, the indicator included only actual funds recovered.

Table 6. Indicators That Are Used by the HHS Components to Assess Health Care Fraud and Abuse Control Program Activities, Source of Indicators, and Outcomes/Outputs for Associated Indicator, for Fiscal Year 2012

		Source of indicator		
HHS Component	**Indicators used by agencies to assess activities**	**FY 2012 HCFAC report**	**Other**	**Outcomes/outputs of indicator for Fiscal Year 2012**[a]
Administration for Community Living (ACL) – Senior Medicare Patrol programs[b]	Total number of active volunteers, number of volunteer training hours, and number of volunteer work hours	√	■	5,137 active volunteers, 39,257 training hours, and 120,953 work hours in calendar year 2012
	Number of media airings	√	■	188,199 media airings in calendar year 2012
	Number of community outreach education events conducted and estimated number of people reached by events	√	■	10,032 education events in which 996,040 people were reached in calendar year 2012
	Number of group education sessions for beneficiaries and number of beneficiaries who attended	√	■	14,748 sessions attended by 449,509 beneficiaries in calendaryear 2012
	Number of one-on-one counseling sessions held with or on behalf of a beneficiary	√	■	113,457 sessions in calendar year 2012
	Total number of simple inquiries received and number of simple inquiries resolved	√	■	84,061 inquiries received and 83,856 inquiries resolved in calendar year 2012
	Number of inquiries involving complex issues received and number of complex issue inquiries referred for further action	√	■	2,270 inquiries received and 908 inquiries referred for further action in calendar year 2012
	Total dollar amount referred for further action	√	■	$27,529,968 in calendar year 2012
	Number of complex issues resolved and number of complex issues pending further action	√	■	1,748 issues resolved and 2,585 issues pending in calendaryear 2012
	Cost avoidance on behalf of Medicare, Medicaid, beneficiaries, or others Additionally, expected recoveries or savings, including: • Expected Medicare funds recovered attributable to the projects,	√[c]	■	In calendar year 2012: • $113,692 in cost avoidance Additionally: • $5,957,910 in expected Medicare funds

		Source of indicator		
HHS Component	**Indicators used by agencies to assess activities**	**FY 2012 HCFAC report**	**Other**	**Outcomes/outputs of indicator for Fiscal Year 2012[a]**
	• Expected Medicaid funds recovered attributable to the projects, • Savings to beneficiaries attributable to the projects, • Other savings attributable to the projects (e.g., Supplemental Insurance), and • Total savings attributable to the projects (which is the sum of expected Medicare funds, expected Medicaid funds, savings to beneficiaries, and other savings attributable to the projects)			• $102,000 in expected Medicaid funds • 130,796 in savings to beneficiaries • $3,175 in other savings • $6,193,881 in total savings
Centers for Medicare & Medicaid Services (CMS)	Estimated amount of the federal share of Medicaid funds that were removed as a result of CMS's financial oversight of Medicaid and Children's Health Insurance Program (CHIP), including approximate amount recovered and approximate amount resolved	√[c]		Estimated $895 million removed, including $451 million recovered and $444 million resolved
	Estimated amount of the federal share of Medicaid funds (in questionable reimbursement) that were averted due to preventive work with states from Medicaid and CHIP financial management project	√[c]		Estimated $128 million averted
	For the community mental health centers project, which uses data analytics to identify fraud in community mental health centers in 3 states			CMS officials indicated that because the project has recently started, CMS does not yet have indicators to assess it. CMS officials reported that they may consider using indicators similar to those used to assess the Fraud Prevention System, such as cost avoided as a result of the project.

Table 6. (Continued)

		Source of indicator		
HHS Component	**Indicators used by agencies to assess activities**	**FY 2012 HCFAC report**	**Other**	**Outcomes/outputs of indicator for Fiscal Year 2012[a]**
Food and Drug Administration (FDA) – Pharmaceutical Fraud Program	Number of criminal investigations opened since the inception of the Pharmaceutical Fraud Program	√[c]		42 criminal investigations
	Number of criminal investigations opened during fiscal year, including a description of the types of cases opened	√[c]		17 criminal investigations
	Type of judicial actions related to the investigations (such as number of individuals convicted from investigations) and outcomes (including amount of jail time, probation, or amount of restitution)	√[c]		1 investigation resulted in conviction of 2 individuals, who received 12 months probation and were ordered to pay $36,040in restitution
Office of General Counsel (OGC)	Amount of recoveries for the government from: • False Claims Act and related matters in which OGC participated, • Civil Monetary Penalties that OGC established the right to recover, and • Money that OGC petitioned law enforcement agencies to seize as a result of criminal and civil litigation matters.	√[c]		• Over $2.6 billion in recoveries under False Claims Act and related matters; • Over $4.5 million in Civil Monetary Penalties; • About $5.4 million in seizures
	Number of physician self-referral disclosures in which OGC advised CMS on how to resolve	√[c]		Over 100 disclosures
	Amount of money that OGC established the right to recover under the Medicare Secondary Payer provisions and amount involving bankrupt providers that OGC established the right to collect	√[c]		Over $17 million recovered under Medicare Secondary Payer provisions and over $4.9 million collected from bankrupt providers

Legend:

√ indicates that measure is included in Fiscal Year 2012 annual HCFAC report

■ indicates that measure is included in Department of Health and Human Services' Office of Inspector General (HHS-OIG) July 2013 report on Senior Medicare Patrol programs.

Source: Agency reports, including fiscal year 2012 annual HCFAC report, and interviews with HHS officials.

[a] Unless otherwise noted, the information on outcomes/output for each measure is for fiscal year 2012.

[b] For the outcomes and outputs for indicators associated with ACL's Senior Medicare Patrol program, we used the most currently available data, which was calendar year 2012 data obtained from the July 2013 HHS-OIG report on the Senior Medicare Patrol program. The outcomes and output for these indicators is also included in the fiscal year 2012 HCFAC report; however, the outcomes and output is calendar year 2011 data.

[c] In HHS-OIG's July 2013 report on Senior Medicare Patrol program, this indicator for Medicare and Medicaid funds recovered attributable to the programs was expanded to account for both expected and actual funds recovered. However, in the fiscal year 2012 report, the indicator included only actual funds recovered.

Table 7. Indicators That Are Used by the Department of Health and Human Services Office of Inspector General (HHS-OIG) to Assess Health Care Fraud and Abuse Control (HCFAC) Program Activities, Source of Indicators, Associated Target (if any), and Outcomes/Outputs for Associated Indicator, for Fiscal Year 2012

		Source of indicator		
HHS-OIG Component	Indicators used by agencies to assess activities (Associated target, if applicable)	FY 2012 HCFAC report	Other	Outcomes/outputs of indicators for Fiscal Year 2012
Collective indicators in which more than one HHS-OIG component contributes	Number of prosecutions or settlements that resulted from investigations or other inquiries conducted by HHS-OIG	√		1,145 prosecutions or settlements of which 1,047 were health care cases
	Amount of health care savings attributable to statutory changes enacted and administrative actions taken in response to HHS-OIG investigations, audits, and evaluations, including: amount of savings to Medicare and Medicaid	√	■	$8.5 billion in total; $8 billion in Medicare savings and $525 million in savings to the federal share of Medicaid
	Examples of audits and evaluations by topic area	√		Audits and evaluations covering a number of topics, including Medicaid drugs, Medicaid managed care, Medicare physicianservices, community mental health centers, and Medicare Advantage organizations

Table 7. (Continued)

		Source of indicator		
HHS-OIG Component	Indicators used by agencies to assess activities (Associated target, if applicable)	FY 2012 HCFAC report	Other	Outcomes/outputs of indicators for Fiscal Year 2012
	Amount of HHS-OIG Audit Disallowances recovered in Medicare and Medicaid	√		$89,667,376 in Medicare and $275,559,307 in Medicaid recovered audit disallowances
	Amount of expected recoveries, including audit receivables and investigative receivables and non-HHS investigative receivables resulting from work in areas such as states' shares of Medicaid restitution		■	$6.9 billion consisting of $923.8 million in audit receivables and $6 billion in investigative receivables (which includes $1.7 billion in non-HHS investigative receivables resulting from work in areas such as the states' shares of Medicaid restitution)
	Ratio of expected return on investment measuring the efficiency of HHS-OIG's health care oversight efforts (Target: $12.0)		□	$17.9
	Number of quality and management improvement recommendations that HHS program managers accepted		□	190 recommendations
	Number of audit reports with funds to be put to better use		■	19 reports
	Examples of recently completed cases and settlements by specific types		■	Examples cover many types, including medical equipment and supplies, pharmaceutical companies, laboratories, hospitals, and hospice care

		Source of indicator		
HHS-OIG Component	Indicators used by agencies to assess activities (Associated target, if applicable)	FY 2012 HCFAC report	Other	Outcomes/outputs of indicators for Fiscal Year 2012
	Number of sanctions administered in the form of program exclusions or administrative actions		□	1,911 sanctions administered in theform of program exclusions or administrative actions for alleged fraud or abuse or other activities that posed a risk to federal health care programs and their beneficiaries
	Amount of civil monetary penalties and assessments from cases in which OIG was involved		□	$6.7 million
	Amount of HHS receivables from self-disclosure cases in which HHS-OIG was involved		■	$53.3 million in HHS receivables
Office of Audit Services (OAS)	Number of audit starts by program area		□	472 reports started, 337 of which were health care-related
	Number of final reports issued by program area		□	438 reports issued, 303 of which were health care-related
	Questioned cost recommendations (dollar value)		■	$860.6 million
	Funds put to better use recommendations		■	$1,659.2 billion
	Timeliness of draft reports (or final reports if issued without a draft) (Target: 63 percent)		□	72 percent
	Single Audits (A-133 audits) reviewed and transmitted to agencies for resolution		■	3,280 audits, which included 8,276 recommendations
	Audit receivables (disallowed questioned cost recommendations)		■ □	$923.8 million
	Accepted management and quality improvement recommendations		□	83 recommendations, 18 of which were implemented

Table 7. (Continued)

		Source of indicator		
HHS-OIG Component	Indicators used by agencies to assess activities (Associated target, if applicable)	FY 2012 HCFAC report	Other	Outcomes/outputs of indicators for Fiscal Year 2012
Office of Counsel to the Inspector General (OCIG)	Number of compliance roundtable meetings held and number of companies represented	√		2 roundtables held with officials representing 55 companies
	Indicators involving Civil Monetary Penalties (CMP), including dollar value of penalties and assessments for CMPs		□	$20,980,462.53
	Indicators related to Corporate Integrity Agreements (CIA) or other similar agreements, including:			214 agreements monitored
	Number of Corporate Integrity Agreements, Integrity Agreements, or other similar agreements monitored for compliance in fiscal year	√	□	35 agreements
	Number of Corporate Integrity Agreements entered		□	
	Indicators related to advisory opinions, including: Number of advisory opinions issued and number modified, including the number issued since inception of HCFAC program	√	□	19 advisory opinions issued and 2 modifications of advisory opinions in fiscal year 2012; 276 opinions have been issued sinceinception of HCFAC program
	Advisory opinion requests received		□	61 opinions received
Office of Evaluation and Inspections (OEI)	Number of evaluations started (Target: 57 evaluations)		□	83 evaluations
	Number of reports issued		□	59 reports
	Percentage of final reports completed within a year (Target: 55 percent)		□	51 percent

		Source of indicator		
HHS-OIG Component	Indicators used by agencies to assess activities (Associated target, if applicable)	FY 2012 HCFAC report	Other	Outcomes/outputs of indicators for Fiscal Year 2012
Office of Investigations (OI)	Number of individuals and entities excluded from participation in federal health care programs, including by the top reasons for exclusion	√	■	3,131 individuals and entities excluded
	Complaints received (Target: 6,290 complaints)		□	4,827 complaints received
	Cases opened		□	2,369 cases
	Cases closed		□	2,105 cases

Legend:

√ indicates that the indicator is included in Fiscal Year 2012 annual HCFAC report.

■ indicates that the indicator is included in at least one of the two HHS-OIG's Semiannual Report to Congress for fiscal year 2012.

□ indicates that the indicator is included in HHS-OIG's Fiscal Year 2014 Justification of Estimates for Appropriations Committees, which includes outcomes/output of indicators for fiscal year 2012.

Source: Agency reports, including fiscal year 2012 annual HCFAC report, and information from HHS-OIG officials.

Notes: In addition to the indicators listed in the annual HCFAC reports and other HHS-OIG reports, officials indicated that they use additional indicators internally to manage and assess the work they conduct related to identifying and reducing health care fraud and abuse.

Table 8. Indicators That Are Used by the Department of Justice (DOJ) Components to Assess Health Care Fraud and Abuse Control (HCFAC) Program Activities, Source of Indicators, Associated Targets (if any), and Outcomes/Outputs for Associated Indicator, for Fiscal Year 2012

		Source of indicator		
DOJ Component	Indicators used by agencies to assess activities (Associated target, if applicable)	FY 2012 HCFAC report	Other	Outcomes/outputs of indicators for fiscal year 2012[a]
Civil Division	Amount obtained through settlements and judgments	✓		Over $3 billion in settlements and judgments
	Number of new civil health care fraud investigations opened	✓		885 new civil investigations[b]
	Number of civil health care fraud matters pending at the end of the fiscal year	✓		1,023 civil investigations pending[b]
	Number of investigations completed per Department of Justice attorney working on financial fraud and health care fraud cases[c] (Target: 11.92 investigations per attorney)		♦	10.28 investigations per attorney for fiscal year 2012

Table 8. (Continued)

		Source of indicator		
DOJ Component	Indicators used by agencies to assess activities (Associated target, if applicable)	FY 2012 HCFAC report	Other	Outcomes/outputs of indicators for fiscal year 2012[a]
	Percentage of civil cases favorably resolved for litigating divisions[c] (Target: 80 percent of civil cases favorably resolved)		♦	81 percent of civil cases favorably resolved
Civil Rights Division	Number of health care facilities reviewed (regarding conditions and services), including: •Number of health care facilities for persons with intellectual and developmental disabilities and/or mental illness found to violate residents' statutory rights •Number of investigations continued for residential facilities for persons with intellectual and developmental disabilities •Number of investigations continued for residential facilities for persons with mental illness •Number of investigations continued for nursing facilities	✓		•Conditions and practices at 12 state facilities for persons with intellectual and developmental disabilities and/or mental illness were found to violate residents' rights •Investigations of 10 residential facilities for persons with intellectual and developmental disabilities that were continued •Investigations of 3 facilities for persons with mental illness that were continued •Investigations of 2 nursing facilities that were continued
	Number of states where reviewed health care facilities are located	✓		Reviewed conditions and services at 19 health care facilities in 16 states
	Number of formal investigations opened or continued and remedial agreements entered or monitored at facilities	✓		62 health care facilities in 19 states, the District of Columbia, and the Commonwealth of Puerto Rico

		Source of indicator		
DOJ Component	Indicators used by agencies to assess activities (Associated target, if applicable)	FY 2012 HCFAC report	Other	Outcomes/outputs of indicators for fiscal year 2012[a]
	Number of existing remedial agreements monitored, including: •Number of remedial agreements monitored for facilities for persons with intellectual and developmental disabilities •Number of remedial agreements monitored for state-operated residential facilities for persons with mental illness •Number of remedial agreements monitored for nursing facilities	✓		Remedial agreements for 17 facilities for persons with intellectual and developmental disabilities monitored Remedial agreements regarding 18 state-operated residential facilities for persons with mental illness monitored Remedial agreements at 2 nursing facilities monitored
	Number of actions involving unjustified institutionalization of a disabled individual in which the Civil Rights Division intervened	✓		2 actions involving unjustified institutionalization of a disabled individual where the division movedto intervene
	Number of statements of interest or *amicus*briefs in litigation filed	✓		10 statements of interest or *amicus*briefs filed
	Number of cases favorably resolved for litigating components[c] (Target: 80 percent of civil cases favorably resolved)		♦	81 percent of civil cases favorably resolved
Criminal Division	Number of new health care fraud cases	✓		136 health care fraud cases
	Number of defendants charged and amount that was collectively billed to Medicare and Medicaid	✓		110 defendants charged who collectively billed Medicare and Medicaid for more than $1.3 billion
	Number of guilty pleas obtained	✓		99 guilty pleas
	Number of jury trials litigated	✓		10 jury trials litigated
	Number of guilty verdicts obtained against number of defendants	✓		Guilty verdicts for 21 defendants

Table 8. (Continued)

		Source of indicator		
DOJ Component	Indicators used by agencies to assess activities (Associated target, if applicable)	FY 2012 HCFAC report	Other	Outcomes/outputs of indicators for fiscal year 2012[a]
	Average number of months of prison sentences in health care fraud cases	✓		56 months
	Amount secured through court-ordered restitution, forfeiture, and fines	✓		$373 million
	Number of investigations completed per Department of Justice attorney working on financial fraud and health care fraud cases[c] (Target: 11.92 investigations per attorney)		♦	10.28 investigations per attorney for fiscal year 2012
	Percentage of criminal cases favorably resolved for litigating divisions[c] (Target: 90 percent of criminal cases favorably resolved)		♦	92 percent of criminal cases favorably resolved
Federal Bureau of Investigation (FBI)	Number of operational disruptions of criminal fraud organizations	✓		329 criminal enterprises disrupted
	Number of dismantlements of criminal hierarchy of health care fraud enterprises	✓		More than 83 criminal enterprises dismantled
	Number of new health care fraud investigations initiated by the FBI (Targets vary by field office)	✓		817 new investigations
	Number of pending health care fraud investigations (Targets vary by field office)	✓		2,835 pending investigations
	Number of criminal health care fraud convictions	✓		1,096 criminal convictions
	Number of indictments and informations filed	✓		909 indictments and informations filed
	Number of FBI health care fraud investigators and analysts that received training (Targets vary by field office)	✓		More than 400 FBI health care fraud investigators and analysts received training
	Number of dismantled criminal enterprises engaging in white-collar crime (Target: 360 criminal enterprises)		♦	409 criminal enterprises

		Source of indicator		
DOJ Component	Indicators used by agencies to assess activities (Associated target, if applicable)	FY 2012 HCFAC report	Other	Outcomes/outputs of indicators for fiscal year 2012[a]
	Amounts received for restitutions, fines, seizures, civil restitution, and civil settlements		⊙	In fiscal year 2011: $1.2 billion in restitutions; $1 billionin fines; $96 million in seizures; $320 million in civil restitution; and over $1 billion in civil settlements.
United States Attorneys' Offices (USAOs)	Number of new criminal matters received and defendants involved with those new matters	✓		1,131 new criminal matters involving 2,148 defendants
	Number of health care fraud criminal matters pending and defendants involved	✓		2,032 criminal matters pending involving 3,410 defendants
	Number of criminal charges filed and defendants involved	✓		Charges filed in 452 cases involving 892 defendants
	Number of Federal health care fraud related convictions	✓		826 convictions
	Number of new civil health care fraud investigations opened	✓		885 new civil investigations[b]
	Number of civil health care fraud investigations pending	✓		1,023 civil investigations pending[b]
	Number of investigations completed per Department of Justice attorney working on financial fraud and health care fraud cases[c] (Target: 11.92 investigations per attorney)		♦	10.28 investigations per attorney
	Percentage of criminal cases favorably resolved for litigating divisions[c] (Target: 90 percent of criminal cases favorably resolved; 80 percent of civil cases favorably resolved)		♦	92 percent of criminal cases favorably resolved; 81 percent of civil cases favorably resolved

Table 8. (Continued)

		Source of indicator		
DOJ Component	Indicators used by agencies to assess activities (Associated target, if applicable)	FY 2012 HCFAC report	Other	Outcomes/outputs of indicators for fiscal year 2012[a]
	Percent of white collar crimes cases concerning mortgage fraud, health care fraud, and official corruption favorably resolved[c] (Target: 90 percent of white collar cases favorably resolved)		O	92.2 percent of white collar crimecases favorably resolved in fiscalyear 2010

Legend:

✓ indicates that measure is included in Fiscal Year 2012 annual HCFAC report

♦ indicates that measure is in DOJ's Performance and Accountability report

O indicates that the measure is in DOJ's Performance Plan for Fiscal Year 2012

⊙ indicates that the measure is in FBI's Financial Crimes Report to the Public for Fiscal Years 2010 – 2011.

Source: Agency reports, including fiscal year 2012 annual HCFAC report, and interviews with DOJ officials.

[a] Unless otherwise noted, the information on outcomes/output for each measure is for fiscal year 2012.

[b] The outputs for these indicators are included in the summary of the HCFAC report and in the section regarding USAO activities. We report the outputs in the Civil Division section and USAO section of this table because the outputs include civil matters handled by the USAOs and/or Civil Division.

[c] These measures are reported at the departmental level for DOJ, in which several DOJ components contribute, and include health care fraud cases in addition to other cases.

Appendix IV: Key Outcomes and Outputs of Health Care Fraud and Abuse Control (HCFAC) Program Activities

Table 9. Key Program Outcomes/Outputs of Health Care Fraud and Abuse Control (HCFAC) Program Activities, Fiscal Years 2008 through 2012

HCFAC Key Program Outcomes/Outputs in Selected Years					
Program outcome/output	Fiscal year 2008	Fiscal year 2009	Fiscal year 2010	Fiscal year 2011	Fiscal year 2012
Approximate amount won or negotiated through health care fraud judgments and settlements	$1 billion	$1.63 billion	$2.5 billion	$2.4 billion	$3 billion
Approximate amount deposited with the Department of Treasury and Centers for Medicare & Medicaid Services, transferred to other federal agencies or paid to private persons (result of fiscal year efforts as well as efforts from previous fiscal years)	$2.14 billion	$2.576 billion	$4.02 billion	$4.1billion	$4.2 billion

HCFAC Key Program Outcomes/Outputs in Selected Years					
Program outcome/output	Fiscal year 2008	Fiscal year 2009	Fiscal year 2010	Fiscal year 2011	Fiscal year 2012
Estimated amount in health care savings attributed to legislative or administrative actions to make funds available for better use (taken in response to HHS-OIG investigations, audits, and evaluations)	$16.7 billion	$16.47 billion	$21.0 billion	$19.8 billion	$8.5 billion
Number of new criminal health care fraud investigations opened	957	1,014	1,116	1,110	1,131
Number of cases where criminal charges were filed	502	481	488	489	452
Number of defendants in cases where criminal charges were filed	797	803	931	1,430	892
Number of defendants convicted of health care fraud-related crimes	588	583	726	743	826
Number of new civil health care fraud investigations opened	843	886	942	977	885
Outcomes/outputs associated with Strike Force teams[a]					
Number of defendants charged	65	209	284	323	278
Number of defendants convicted	75	104	240	198	280
Number of defendants sentenced to prison	71	77	146	175	201
Estimated total amount billed to Medicare in alleged Strike Force cases	$140 million	$253 million	$590 million	$1 billion	$1.5 billion
Number of individuals and entities excluded by HHS-OIG	3,129	2,556	3,340	2,662	3,131
Return-on-investment (3-year moving average)	$4.9:1	$5.1:1	$6.8:1	$7.2:1	$7.9:1
HCFAC mandatory obligations	$354,970, 390	$366,075, 050	$387,037, 433	$395,868, 822	$452, 924,566
HCFAC discretionary obligations	—	$39,085, 681	$32,598 ,092	$78,403, 309	$63,501, 482
Program outcome/output	Fiscal year 2008	Fiscal year 2009	Fiscal year 2010	Fiscal year 2011	Fiscal year 2012
Obligations of other appropriations	$67,274, 025	$80,799, 515	$75,075, 212	$91,473, 384	$67,165, 097
Total obligations	$422,244, 416	$485,960, 246	$494,710, 737	$565,745, 516	$583, 591,144

Source: GAO analysis of annual HCFAC reports for fiscal years 2008 through 2012, return-on-investment data for fiscal years 2008-2012 reported to GAO by the Department of Justice, and HCFAC obligations reported to GAO by Department of Justice, Department of Health and Human

Services (HHS), and HHS Office of Inspector General (HHS-OIG) for fiscal years 2008 through 2012.

[a] Some of the outcomes/outputs associated with the Strike Force teams are subsets of outcomes/outputs reported for the HCFAC program as a whole. For example, the number of defendants charged in Strike Force cases is a subset of the total number of defendants in health care fraud-related cases where criminal charges were filed. As a result, the outcomes/outputs reported in this table may be duplicative.

End Notes

[1] GAO, *High-Risk Series: An Update*, GAO-11-278 (Washington, D.C.: February 2011). Fraud represents intentional acts of deception with knowledge that the action or representation could result in an inappropriate gain. Abuse represents actions inconsistent with acceptable business or medical practices.

[2] Pub. L. No. 104-191, § 201, 110 Stat. 1936, 1992 (Aug. 21, 1996) (codified at 42 U.S.C. §§ 1320a-7c, 1395i(k)).

[3] Medicare is the federal health insurance program for persons aged 65 and over, certain disabled individuals, and individuals with end-stage renal disease. Medicaid and CHIP are joint federal-state programs that finance health insurance coverage for certain categories of low-income adults and children.

[4] In this report, we refer to the agencies, divisions, and offices within HHS and DOJ as components.

[5] In addition to HCFAC mandatory and discretionary funding appropriated to HHS, HHSOIG, and DOJ, over $250 million in discretionary HCFAC funding was appropriated to CMS to support program integrity activities in Medicare and Medicaid for fiscal year 2012.

[6] See GAO, *Medicare: Progress Made to Deter Fraud, but More Could Be Done,* GAO-12-801T (Washington, D.C.: June 8, 2012).

[7] Mandatory funding refers to budgetary resources controlled by laws other than appropriations acts. Discretionary funding refers to budgetary resources provided in annual appropriations acts, other than those that fund mandatory programs. HHS and DOJ receive mandatory funding as well as discretionary funding for the HCFAC program. The FBI receives mandatory funding to support HCFAC activities.

[8] HHS's components that received HCFAC funding in fiscal year 2012 were: Administration for Community Living (ACL), CMS, Food and Drug Administration (FDA), and Office of General Counsel (HHS-OGC). HHS-OIG's components that received HCFAC funding in fiscal year 2012 were: Office of Audit Services (OAS), Office of Counsel to the Inspector General (OCIG), Office of Evaluation and Inspections (OEI), Office of Investigations (OI), and Office of Management and Policy (OMP). DOJ's components that received HCFAC funding were: DOJ's Civil Division, Civil Rights Division, Criminal Division, Executive Office for United States Attorneys (EOUSA)—which provides administrative support for the 94 USAOs—the Justice Management Division (JMD), and the FBI.

[9] The Medicare Trust Funds refer to the Hospital Insurance Trust Fund and the Supplementary Medical Insurance Trust Fund, which finance Medicare.

[10] The HCFAC funding appropriated to CMS that we included in our review supports a Medicaid and CHIP financial management oversight project, a pilot project using data analytics to identify fraud in community mental health centers in 3 states, and some of CMS's contributions to the Medicare Strike Force teams, which provide additional investigative and prosecutorial resources in high fraud cities. The funding included in our review is a small portion of the HCFAC funding that CMS receives. In fiscal year 2012, CMS received over $250 million in discretionary HCFAC funding, and CMS officials told us that most of this funding was used to support program integrity activities in Medicare Parts C and D.

[11] In July 2011, we issued a report on how CMS used its Medicare Integrity Program (MIP) funding to support the program's activities in fiscal years 2006 through 2010, how CMS assessed the effectiveness of MIP, and the factors CMS considered when allocating MIP funding. See GAO, *Medicare Integrity Program: CMS Used Increased Funding for New Activities but Could Improve Measurement of Program Effectiveness*, GAO-11-592 (Washington, D.C.: July 29, 2011). CMS concurred with our recommendations that CMS update the return-on-investment calculation when program expenditure data are updated and implement data system changes that will permit CMS to capture accurate spending data.

[12] An obligation is a definite commitment that creates a legal liability of the government for payment of goods and services ordered or received. Obligations can be paid immediately or in the future.

[13] We requested that HHS, HHS-OIG, and DOJ report their information within five categories of expenses: (1) personnel compensation and benefits; (2) contractual services and supplies (including rent, transportation, printing, and supplies); (3) acquisition of assets; (4) grants; and (5) other expenses. In addition to fiscal year 2012, we obtained information for fiscal years 2008 through 2011, which is included in appendix II.

[14] Two HHS components, the Office of the Assistant Secretary for Public Affairs and the Office of the Assistant Secretary for Planning and Evaluation, had HCFAC obligations for fiscal year 2011 only.

[15] For the purposes of our report, we refer to HHS-OIG and its components separately from HHS and its agencies. Several HHS and DOJ components obligated funds not specifically appropriated for the HCFAC program in addition to HCFAC appropriations to carry out activities related to health care fraud and abuse. For example, DOJ's USAOs used other appropriations, including direct appropriations, to support HCFAC activities.

[16] The return-on-investment calculation compares the amount of funding returned as a result of HCFAC activities with the funding appropriated to conduct those activities.

[17] We selected these experts through our literature review.

[18] Safe harbors identify payment or business practices that are protected from enforcement under federal laws that prohibit such payment or business practices.

[19] *See, e.g.*, Omnibus Appropriations Act, 2009, Pub. L. No. 111-8, 123 Stat. 524, 773 (Mar. 11, 2009). In addition to appropriating discretionary HCFAC funds, this law and subsequent annual appropriations laws have required that the annual HCFAC report include measures of operational efficiency and impact on fraud, waste, and abuse in Medicare, Medicaid, and CHIP for the funds provided by these appropriations. Starting in fiscal year 2010, the annual HCFAC report has included a return-on-investment calculation. The calculation is estimated by dividing the monetary results (such as deposits and transfers to the Medicare Trust Funds) by the annual HCFAC appropriation in a given year.

[20] The Patient Protection and Affordable Care Act and the Health Care and Education Reconciliation Act of 2010 provided additional mandatory appropriations from the Medicare Trust Funds for the HCFAC program for fiscal years 2011 through 2020. The additional fiscal year 2012 mandatory appropriation is reflected in figure 1. Patient Protection and Affordable Care Act, Pub. L. No. 111-148, § 6402(i), 124 Stat. 119, 760 (Mar. 23, 2010); Health Care Education and Reconciliation Act of 2010, Pub. L. No. 111- 152, § 1303(a), 124 Stat. 1029, 1057 (Mar. 30, 2010).

[21] In fiscal year 2012, CMS was appropriated over $250 million in discretionary HCFAC funding and CMS officials told us that most of this funding was used to support program integrity activities in Medicare Parts C and D. In addition to HCFAC funding, CMS also received about $863 million in funding for the Medicare Integrity Program in fiscal year 2012.

[22] The False Claims Act prohibits certain actions, including the knowing presentation of a false claim for payment by the federal government. Such claims may be brought by the United States or a private person—known as a relator or whistleblower—on behalf of him or herself and the United States, alleging the submission of false claims for payments by the federal government. DOJ may intervene in such an action, known as a "qui tam" action, and litigate the case along with the private party. 31 U.S.C. §§ 3729-3733.

[23] Percentages do not add to 100 due to rounding.

[24] An obligation is a definite commitment that creates a legal liability of the government for payment of goods and services ordered or received. Obligations can be paid immediately or in the future.

[25] In addition to mandatory and discretionary HCFAC funding, we requested that HHS, HHS-OIG, and DOJ components identify other appropriations used to support HCFAC activities. For the purposes of this report, we define "HCFAC obligations" to be obligations used to support HCFAC activities, which includes obligations of HCFAC mandatory and discretionary appropriations, obligations of FBI mandatory appropriations provided under HIPAA for health care fraud and abuse activities, and obligations of other appropriations not specific to the HCFAC program.

[26] As a component of DOJ, the FBI's obligations are included with DOJ HCFAC obligations, even though it receives its mandatory funding for health care fraud and abuse activities from the U.S. Treasury's general fund and not the Medicare Trust Funds. The FBI includes a description of its activities in an appendix to the annual HCFAC report and its funding is included in the HCFAC return-on-investment calculation.

[27] The Patient Protection and Affordable Care Act and the Health Care and Education Reconciliation Act of 2010, which provide additional mandatory HCFAC appropriations for fiscal years 2011 through 2020, require that these additional appropriations be allocated in the same proportion as the wedge fund was allocated in fiscal year 2010. The agencies have applied this allocation to the entire wedge appropriation since fiscal year 2010.

[28] CMS's efforts related to the Strike Force teams were funded with HCFAC discretionary appropriations.

[29] OMP provides management, guidance, and resources in support of the other HHS-OIG components.

[30] HHS-OGC's reported estimated obligations of other appropriations, which also included reimbursements for attorney services provided to OGC clients within HHS that supported HCFAC activities.

[31] Deficit Reduction Act of 2005, Pub. L. No. 109-171, § 6034(c), 120 Stat. 4, 77 (Feb. 8, 2006).

[32] Although some DOJ components reported obligating funds from other appropriations for HCFAC activities, they also reported carrying over some of their HCFAC funding into other fiscal years. A DOJ official told us that funds are often carried over to a new fiscal year, such as in the situation of a continuing resolution, which may shorten the number of months in which they are able to obligate the appropriated funds.

[33] Section 11013 of the 21st Century Department of Justice Appropriations Authorization Act authorized the Attorney General to credit, as an offsetting collection, to the Department of Justice Working Capital Fund—a revolving fund that is authorized by Congress, as a form of permanent appropriation, to maintain moneys from certain sources for specific purposes—up to 3 percent of all amounts collected pursuant to DOJ's civil debt collection litigation activities. DOJ refers to this appropriation as "Three Percent Funds." Pub. L. No. 107-273, § 11013, 116 Stat. 1758, 1823 (Nov. 2, 2002).

[34] A qui tam case is a civil action brought under the False Claims Act by an individual— known as a relator or whistleblower—on behalf of him or herself and the United States, alleging the submission of false claims for payment by the federal government. In these qui tam cases, the relator may be eligible to receive a portion of the proceeds of the action or settlement, and reasonable expenses and attorneys' fees and costs. 31 U.S.C. § 3730(b),(d).

[35] We requested that HHS, HHS-OIG, and DOJ report their HCFAC obligations within five categories of expenses. These categories were personnel compensation and benefits; contractual services and supplies (including rent, transportation, printing, supplies); acquisition of assets; grants; and other expenses.

[36] HHS-OIG found that three South Florida counties (Miami-Dade, Broward, and Palm Beach) accounted for half of the submitted charges totaling $976 million, and 79 percent of the amount for drugs, billed nationally for Medicare beneficiaries with HIV/AIDs in the last half of 2006. In addition, HHS-OIG found that CMS and its contractors' efforts to control these inappropriate payments through multiple approaches—such as payment suspensions, provider revocations, and claims-processing edits—resulted in limited success in controlling the aberrant billing. See HHS-OIG, *Aberrant Billing in South Florida For Beneficiaries with HIV/AIDs*, OEI-09-07-0030 (Washington, D.C., Sept. 2007).

[37] HHS-OIG's report on the Senior Medicare Patrol (SMP) programs presents performance data for each SMP program. HHS-OIG collects the data every 6 months, reports annually, and has done so since 1997.

[38] According to the fiscal year 2012 HCFAC report, OGC advised CMS on the new voluntary Self Referral Disclosure Protocol established by the Patient Protection and Affordable Care Act. Pub. L. No. 111-148, § 6409(a), 124 Stat. at 772. Under this protocol, providers of services and supplies may self-disclose actual or potential violations of the physician self-referral law, commonly known as the Stark law. The Stark law prohibits physicians from making certain referrals for "designated health services" paid for by Medicare to entities with which the physician (or immediate family members) has a financial relationship, unless the arrangement complies with a specified exception, such as in-office ancillary services. 42 U.S.C. § 1395nn(a)(1), (b)(2).

[39] Corporate integrity agreements outline conditions or requirements an entity agrees to as a part of a civil settlement. An entity agrees to the corporate integrity agreement's requirements in exchange for HHS-OIG's agreement that it will not seek to exclude the entity from participation in federal health care programs. HHS-OIG's Office of Counsel to the Inspector General monitors the compliance with these agreements.

[40] GAO, *2013 Annual Report: Actions Needed to Reduce Fragmentation, Overlap, and Duplication and Achieve Other Financial Benefits*, GAO-13-279SP, (Washington, D.C.: April 2013); *Medicare Integrity Program: CMS Used Increased Funding for New Activities but Could Improve Measurement of Program Effectiveness*, GAO-11-592 (Washington, D.C.: July 2011); and *Opportunities to Reduce Potential Duplication in Government Programs, Save Tax Dollars, and Enhance Revenue*, GAO-11-318SP (Washington, D.C.: March 2011).

[41] For example, officials told us that although a defendant convicted of health care fraud may be ordered to pay restitution and penalties in a specific amount, the defendant may pay less than what is ordered as the ability to pay often affects how much is actually received.

[42] Many cases discussed in the annual HCFAC report include settlements reached with pharmaceutical and device manufacturers for criminal and civil liabilities. For example, the fiscal year 2012 HCFAC report describes many settlements reached with pharmaceutical and device manufacturers and the settlements ranged from about $200,000 to $3 billion.

[43] The CMS activities for which funding is included are financial management oversight of the Medicaid program and CHIP; a pilot project related to payments for partial hospitalization programs made to community mental health centers (which is designed to use predictive modeling to prevent fraud in community mental health centers in Florida, Texas, and Louisiana); and for CMS support for the Medicare Strike Force teams. The return-on-investment calculation does not include the remaining HCFAC funding that CMS receives because it generally supports program integrity activities in Medicare Parts C and D.

[44] Mandatory HCFAC appropriations are available until expended. Discretionary HCFAC appropriations are available for two years.

[45] GAO, *Intellectual Property: Federal Enforcement Has Generally Increased, but Assessing Performance Could Strengthen Law Enforcement Efforts*, GAO-08-157 (Washington, D.C.: Mar. 11, 2008).

[46] According to one DOJ official, some of the department's indicators have targets that focus on the quality or efficiency of its work, rather than focusing on the number of cases opened or criminal charges filed. For example, DOJ has department-wide measures for the percentage of cases favorably resolved, that is, a judgment in favor of the U.S. government or a settlement. The target rate of cases favorably resolved is 90 percent for criminal cases and 80 percent for civil cases, which incorporate all of DOJ's cases (including health care fraud cases as well as other cases).

[47] A. Rashidian, H. Joudaki, and T. Vian, "No Evidence of the Effect of the Interventions to Combat Health Care Fraud and Abuse: A Systematic Review of Literature," PLoS ONE, vol. 7, no. 8 (2012).

[48] See GAO, *Medicare: Progress Made to Deter Fraud, but More Could Be Done,* GAO-12-801T (Washington, D.C.: June 8, 2012).

[49] For example, DOJ Criminal Division officials reported that home health billings in Florida dropped from $3.4 billion in 2009 to $2.3 billion in 2011.

[50] DOJ officials reported that they compared claims submitted to Medicare for group psychotherapy during the six-month period between January 1, 2011 and June 30, 2011 to claims submitted to Medicare for those same services during the six-month period between July 1, 2012 and December 31, 2012.

In: The Health Care Fraud and Abuse Control Program
Editor: Curtis Wood
ISBN: 978-1-63463-693-3

Chapter 2

HEALTH CARE FRAUD AND ABUSE CONTROL PROGRAM ANNUAL REPORT FOR FISCAL YEAR 2013*

Department of Health and Human Services and Department of Justice

EXECUTIVE SUMMARY

The Health Insurance Portability and Accountability Act of 1996 (HIPAA) established a national Health Care Fraud and Abuse Control Program (HCFAC or the Program) under the joint direction of the Attorney General and the Secretary of the Department of Health and Human Services (HHS)[1], acting through the Inspector General, designed to coordinate Federal, state and local law enforcement activities with respect to health care fraud and abuse. In its seventeenth year of operation, the Program's continued success confirms the soundness of a collaborative approach to identify and prosecute the most egregious instances of health care fraud, to prevent future fraud and abuse, and to protect program beneficiaries.

Monetary Results

During Fiscal Year (FY) 2013, the Federal government won or negotiated over $2.6 billion in health care fraud judgments and settlements[2], and it attained additional administrative impositions in health care fraud cases and proceedings. As a result of these efforts, as well as those of preceding years, in FY 2013, approximately $4.3 billion was deposited with the Department of the Treasury and the Centers for Medicare & Medicaid Services (CMS), transferred to other Federal agencies administering health care programs, or paid to private persons during the fiscal year. Of this $4.3 billion, the Medicare Trust Funds[3] received transfers of approximately $2.85 billion during this period, and over $576 million in Federal Medicaid money was similarly transferred separately to the Treasury as a result of

* This is an edited, reformatted and augmented version of a report issued February 2014.

these efforts. The HCFAC account has returned over $25.9 billion to the Medicare Trust Funds since the inception of the Program in 1997.

Enforcement Actions

In FY 2013, the Department of Justice (DOJ) opened 1,013 new criminal health care fraud investigations involving 1,910 potential defendants. Federal prosecutors had 2,041 health care fraud criminal investigations pending, involving 3,535 potential defendants, and filed criminal charges in 480 cases involving 843 defendants. A total of 718 defendants were convicted of health care fraud-related crimes during the year. Also in FY 2013, DOJ opened 1,083 new civil health care fraud investigations and had 1,079 civil health care fraud matters pending at the end of the fiscal year. In FY 2013, Federal Bureau of Investigation (FBI) health care fraud investigations resulted in the operational disruption of 425 criminal fraud organizations and the dismantlement of the criminal hierarchy of more than 115 criminal enterprises engaged in health care fraud.

In FY 2013, HHS' Office of Inspector General (HHS-OIG) investigations resulted in 849 criminal actions against individuals or entities that engaged in crimes related to Medicare and Medicaid; and 458 civil actions, which include false claims and unjust-enrichment lawsuits filed in Federal district court, civil monetary penalties (CMP) settlements, and administrative recoveries related to provider self-disclosure matters. HHS-OIG also excluded 3,214 individuals and entities. Among these were exclusions based on criminal convictions for crimes related to Medicare and Medicaid (1,132) or to other health care programs (311); for patient abuse or neglect (180); and as a result of licensure revocations (1,324). HHS-OIG also issued numerous audits and evaluations with recommendations that, when implemented, would correct program vulnerabilities and save program funds.

Impact of Sequestration

Due to sequestration in 2013, there were fewer resources for DOJ and HHS to fight fraud and abuses against Medicare, Medicaid, and other healthcare programs. A total of $30.6 million was sequestered from the HCFAC program in FY 2013.

INTRODUCTION

Annual Report of the Attorney General and the Secretary Detailing Expenditures and Revenues Under the Health Care Fraud and Abuse Control Program for Fiscal Year 2013

As Required by Section 1817(k)(5) of the Social Security Act

STATUTORY BACKGROUND

The Social Security Act Section 1128C(a), as established by the Health Insurance Portability and Accountability Act of 1996 (P.L. 104-191, HIPAA or the Act), created the Health Care Fraud and Abuse Control Program, a far-reaching program to combat fraud and abuse in health care, including both public and private health plans.

As was the case before HIPAA, amounts paid to Medicare in restitution or for compensatory damages must be deposited in the Medicare Trust Funds. The Act requires that an amount equaling recoveries from health care investigations – including criminal fines, forfeitures, civil settlements and judgments, and administrative penalties – also be deposited in the Trust Funds.

The Act appropriates monies from the Medicare Hospital Insurance Trust Fund to an expenditure account, called the Health Care Fraud and Abuse Control Account (the Account), in amounts that the Secretary and Attorney General jointly certify as necessary to finance anti-fraud activities. The maximum amounts available for certification are specified in the Act. Certain of these sums are to be used only for activities of the HHS-OIG, with respect to the Medicare and Medicaid programs. In FY 2006, the Tax Relief and Health Care Act (TRHCA) (P.L 109-432, §303) amended the Act so that funds allotted from the Account are "available until expended." TRHCA also allowed for yearly increases to the Account based on the change in the consumer price index for all urban consumers (all items; United States city average) (CPI-U) over the previous fiscal year for fiscal years for 2007 through 2010.[4] In FY 2010, the Patient Protection and Affordable Care Act, as amended by the Health Care and Education Reconciliation Act, collectively referred to as the Affordable Care Act (P.L. 111-148, ACA) extended permanently the yearly increases to the Account based upon the change in the consumer price index for all urban consumers or CPI-U.

In FY 2013, the Secretary and the Attorney General certified $295.1 million in mandatory funding for appropriation to the Account. Additionally, Congress appropriated $309.1 million in discretionary funding. A detailed breakdown of the allocation of these funds is set forth later in this report. HCFAC appropriations generally supplement the direct appropriations of HHS and DOJ that are devoted to health care fraud enforcement and funded approximately three-fourths of HHS-OIG's appropriated budget in FY 2013. (Separately, the FBI received $128.1 million from HIPAA which is discussed in the Appendix.)

Under the joint direction of the Attorney General and the Secretary, the Program's goals are:

(1) to coordinate Federal, state and local law enforcement efforts relating to health care fraud and abuse with respect to health plans;
(2) to conduct investigations, audits, inspections, and evaluations relating to the delivery of and payment for health care in the United States;
(3) to facilitate enforcement of all applicable remedies for such fraud;
(4) to provide education and guidance regarding complying with current health care law; and

(5) to establish a national data bank to receive and report final adverse actions against health care providers and suppliers.

The Act requires the Attorney General and the Secretary to submit a joint annual report to the Congress which identifies both:

(1) the amounts appropriated to the Trust Funds for the previous fiscal year under various categories and the source of such amounts; and
(2) the amounts appropriated from the Trust Funds for such year for use by the Attorney General and the Secretary and the justification for the expenditure of such amounts.

This annual report fulfills the above statutory requirements.

Additionally, this report fulfills the requirement in the annual discretionary HCFAC appropriation (Public Law 112-74 "Consolidated Appropriations Act of 2012") that this report "include measures of the operational efficiency and impact on fraud, waste, and abuse in the Medicare, Medicaid, and CHIP programs for the funds provided by this appropriation."

MONETARY RESULTS

As required by the Act, HHS and DOJ must detail in this Annual Report the amounts deposited to the Medicare Trust Funds and the source of such deposits. In FY 2013, approximately $4.3 billion was deposited with the Department of the Treasury and CMS, transferred to other Federal agencies administering health care programs, or paid to private persons during the fiscal year. The following chart provides a breakdown of the transfers/deposits:

Total Transfers/Deposits by Recipient FY 2013	
Department of the Treasury	
Deposits to the Medicare Trust Funds, as required by HIPAA	
Gifts and Bequests	$95
Amount Equal to Criminal Fines	$708,406,030
Civil Monetary Penalties	$14,483,916
Asset Forfeiture	$30,166,006
Penalties and Multiple Damages	$1,363,761,885
Subtotal	**$2,116,817,933**
Centers for Medicare & Medicaid Services	
HHS-OIG Audit Disallowances – Recovered -Medicare	$61,717,799
Restitution/Compensatory Damages	$677,300,987
Subtotal*	**$739,018,786**
Grand Total of Amounts Transferred to the Medicare Trust Funds	**$2,855,836,718**
Restitution/Compensatory Damages to Federal Agencies	
TRICARE	$41,597,410
Department of Veterans Affairs	$40,896,098
HHS-OIG Cost of Audits, Investigations and Compliance Monitoring	$9,888,585

Office of Personnel Management	$43,286,981
Other Agencies	$10,065,851
Centers for Medicare and Medicaid Services	
Federal Share of Medicaid	$576,540,583
HHS-OIG Audit Disallowances – Recovered -Medicaid	$431,249,581
Subtotal	**$1,153,525,089**
Relators= Payments**	**$324,194,039**
TOTAL ***	**$4,333,555,846**

* Restitution, compensatory damages, and recovered audit disallowances include returns to both the Medicare Hospital Insurance (Part A) Trust Fund and the Supplemental Medical Insurance (Part B) Trust Fund.

**These are funds awarded to private persons who file suits on behalf of the Federal government under the *qui tam* provisions of the False Claims Act, 31 U.S.C. ' 3730(b).

***State funds are also collected on behalf of state Medicaid programs; only the Federal share of Medicaid funds transferred to CMS are represented here.

The above transfers include certain collections, or amounts equal to certain collections, required by HIPAA to be deposited directly into the Medicare Trust Funds. These amounts include:

(1) Gifts and bequests made unconditionally to the Trust Funds, for the benefit of the Account or any activity financed through the Account;
(2) Criminal fines recovered in cases involving a Federal health care offense, including collections under section 24(a) of Title 18, United States Code (relating to health care fraud);
(3) Civil monetary penalties in cases involving a Federal health care offense;
(4) Amounts resulting from the forfeiture of property by reason of a Federal health care offense, including collections under section 982(a)(7) of Title 18, United States Code; and
(5) Penalties and damages obtained and otherwise creditable to miscellaneous receipts of the general fund of the Treasury obtained under sections 3729 through 3733 of Title 31, United States Code (known as the False Claims Act, or FCA), in cases involving claims related to the provision of health care items and services (other than funds awarded to a relator, for restitution or otherwise authorized by law).

PROGRAM ACCOMPLISHMENTS

Expenditures

In the seventeenth year of operation, the Secretary and the Attorney General certified $295.1 million in mandatory funding as necessary for the Program. Additionally, Congress appropriated $309.2 million in discretionary funding. Sequestration reductions, as required by law, were taken against the mandatory and discretionary HCFAC accounts. The following chart gives the allocation by recipient:

FY 2013 ALLOCATION OF HCFAC APPROPRIATION				
Organization	**Mandatory Allocation**[5]	**Discretionary Allocation**	**Funds Sequester**	**Total Allocation**
Department of Health and Human Services				
Office of Inspector General[6]	197,109,153	29,614,462	(11,503,999)	215,219,616
Office of the General Counsel	8,887,870	0		8,887,870
Administration for Community Living	10,548,259	0		10,548,259
Food and Drug Administration	3,377,220	0		3,377,220
Centers for Medicare & Medicaid Services	12,005,774	249,941,882	(12,598,773)	249,348,883
Unallocated Funding	1,914,767	0	(1,914,767)	0
Subtotal	**233,843,043**	**279,556,344**	**(26,017,539)**	**487,381,848**
Department of Justice				
United States Attorneys	31,400,000	10,610,752		42,010,752
Civil Division	18,972,139	8,113,000		27,085,139
Criminal Division	1,580,000	6,594,000		8,174,000
Civil Rights Division	2,376,000	1,741,493		4,117,493
Nursing Home and Elder Justice Initiative	1,000,000	0		1,000,000
Justice Management Division	200,000	0		200,000
Department of Justice – Other	5,761,684	2,555,217	(4,618,552)	3,698,349
Subtotal	**61,289,823**	**29,614,462**	**(4,618,552)**	**86,285,733**
TOTAL[7]	**295,132,866**	**309,170,806**	**(30,636,091)**	**573,667,581**

Accomplishments

Overall Recoveries

During this fiscal year, the Federal government won or negotiated approximately $4.33 billion in judgments and settlements, and it attained additional administrative impositions in health care fraud cases and proceedings. The Medicare Trust Funds received transfers of approximately $2.85 billion during this period as a result of these efforts, as well as those of preceding years; and another $576 million in Federal Medicaid money was transferred to the Treasury separately as a result of these efforts. [8]

In addition to these enforcement actions, numerous audits, evaluations and other coordinated efforts yielded recoveries of overpaid funds, and prompted changes in Federal health care programs that reduce vulnerability to fraud.

The return-on-investment (ROI) for the HCFAC program over the last three years (2011-2013) is $8.1 returned for every $1.00 expended. This is $2.7 higher than the average ROI for the life of the HCFAC program since 1997. Due to the fact that the annual ROI can vary from year to year depending on the number of cases that are settled or adjudicated during that year, DOJ and HHS use a three-year rolling average ROI for results contained in the report. Additional information on how the ROI is calculated can be found in the Appendix.

Departmental Collaboration

Health Care Fraud Prevention & Enforcement Action Team (HEAT)

The Attorney General and the Secretary maintain regular consultation at both senior and staff levels to accomplish the goals of the HCFAC Program. On May 20, 2009, Attorney General Holder and Secretary Sebelius announced the Health Care Fraud Prevention & Enforcement Action Team (HEAT), a new effort with increased tools and resources, and a sustained focus by senior level leadership to enhance collaboration between the Departments of Health and Human Services and Justice. With the creation of the new HEAT effort, DOJ and HHS pledged a cabinet- level commitment to prevent and prosecute health care fraud. HEAT, which is jointly led by the Deputy Attorney General and HHS Deputy Secretary, is comprised of top level law enforcement agents, prosecutors, attorneys, auditors, evaluators, and other staff from DOJ and HHS and their operating divisions, and is dedicated to joint efforts across government to both prevent fraud and enforce current anti-fraud laws around the country. The Medicare Fraud Strike Force teams are a key component of HEAT.

The mission of HEAT is:

- **To marshal significant resources across government to prevent waste, fraud and abuse in the Medicare and Medicaid programs** and crack down on the fraud perpetrators who are abusing the system and costing us all billions of dollars.
- **To reduce skyrocketing health care costs and improve the quality of care** by ridding the system of perpetrators who are preying on Medicare and Medicaid beneficiaries.
- **To highlight best practices by providers and public sector employees** who are dedicated to ending waste, fraud, and abuse in Medicare.
- **To build upon existing partnerships between DOJ and HHS, such as our Medicare Fraud Strike Force Teams,** to reduce fraud and recover taxpayer dollars.

Since its creation in May 2009, HEAT has focused on key areas for coordination and improvement. HEAT members are working to identify new enforcement initiatives and areas for increased oversight and prevention to increase efficiency in areas such as pharmaceutical and device investigations. DOJ and HHS have expanded data sharing and improved information sharing procedures in order to get critical data and information into the hands of law enforcement to track patterns of fraud and abuse, and increase efficiency in investigating and prosecuting complex health care fraud cases. The departments established a cross-government health care fraud data intelligence sharing workgroup to share fraud trends, new initiatives, ideas, and success stories to improve awareness across the government of issues relating to health care fraud.

Both departments also have developed training programs to prevent honest mistakes and help stop potential fraud before it happens. This includes CMS compliance training for providers, HHS- OIG's HEAT Provider Compliance Training initiative, and on-going meetings at U.S. Attorneys' Offices (USAOs) with the public and private sector, and increased efforts by HHS to educate specific groups – including elderly and immigrant communities – to help protect them. In addition, DOJ conducts, with the support of HHS, a Medicare Fraud Strike Force training program designed to teach the Strike Force concept and case model to prosecutors, law enforcement agents, and administrative support teams.

To achieve the mission and objectives of HEAT, the Attorney General and the Secretary promoted several HEAT initiatives during the fiscal year:

- In October 2012, Medicare Fraud Strike Force operations in seven cities led to charges against 91 individuals – including doctors, nurses and other licensed medical professionals– for their alleged participation in Medicare fraud schemes involving approximately$429.2 million in false billing. The coordinated nationwide takedown encompassed indictments charging more than $230 million in home health care fraud; more than $100 million in mental health care fraud and more than $49 million in ambulance transportation fraud; and millions more in other frauds. HHS also suspended or took other administrative action against 30 health care providers.
- In May 2013, a nationwide takedown by Medicare Fraud Strike Force operations in eight cities resulted in charges against 89 individuals, including doctors, nurses and other licensed medical professionals, for their alleged participation in Medicare fraud schemes involving approximately $223 million in false billings. The defendants charged were accused of various health care fraud-related crimes, including conspiracy to commit health care fraud, violations of the anti-kickback statutes and money laundering. The charges were based on a variety of alleged fraud schemes involving various medical treatments and services, primarily home health care, but also mental health services, psychotherapy, physical and occupational therapy, durable medical equipment (DME) and ambulance services. This coordinated takedown was the sixth national Medicare fraud takedown in Strike Force history.

Healthcare Fraud Prevention Partnership (HFPP)

The Healthcare Fraud Prevention Partnership (HFPP) is the groundbreaking public/ private partnership between the government and private sector insurance payers. The purpose of the partnership is to exchange data and information between the partners to help improve capabilities to fight fraud, waste and abuse in the health care industry. Current partners include federal (HHS- OIG, DOJ, FBI, CMS), states, private plans and associations. The Partnership's first information sharing study included exchanging codes and code combinations frequently associated with fraud, waste or abuse, as well as fraud schemes and descriptions. Additional studies are underway and the Partnership is poised for the procurement of the data-exchange entity, the Trusted Third Party (TTP), as well as expansion to new partners.

The HFPP is a demonstrated example of effective departmental collaboration between HHS and DOJ, working together to create a strong partnership with the states and private payers to detect fraud, waste, and abuse.

During FY 2013, the many significant HCFAC Program accomplishments included the following:

Medicare Fraud Strike Force

The first Medicare Fraud Strike Force (Strike Force) was launched in March 2007 as part of the South Florida Initiative, a joint investigative and prosecutorial effort against Medicare fraud and abuse among Durable Medical Equipment (DME) suppliers and Human Immunodeficiency Virus (HIV) infusion therapy providers in South Florida. The Strike Force teams use advanced data analysis techniques to identify high-billing levels in health care fraud hot spots so that interagency teams can target emerging or migrating schemes along with chronic fraud by criminals masquerading as health care providers or suppliers. Based on the success of these efforts and increased appropriated funding for the HCFAC program from Congress and the Administration, DOJ and HHS expanded the Strike Force to include teams of investigators and prosecutors in a total of nine locations – Miami, FL; Los Angeles, CA; Detroit, MI; Houston, TX; Brooklyn, NY; South Louisiana (South Louisiana and New Orleans, LA)[9]; Tampa, FL; Chicago, IL; and Dallas, TX.

Each Medicare Fraud Strike Force team combines the data analysis and administrative action capabilities of CMS, the investigative resources of the FBI and HHS-OIG, and the prosecutorial resources of the Criminal Division's Fraud Section and the USAOs. Strike Force accomplishments from cases prosecuted in all nine cities during FY 2013 include[10]:

- 137 indictments, informations and complaints involving charges filed against 345 defendants who allegedly collectively billed the Medicare program more than $1.1 billion;
- 234 guilty pleas negotiated and 34 jury trials litigated, with guilty verdicts against 48 defendants; and
- Imprisonment for 229 defendants sentenced during the fiscal year, averaging more than 52 months of incarceration.

In the six and a half years since its inception, Strike Force prosecutors filed more than 788 cases charging more than 1,727 defendants who collectively billed the Medicare program more than $5.5 billion; 1,137defendants pleaded guilty and 148 others were convicted in jury trials; and 1087 defendants were sentenced to imprisonment for an average term of approximately 47 months.[11]

Although multiple factors may be in play, there has been a measurable decrease in Medicare reimbursements for certain medical services that have also been targeted by the Medicare Strike Force. For instance:

> **Miami: Medicare Payments for DME**. The Strike Force initially started in Miami precisely to respond to an epidemic of a particular type of fraud involving claims for DME. The law enforcement activity response to DME fraud in the Miami area was overwhelming. Hundreds of defendants were charged and convicted of DME fraud by the Miami Medicare Fraud Strike Force. Law enforcement prosecution of DME fraud, while diminished from its height, continues.
> During this same time period, CMS implemented an aggressive and multifaceted strategy to address DME fraud, waste, and abuse without any loss of access or quality for Medicare beneficiaries. In 2009, CMS began to require DME suppliers to become accredited and possess a surety bond of at least $50,000. Based upon these new requirements, 10,533 DME suppliers were revoked between October 2009 and December 2009. In addition to those revoked, approximately 1,500 more suppliers voluntarily terminated their enrollment between September 2009 and December 2009, likely to avoid facing revocation actions until they could procure a surety bond or obtain accreditation.[12] Also in 2009, CMS developed the DME Stop Gap Plan. This two year project enhanced detection and prevention in seven high risk states, including Florida, and resulted in the implementation of claims processing edits that

denied millions in claims, and the revocation or deactivation of hundreds of providers. Finally, on January 1, 2011, CMS implemented the competitive bidding program for DME in nine areas, including Miami. Competitive bidding plays an important part in the oversight of the DME benefit. As a new payment methodology and process, DME competitive bidding was devised due to concerns about program integrity. The revisions to program administration and payment established by competitive bidding have resulted in program integrity changes.

Law enforcement activity combined with various measures taken by CMS, which themselves were prompted by enforcement activity, appear to have contributed to even further declines in Medicare payments for DME in Miami over time, as indicated by the chart below. Payments by Medicare for DME in Miami-Dade County[13] alone hit an all- time high in the third-quarter of 2006, when payments exceeded $73 million, those payments have decreased over time, and in the first-quarter of 2013 payments were under $15 million

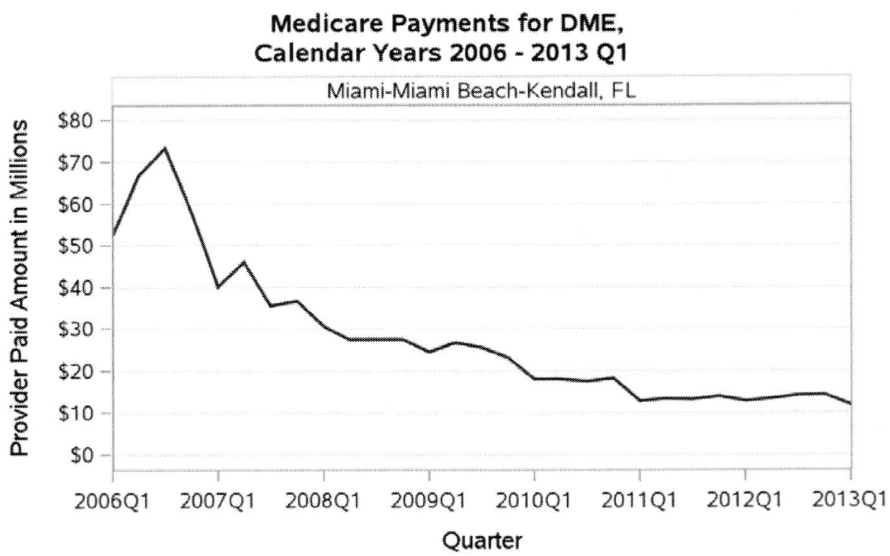

Note: The results of this analysis are subject to change as claims are adjusted or deleted. Medicare timely filing requires providers to submit their claims within 12 months of the date of service. Medicare Claims Processing Manual, Chapter 1, Section 70.1.

Miami: Medicare Payments for Home Health. The Miami Medicare Fraud Strike Force began to focus on home health care fraud in 2009. On June 23, 2009, the Strike Force indicted the first large home health care case, *United States v. Zambrana et al.* The *Zambrana* case led law enforcement to discover how criminals operating home health care companies in South Florida were cheating Medicare. To qualify for home health care, which involves a nurse or other skilled medical professional providing services in a beneficiary's home, a beneficiary must be homebound. Medicare makes additional payments, known as outlier payments, to home health providers that supply services to beneficiaries who incur unusually large costs. Criminals in South Florida took advantage of the outlier payment system by falsely claiming that almost every service qualified for an outlier payment. During calendar year 2009, Medicare paid over $976 million to home health agencies in the Miami area. More than half of these home health payments -- $558 million -- were for "outliers." Since 2009, the Miami Strike Force has charged over 202 defendants, and convicted 191 for their roles in falsely billing Medicare over $570 million for home health care services.

Following the issuance of a report by the Inspector General for HHS describing the scheme,[14] CMS put into effect a limit on the percentage of outlier payments that each home health agency can claim to address abuses of these payments. The CMS field office also ran a home health special project in Miami in 2009 and 2010 to identify beneficiaries that were not homebound. As a result of this project, 32 home health agencies had their payments suspended, additional automated payment edits saved $9.6 million, and $5.5 million in costs were avoided as a result of the payment suspensions. On July 30, 2013, CMS implemented a temporary enrollment moratorium on new HHAs in Miami-Dade and certain bordering counties to further the fight against fraud in this area.

The coordination between the Strike Force and CMS appears to have contributed to a dramatic decline in payment for home health care in Miami and throughout Florida. In 2009, claims to Medicare for home health services in Florida were $3.4 billion, and Medicare paid approximately $2.9 billion for home health care services. Just two years later, in 2011, billings to Medicare had dropped precipitously to $2.3 billion, a difference of $1.1 billion. Payments by Medicare had dropped to $2.4 billion, a difference of approximately $500 million. Payments have essentially flat-lined since that time.

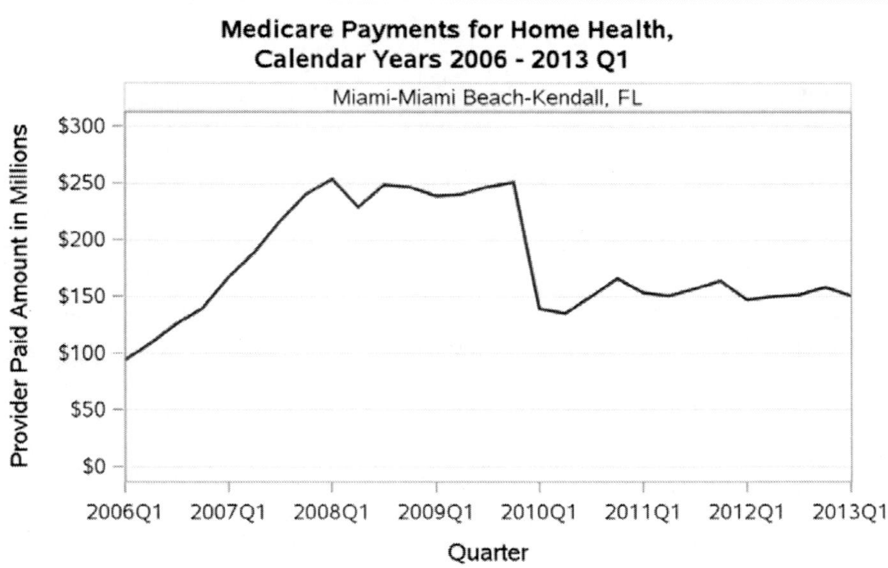

Note: The results of this analysis are subject to change as claims are adjusted or deleted. Medicare timely filing requires providers to submit their claims within 12 months of the date of service. Medicare Claims Processing Manual, Chapter 1, Section 70.1.

Detroit: Medicare Payments for Home Health. The first large home health care prosecution in Detroit commenced in January 2010 with the indictment of thirteen individuals who participated in a home health care fraud at Patient Choice Home Health Care and All American Home Health Care. Since that time, prosecution of home health care fraud in Detroit has led to the charging of 84 individuals who in aggregate submitted approximately $150 million in allegedly fraudulent home health care claims to Medicare. To date, the Detroit Strike Force has obtained the conviction of 47 of those individuals. The Strike Force has also coordinated with CMS to ensure that payments are cut off at the earliest possible time. For example, in May 2012, simultaneous with a Detroit Strike Force takedown of home health care fraudsters, CMS suspended payments to 18 associated home health agencies. As shown in the following chart, Medicare payments for home health care services have declined steadily since 2009.[15]

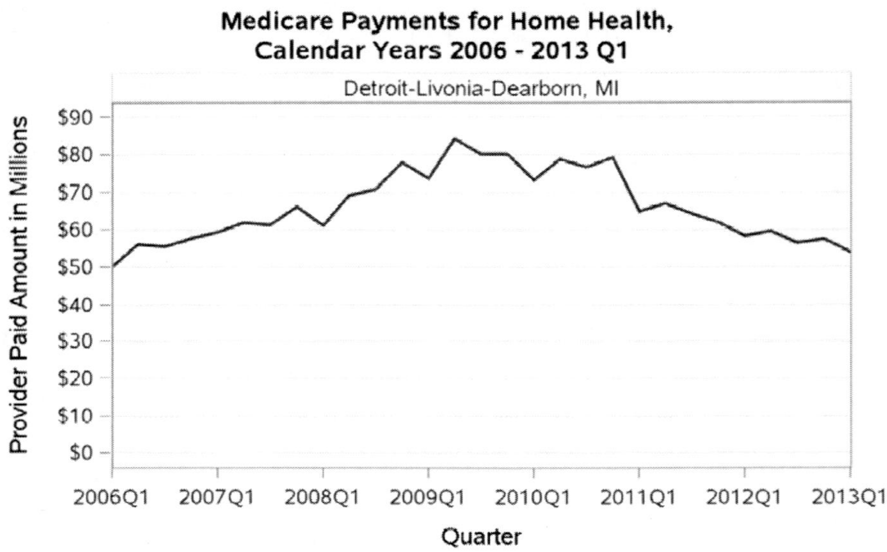

Note: The results of this analysis are subject to change as claims are adjusted or deleted. Medicare timely filing requires providers to submit their claims within 12 months of the date of service. Medicare Claims Processing Manual, Chapter 1, Section 70.1.

Nationwide: Medicare Payments for Community Mental Health Center (CMHC). Strike Force and CMS activity targeting CMHC fraud began in 2008, accelerated in 2010 and culminated in prosecutions in Miami in 2010 and 2011, the suspension of CMHC providers in Baton Rouge and Houston in 2011, and the prosecution of owners and operators of CMHCs in Baton Rouge and Houston in 2012. The enforcement activity was purposefully aimed at the CMHCs that billed Medicare the most, and were paid the most. The actions correspond to a national decline in CMHC billing to Medicare that has persisted to the present time as indicated in the chart below. Total payments by Medicare to CMHCs, which peaked in 2008 at more than $70 million per quarter, are now well under $10 million per quarter, a savings to the Trust Fund exceeding $60 million per quarter.

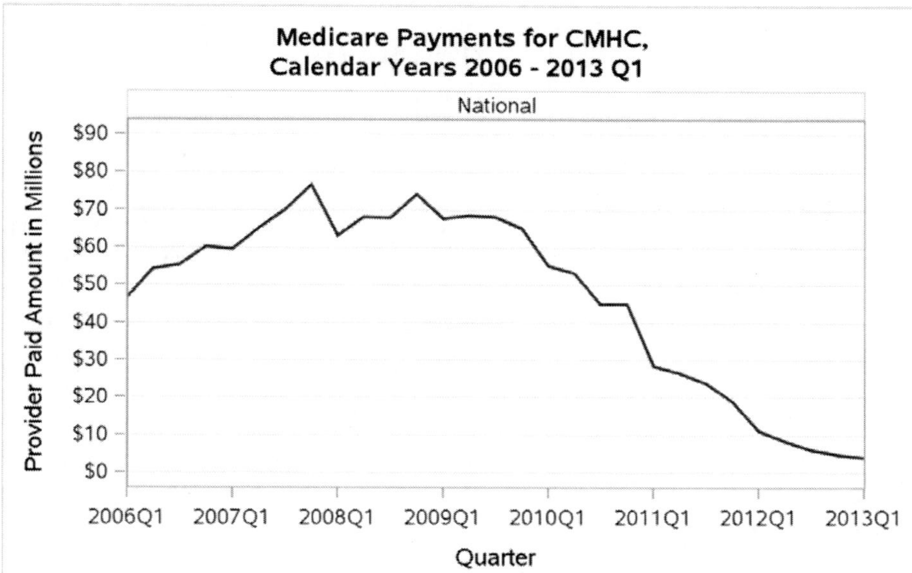

Note: The results of this analysis are subject to change as claims are adjusted or deleted. Medicare timely filing requires providers to submit their claims within 12 months of the date of service. Medicare Claims Processing Manual, Chapter 1, Section 70.1.

Based on these examples, Strike Force and HEAT prevention and enforcement operations appear to have had a real and lasting impact on Medicare payments.

Examples of successful cases initiated or concluded in districts where Strike Force prosecution teams were operational during FY 2013, as well as other successful cases are provided below. Summaries of additional successful prosecutions and settlements follow, organized by fraud type.

Phase 1: Miami (Southern District of Florida)

- In June 2013 in the Southern District of Florida, the chief executive officer (CEO) of a state-licensed psychiatric hospital and three other hospital executives were convicted at trial in connection with a $67 million Medicare fraud scheme. This was the first Strike Force case involving charges against executives of a licensed hospital. According to trial evidence, the defendants and their co-conspirators paid illegal bribes and kickbacks to patient brokers in order to obtain Medicare beneficiaries as patients. The defendants then caused the submission of fraudulent Medicare claims for treatments for which these beneficiaries were not eligible. To cover up the fraudulent claims, employees of the hospital falsified patient charts and even administered unnecessary psychotropic medications to make it appear as if Medicare beneficiaries attending the hospital needed intensive mental health services. A fifth defendant, a patient recruiter, had pled guilty prior to trial. On September 10, 2013, a federal district judge sentenced the CEO to 25 years in prison for her leading role in the fraud, and two other executives to 15 years and 12 years in prison, respectively for their conduct.
- Between October 2012 and July 2013, 11 individuals were convicted, including one at trial, and thirteen were sentenced for their role in a $63 million health care fraud

scheme. On July 17, 2013, a psychiatrist and six additional therapists were also charged in the case, bringing the total number of defendants charged in the case to twenty. According to court documents, the defendants caused the submission of fraudulent claims to Medicare and Medicaid through a company that operated community mental health centers in Miami, FL, and North Carolina. The company paid kickbacks to the owners and operators of assisted living facilities in order to obtain Medicare beneficiaries for purported partial hospitalization program (PHP) services that were unnecessary, and, in many instances, not provided. The scheme operated from 2004 through 2011, and billed Medicare and Florida Medicaid $63.4 million of which they paid $28.1 million. All of the sentenced defendants received prison time, ranging from 168 months to 24 months; eight individuals received over five years in prison for their conduct. In addition, defendants were ordered to pay restitution in excess of $28 million.

- Twelve defendants have been sentenced related to a $56 million health care fraud scheme. Health Care Solutions Network, Inc. (HCSN), operated community mental health centers (CMHCs) in Florida (HCSN-FA) and North Carolina (HCSN-NC). These CMHCs allegedly provided partial hospitalization program (PHP) services to individuals suffering from mental illness. The clinical director of the PHP at HCSN-FL submitted claims to Medicare under her personal Medicare provider number for individual therapy she purportedly provided, while knowing that HCSN-FL was simultaneously billing for PHP services for the same patients. In addition the defendants paid illegal kickbacks to owners and operators of Miami-Dade County Assisted Living Facilities (ALF) in exchange for referring patients to the HCSN-FL PHP. Many of the ALF referral patients were ineligible for PHP services because they suffered from mental retardation, dementia, and Alzheimer's disease. To date, co-conspirators have been sentenced to a combined 70 years of incarceration and ordered to pay $186 million in joint and several restitution.
- In April 2013, the owner of a mental health clinic in Miami, FL and three other participants in a $50 million fraud were sentenced to 30 years in prison, 25 years in prison, 262 months in prison, and 1 year probation following their August 2012 trial convictions. The defendants caused the submission of over $50 million in false and fraudulent claims to Medicare for purported PHP services at a fraudulent clinic. The defendants paid patient recruiters to refer ineligible Medicare beneficiaries to the clinic for services that were never provided or were not reimbursable under applicable Medicare rules. In December 2012, the former clinical director of the facility was sentenced to 100 months in prison and ordered to pay $5.6 million in restitution for his role in the offense.
- From October 2012 through January 2013, nine defendants were sentenced and one defendant was convicted at trial in connection with a Medicare fraud scheme involving over $205 million in fraudulent billing through a mental health care corporation and related companies. The corporation purported to operate community mental health centers at seven different locations throughout South Florida and Orlando, which purported to provide PHP services. A related company purported to provide diagnostic sleep disorder testing. According to court documents, the corporation paid kickbacks to the owners and operators of assisted living facilities, half-way houses, and patient brokers in exchange for delivering ineligible patients for

treatment. In some cases, the patients received a portion of the kickbacks. Throughout the conspiracy, millions of dollars in kickbacks were paid in exchange for Medicare beneficiaries to attend treatment programs at the centers; the companies would then bill Medicare for these medically unnecessary services. To obtain the cash required to support the kickbacks, the co-conspirators laundered millions of dollars of payments from Medicare.
All of the sentenced defendants received a prison sentence, ranging in time from 120 months to 36 months. Additionally, defendants were ordered to pay up to $87.4 million in restitution.

- In April 2013, a co-owner of Ideal Home Health, Inc., was sentenced to 14 years of imprisonment and ordered to pay $30 million in restitution after pleading guilty to charges of conspiracy to commit health care fraud and conspiracy to pay health care kickbacks. Ideal Home Health purportedly provided skilled nursing services and home health aide to Medicare beneficiaries. According to the indictment, the co-owner offered and paid kickbacks and bribes to recruiters and its own employees for recruiting Medicare beneficiaries for the purpose of billing Medicare for home health services that were not medically necessary and not provided.
- In October 2012, the owner of a home health agency in Miami was sentenced to 10 years in prison and ordered to pay $26 million in restitution, joint and several, after pleading guilty to charges of conspiracy to commit health care fraud. The agency, Willsand Home Health Services, Inc. (Willsand), purportedly provided home health care and physical therapy services to Medicare beneficiaries. According to court documents, the owner paid kickbacks to patient recruiters for enrolling Medicare beneficiaries to be placed at Willsand and signed false documents stating that they received home health care services. He also paid kickbacks to physicians in return for signing false prescriptions for these patients. From approximately January 2006 through November 2009, Willsand submitted more than $40 million in claims to Medicare for home health services it purportedly provided to beneficiaries when, in fact, the patients were not homebound and/or had no medical necessity for the services.
- In February 2013, the co-owner and operator of three Miami, Florida-based pharmacies was sentenced to 168 months in prison, ordered to forfeit over $23 million, and ordered to pay a $100,000 fine on his December 2012 guilty plea to conspiracy to pay health care kickbacks and conspiracy to commit health care fraud. According to court documents, from 2007 to September 2012, the defendant paid illegal kickbacks to guarantee a stream of beneficiary information, which was used to submit false and fraudulent claims by the pharmacies to Medicare and Medicaid.

Phase 2: Los Angeles (Central District of California)

- On October 4, 2012, the U.S. District Court for the Central District of California unsealed an indictment charging four defendants with conspiracy to commit health care fraud, health care fraud, and conspiracy to obstruct a federal auditor. The charges stemmed from a Medicare fraud scheme regarding purported ambulance transportation services involving Alpha Ambulance. According to the indictment, the defendants conspired to defraud Medicare by providing ambulance services to ineligible Medicare beneficiaries. From June 2008 to July 2012, Alpha submitted

Medicare claims totaling approximately $49.3 million for purported ambulance transportation and related services, and Medicare paid Alpha approximately $13.3 million on those claims. In addition, the indictment alleges that the defendants obstructed a Medicare audit of Alpha's false and fraudulent claims by altering patient files and records that otherwise showed ambulance transportation services provided by Alpha were not medically necessary, and therefore not reimbursable by Medicare.

- A former officer of Fendih Medical Supply, Inc., a medical supply company, was sentenced in September 2013 to serve 51 months in prison for his role in a fraud scheme that resulted in $1.5 million in fraudulent claims to Medicare. In addition, a physician was sentenced to 27 months in prison for his role in the scheme. In April 2013, a jury in Los Angeles federal court found the two defendants, as well as another health care professional, guilty of conspiracy to pay and receive kickbacks and of conspiracy to commit health care fraud. Trial evidence showed that the owner of the DME company fraudulently billed Medicare for DME that was either never provided to its Medicare beneficiaries or was not medically necessary. The defendant physician provided medically unnecessary power wheelchair prescriptions in exchange for cash kickbacks. This fraud scheme caused the submission of approximately $1.5 million in false and fraudulent claims to Medicare, of which about $1 million was paid.
- In July 2013 in the Central District of California, the owner and operator of a DME supply company was convicted in connection with an $11 million Medicare fraud scheme. The evidence at trial revealed that the defendant submitted false and fraudulent prescriptions for DME by using street-level patient recruiters to find senior citizens with Medicare and Medi-Cal benefits at swap meets and other public places. The recruiters, who were paid about $600 per beneficiary, would convince the seniors to accept power wheelchairs and other DME that they did not need.

Phase 3: Detroit (Eastern District of Michigan)

- In August 2013, a Michigan oncologist/hematologist was charged with health care fraud in wide-ranging and dangerous fraudulent billing scheme. According to the original complaint and subsequent indictment, the doctor alleged provided chemotherapy and other medical treatments to patients who did not need the treatments, including patients who were in remission and did not need chemotherapy, and directed his staff to falsify medical documents to justify the treatments. The allegations raised serious health concerns, particularly given the physical effect of chemotherapy and some of the other treatments the doctor administered to his patients. At the time of arrest, the doctor was treating 1,200 patients. The Criminal Division's Fraud Section, working with the U.S. Attorney's Office for the Eastern District of Michigan, undertook a massive and aggressive effort to make sure that victim witnesses received all necessary support in finding new medical care. Between August 2010 and August 2013, the doctor's business, billed Medicare $225 million and was paid $91 million. In addition, private insurer Blue Cross/Blue Shield also paid the doctor $78 million on claims submitted by the practice.
- In May 2013, two health center owners were sentenced on their October 2012 guilty pleas in connection with an over $13 million Medicare fraud scheme. One owner was sentenced to 100 months in prison and $5.4 million in restitution, while the other was

sentenced to 12 months and one day in prison, and over $500,000 in restitution. The two defendants were also ordered to forfeit $40,717. According to plea documents, the two defendants submitted claims through their health clinics for infusion therapy treatments which were never rendered.

- From May 2013 to July 2013, 2 defendants were sentenced and or pled guilty for their involvement in a $13.8 million home health care Medicare fraud scheme. According to court documents, from June 2009 through September 2011 four companies conspired to defraud Medicare through falsifying documents and submitting fraudulent claims. The two sentenced defendants, the owner/administrator of a home health care company and a physical therapy assistant, were given 30 month and 60 month prison terms, and ordered to pay $1.7 million and $1.3 million in restitution, respectively.
- Between December 2012 and April 2013, four individuals— two owners, a marketer and a registered nurse pled guilty for their involvement in a $24.7 million home health care fraud scheme. According to court documents, the conspirators attempted to defraud Medicare by submitting claims for home health services that were medically unnecessary and/or not provided. The owners oversaw and ran the schemes at multiple home health agencies. The marketer sold the Medicare information of hundreds of Medicare beneficiaries, and the registered nurse fabricated notes and other documentation to give Medicare the impression that she had provided necessary home health care services. In reality, the home health care billed was not needed and/or not provided.

Phase 4: Houston (Southern District of Texas)

- In June 2013, the owner of a DME supply company was sentenced to 97 months in prison and ordered to pay $2.5 million in restitution as the result of a December 2012 conviction in connection with a $6.7 million Medicare fraud scheme. According to court documents and trial evidence, the defendant used his company's Medicare provider number to submit claims to Medicare for DME that was medically unnecessary, and in some cases, never provided.
- In March 2013, a physician was sentenced to 63 months in prison and ordered to pay over $2.9 million in restitution on his December 2012 conviction of conspiracy to commit health care fraud and several counts of false statements relating to heath care matters. Trial evidence showed that the defendant signed plans of care for Medicare beneficiaries who were not under his care and about whose conditions he had no knowledge. Overall, approximately $17.3 million was paid by Medicare for fraudulent home health care services.
- In March 2013, the owner/operator of an ambulance transport company was convicted on conspiracy to commit health care fraud and health care fraud, in connection with a $1.7 million Medicare fraud scheme. Trial evidence showed that the defendant and others conspired to enrich themselves by falsifying patient records in order to bill Medicare for ambulance services that were medically unnecessary and not provided.

Phase 5: Brooklyn (Eastern District of New York)

- In October 2012, nine defendants, including the owner and operator of a fraudulent physical therapy clinic in Brooklyn and its medical director, were charged with participating in a $13 million Medicare fraud scheme. The indictment alleged that the defendants operated a physical therapy clinic in Brooklyn, recruited patients to visit the clinic through the payment of kickbacks and bribes, and billed Medicare for services that were unnecessary and often never provided at all. Between the time of indictment and September 30, 2013, four defendants had pled guilty to participating in the scheme.
- Between October 2012 and July 2013, two physicians and three owners and operators of a fraudulent "medical" clinic pled guilty in connection with an over $12.6 million Medicare fraud scheme. According to plea documents, these individuals in fact provided a variety of spa services, such as massages, facials, lunches, and dancing classes to Medicare beneficiaries in an effort to induce those beneficiaries into allowing their Medicare numbers to be billed for medical services that were never provided and were not medically necessary.
- In December 2012, a board-certified colorectal surgeon was sentenced to 30 months in prison, ordered to pay over $1 million in restitution and forfeit over $1 million on his June 2012 jury conviction on health care fraud and false statements relating to health care matters in connection with a $22.6 million Medicare scheme. Trial evidence demonstrated that from January 2008 to January 2010, the doctor defrauded Medicare and private insurance companies by billing for surgeries, specifically hemorrhoidectomies, and related medical services that he never provided.

Phase 6: South Louisiana (Middle and Eastern Districts of Louisiana)

- In May 2013, five individuals were indicted in the Eastern District of Louisiana for their role in a home health scheme that billed Medicare $51 million. The indictment charges an owner, two doctors and two recruiters with conspiracy to commit health care fraud, conspiracy to pay or receive health care kickbacks and health care fraud. The conduct involves billings by three, related home health agencies in Louisiana which obtained patients through paying patient recruiters and billed by services that were not medically necessary and, sometimes, not provided.
- In October 2012, in the Middle District of Louisiana, an executive of a Mississippi corporation that purportedly provided durable medical equipment to Medicare beneficiaries was sentenced to 72 months in prison and ordered to pay $3 million in restitution on his October 2011 guilty plea in connection with a $9.1 million Medicare fraud scheme. According to court documents, the defendant admitted that from October 2004 through October 2010, he and others conspired to defraud Medicare through the submission of false and fraudulent claims, and by concealing the submission of those claims and the receipt and transfer of the fraud proceeds. The proceeds were diverted to their own personal use or benefit of others.
- In March 2013, two New Orleans residents, the owner of a home health care company and the director of nursing for the same company, were convicted after a six day trial for their involvement in a scheme that fraudulently billed Medicare $17.1 million between 2005 and 2011. According to trial evidence, the defendants paid recruiters to obtain Medicare beneficiary information. The owner paid medical

doctors to sign referrals and certifications for home health services that were not medically necessary, and the nurse falsified and directed others to falsify certification evaluations and other forms to make it appear that the home health services were medically necessary. The owner was sentenced to 180 months, and the director of nursing was sentenced to 60 months.

Phase 7: Tampa (Middle District of Florida)

- Two defendants were indicted on May 7, 2013 on a charge of conspiracy to commit money laundering involving the proceeds of a health care fraud scheme. According to documents filed in the case, the defendants and others conspired to engage in financial and monetary transactions of health care fraud proceeds from Renew Therapy Center of Port St. Lucie LLC (Renew Therapy), a comprehensive outpatient rehabilitation facility. From November 2007 through August 2009, Renew Therapy submitted approximately $10.5 million in fraudulent claims for reimbursement to Medicare for therapy services that were not legitimately prescribed and not legitimately provided to Medicare beneficiaries. As a result of those fraudulent claims, Medicare deposited approximately $6.2 million into a Renew Therapy bank account, approximately $1,847,222 of which was moved through bank accounts and business entities that the defendants controlled. The defendants pled guilty on Oct. 23, 2013 and Oct. 24, 2013.

Phase 8: Dallas (Northern District of Texas)

- In February 2013, the husband and wife owners/operators of a home health care agency were each sentenced to 37 months in prison and ordered to pay over $850,000 on their December 2011 guilty pleas to conspiracy to commit health care fraud. According to court documents, the couple along with a second couple owned a home health care agency that provided care to Medicare and Medicaid beneficiaries. The couple admitted to conspiring with others to defraud Medicare by submitting fraudulent claims home health services on behalf of patients who were ineligible for the services. They also falsified documentation indicating that patients were home bound and eligible for home health services, when in fact they were ineligible, and paid kickbacks to a patient recruiter to recruit Medicare patients so that the agency could increase its Medicare billing and revenue.
- In October 2012, the owner and operator of a home health services company pled guilty to conspiracy to commit health care fraud, in connection with a home health care scheme that billed over $350 million to Medicare and $24 million to Texas Medicaid. According to the court documents, the defendant admitted to directing others to recruit Medicare beneficiaries from Dallas, Texas neighborhoods for home health services they did not need and for which they did not qualify.

Phase 9: Chicago (Northern District of Illinois)

- In September 2013, the owner of numerous outpatient surgery centers and other healthcare-related businesses in Illinois and Indiana, pleaded guilty in the U.S. District Court for the Northern District of Illinois to honest services fraud and tax fraud. The charges stem from a healthcare bribery scheme that included the defendant paying cash to physicians in exchange for the physician referring his patients to or conducting surgeries at the defendant's outpatient surgery centers, rather than at a hospital or competitor surgery center. The indictment, returned by the grand jury in June 2012, alleges that the defendant paid hundreds of thousands of dollars to different physicians, in exchange for the referrals the physicians made to the defendant's facilities, and that the bribery arrangement was not disclosed to the patients, thereby depriving patients of the right to the honest services of their physician. The indictment further alleged that, to obtain cash to pay bribes to doctors, the defendant engaged in a tax fraud scheme with another individual that consisted of the defendant giving Individual A over $2 million in checks written from defendant's healthcare businesses, which were deducted as business expenses, in exchange for which Individual A gave the defendant cash in an amount approximately equal to about 70% of the value of the checks.

- On October 3, 2012, a grand jury returned an indictment charging a Chicago-area dermatologist, with defrauding Medicare and private health insurance companies by submitting false claims for hundreds of patients resulting in millions of dollars of losses. The doctor falsely diagnosed patients with actinic keratosis, or sun-induced skin lesions that have the potential to become cancerous, and then billed Medicare, Blue Cross Blue Shield of Illinois, Aetna, and Humana for treatments that were ineffective and falsely documented. Between 2003 and 2010, the doctor allegedly falsely documented patients' charts to support medically unnecessary, cosmetic treatments that he ordered. In some instances, he falsely documented the removal of more than 1,000 lesions from patients over several years of treatment, according to the indictment. Trial is scheduled for February 2014.
- In September 2013, the owner of numerous outpatient surgery centers and other healthcare-related businesses in Illinois and Indiana, pleaded guilty in the U.S. District Court for the Northern District of Illinois to honest services fraud and tax fraud. The charges stem from a healthcare bribery scheme that included the defendant paying physicians cash in exchange for the physician referring his patients to or conducting surgeries at the defendant's outpatient surgery centers, rather than at a hospital or competitor surgery center. The indictment, returned by the grand jury in June 2012, alleges that the defendant paid hundreds of thousands of dollars to different physicians, in exchange for the referrals the physicians made to the defendant's facilities, and that the bribery arrangement was not disclosed to the patients, thereby depriving patients of the right to the honest services of their physician. The indictment further alleged that, to obtain cash to pay bribes to doctors, the defendant engaged in a tax fraud scheme with another individual that consisted of the defendant giving Individual A over $2 million in checks written from defendant's healthcare businesses, which were deducted as business expenses, in exchange for which Individual A gave the defendant cash in an amount approximately equal to about 70% of the value of the checks.

This case is one of the first in which a healthcare bribery scheme has been charged as honest services fraud under 18 U.S.C. §§ 1341 and 1346, premised upon the defendant (as a third-party) causing a breach of the physician's duty of care and disclosure to a patient. Also representing a departure from ordinary charging theories in healthcare fraud cases, the indictment included Travel Act allegations, *see* 18 U.S.C. § 1951, premised on the defendant causing the travel of patients across state lines and the use of the interstate mail with intent to facilitate commercial bribery in violation of Illinois law. The defendant's sentencing is scheduled for January 2014.

- In 2013, five of ten defendants charged in two separate indictments with conspiracy to violate the Medicare anti-kickback statute pled guilty, including a Doctor who admitted to receiving approximately $324,000 in cash kickbacks in exchange for Medicare patients referrals to Grand Home Health Care, Inc. In all, ten individuals, including the owners of two home health care agencies and three physicians, were charged in two indictments with conspiracy to violate the Medicare anti-kickback statute. The charges stemmed from kickback schemes in which the owners of the two home health care agencies paid cash kickbacks to physicians and other health care professionals in exchange for the referral of Medicare patients. According to the indictments, from 2005 through 2011, the owners of Grand Home Health Care, Inc. paid over $1.1 million in cash kickbacks to approximately twenty doctors, nurses, social workers, and other health care professionals in exchange for the referral of Medicare patients to Grand. During this period, Medicare paid Grand more than approximately $8.3 million on claims for patients illegally referred to Grand in exchange for kickbacks. During this same time period, the owner of Romyst Home Health, Inc. paid approximately $500,000 in cash kickbacks to several doctors in exchange for the referral of Medicare patients to Romyst. Medicare paid Romyst more than approximately $11.7 million on claims for patients illegally referred to Romyst in exchange for kickbacks.

In addition to the Medicare Strike Force matters listed above, our respective Departments successfully pursued the following matters, which are grouped by subject below:

Pharmaceutical and Device Manufacturers and Related Individuals

- In May 2012, Abbott Laboratories pleaded guilty and in October 2012 was sentenced to pay $1.5 billion (including a criminal fine and forfeiture totaling $700 million and federal and state civil settlements totaling $800 million) to resolve criminal and civil liability arising from the company's off-label promotion of the prescription drug, Depakote. In particular, Abbott pleaded guilty to misbranding Depakote by promoting the drug to control agitation and aggression in elderly dementia patients and to treat schizophrenia when neither of these uses was FDA approved. In an agreed statement of facts filed in the criminal action, Abbott admitted that from 1998 through 2006, the company maintained a specialized sales force trained to market Depakote in nursing homes for the control of agitation and aggression in elderly dementia patients, despite the absence of credible scientific evidence that Depakote was safe and effective for that use. Moreover, this settlement resolved FCA allegations that Abbott misled doctors about the safety and efficacy of Depakote for off-label indications, encouraged physicians to circumvent regulations designed to prevent the use of unnecessary drugs in nursing homes, and paid kickbacks to doctors and long-term care pharmacies to prescribe and/or recommend Depakote. As part of this resolution, Abbott also is now subject to court-supervised probation and reporting obligations for Abbott's CEO and Board of Directors.
- In December 2012, Amgen Inc. paid $762 million to resolve criminal and civil FCA liability arising from the improper marketing of certain drugs and biologics. The

company pleaded guilty to a misdemeanor and paid $150 million combined criminal fine and forfeiture for misbranding the anemia drug Aranesp. In addition, the company paid $612 million to resolve FCA allegations that Amgen (1) promoted Aranesp and two other drugs that it manufactured, Enbrel and Neulasta, for off-label uses and doses that were not approved by the FDA and not properly reimbursable by federal insurance programs; (2) offered illegal kickbacks to a wide range of entities in an effort to influence health care providers to select its products for use, regardless of whether they were reimbursable by federal health care programs or were medically necessary; and (3) engaged in false price reporting practices involving several of its drugs. As part of the criminal and civil resolutions, Amgen also executed a Corporate Integrity Agreement (CIA) with HHS-OIG.

- In May 2013, Ranbaxy Laboratories Limited (Ranbaxy) and its subsidiary, Ranbaxy USA, Inc., paid a total of $500 million to resolve criminal and civil liability relating to the manufacture and distribution of certain adulterated drugs made at two of Ranbaxy's manufacturing facilities in India. The settlement included $350 million to resolve FCA allegations that Ranbaxy manufactured, distributed, and sold drugs whose strength, purity, or quality differed from the drug's specifications or that were not manufactured according to the FDA-approved formulation. In addition, Ranbaxy USA pleaded guilty to three felony Food, Drug, and Cosmetic Act (FDCA) counts, and four felony counts of knowingly making material false statements to the FDA. Under the plea agreement, the company will pay $150 million in fines and forfeitures.
- In July 2013, Wyeth Pharmaceuticals Inc. pleaded guilty and paid a total of $490.9 million to resolve its criminal and civil liability arising from the unlawful marketing of the prescription drug Rapamune for uses not approved as safe and effective by the FDA. In particular, Wyeth pleaded guilty to a criminal information charging it with a misbranding violation under the FDCA. The resolution included a criminal fine and forfeiture totaling $233.5 million. In addition, Wyeth paid $257.4 million to resolve FCA allegations that it promoted Rapamune for unapproved uses, some of which were not medically accepted indications and, therefore, were not covered by Medicare, Medicaid and other federal health care programs. These unapproved uses included non-renal transplants, conversion use (switching a patient from another immunosuppressant to Rapamune) and using Rapamune in combination with other immunosuppressive agents not listed on the label.
- In December 2012, Sanofi-Aventis U.S., Inc. and Sanofi-Aventis U.S. LLC, subsidiaries of international drug manufacturer Sanofi (collectively, Sanofi), agreed to pay $109 million to resolve FCA allegations that they provided physicians with free units of Hyalgan, a knee injection, to induce them to purchase and prescribe the product in violation of the Anti-Kickback Statute. The settlement also resolved allegations that Sanofi submitted false average sales price (ASP) reports for Hyalgan that failed to account for the free units distributed contingent on Hyalgan purchases. The Government alleged that the false ASP reports, which were used to set reimbursement rates, caused Government programs to pay inflated amounts for Hyalgan.
- In October 2012, Boehringer Ingelheim Pharmaceuticals Inc. paid $95 million to resolve FCA allegations relating to the improper promotion of the stroke-prevention

drug Aggrenox, the chronic obstructive pulmonary disease (COPD) drugs Atrovent and Combivent, and the hypertension drug Micardis. Boehreinger promoted each of the drugs for uses that were not medically accepted indications and were not covered by federal health care programs. Specifically, the settlement resolves allegations that Boehreinger promoted Aggrenox for certain cardiovascular events such as myocardial infarction and peripheral vascular disease; that Combivent was marketed for use prior to another bronchodilator in treating COPD; and that Micardis was marketed for treatment of early diabetic kidney disease. As part of the resolution, Boehreinger entered into a CIA with HHS/OIG.

- In December 2012, Wyeth Pharmaceuticals Inc. (acquired by Pfizer in October 2009) agreed to a $55 million civil disgorgement settlement to resolve civil FDCA allegations that it illegally introduced and caused the introduction into interstate commerce of a misbranded drug, Protonix, between February 2000 and June 2001. Protonix is a proton pump inhibitor ("PPI") that was used by physicians to treat various forms of gastro- esophageal reflux disease ("GERD"). Wyeth sought and obtained approval from the FDA to promote Protonix for short-term treatment of erosive esophagitis–a condition associated with GERD that can only be diagnosed with an invasive endoscopy. However, Wyeth allegedly promoted Protonix for all forms of GERD, including symptomatic GERD, which is far more common and can be diagnosed without an endoscopy.
- In May 2013, C.R. Bard, Inc. paid $48.26 million to resolve FCA allegations that it paid illegal kickbacks in the form of grants and rebates to doctors and/or hospitals to solicit business from those providers in violation of the Anti-kickback Statute. The hospitals purchased Bard's brachytherapy seeds, the doctors surgically implanted the seeds in prostate cancer patients, and the hospitals then falsely billed Medicare for those seeds in claims the government alleged were rendered false by Bard's illegal kickback conduct. As part of the resolution, Bard also paid $2.2 million to pursuant to a Non-Prosecution Agreement to resolve a related criminal investigation.
- In December 2012, Healthpoint Ltd. agreed to pay $48 million to resolve allegations that it caused false claims to be submitted to Medicare and Medicaid for an unapproved drug, Xenaderm, which was ineligible for reimbursement by those programs. The complaint alleged that Healthpoint's business strategy was to market new prescription drug products modeled after drug products that were on the market before October 1962, in order to avoid the time, effort, and expense of obtaining FDA approval. The complaint further alleged that at no time prior to its introduction of Xenaderm into the market did Healthpoint complete any double-blind placebo-controlled clinical studies that established the safety and effectiveness of Xenaderm. Notwithstanding the lack of FDA approval, the government alleges, Healthpoint actively promoted Xenaderm as a prescription drug that, unlike non-prescription skin ointments such as Vaseline, was "Medicaid reimbursed" and thus cost nursing homes nothing to administer to Medicaid patients.
- In March 2013, Par Pharmaceutical Companies Inc. (Par) pleaded guilty and paid a total of $45 million to resolve its criminal and civil FCA liability arising from the company's promotion of its prescription drug Megace ES for uses not approved as safe and effective by the FDA and not covered by federal health care programs. In particular, Par pleaded guilty to a criminal misdemeanor for misbranding Megace®

ES and paid a fine and forfeiture totaling $22.5 million. Moreover, Par paid an additional $22.5 million to resolve civil allegations that, by promoting the sale and use of Megace® ES for uses that were not FDA-approved and not covered by federal health care programs, Par caused false claims to be submitted to these programs. The government further alleged that Par deliberately and improperly targeted sales to elderly nursing home residents with weight loss, whether or not such patients suffered from AIDS, and launched a long-term care sales force to market to this population. As part of the criminal and civil resolution, Par entered into a CIA with HHS-OIG.

- In May 2013, ISTA Pharmaceuticals, Inc. pleaded guilty and paid a total of $33.5 million to resolve its criminal and civil FCA liability arising from the company's promotion of its prescription drug, Xibrom. In particular, ISTA pled guilty to conspiring to introduce a misbranded drug into interstate commerce and conspiracy to pay illegal remuneration in violation of the federal Anti-Kickback Statute. Under the terms of the plea agreement, ISTA paid $18.5 million, including a criminal fine of $16,125,000 for the conspiracy to introduce misbranded Xibrom into interstate commerce, $500,000 for the conspiracy to violate the Anti-Kickback Statute, and $1,850,000 in asset forfeiture associated with the misbranding charge. In addition, ISTA also paid $15 million to resolve FCA allegations that ISTA promoted the sale and use of Xibrom for certain uses that were not FDA- approved and not covered by the federal health care programs, including prevention and treatment of cystoid macular edema, treatment of pain and inflammation associated with non-cataract eye surgery, and treatment of glaucoma.
- In April 2013, Amgen Inc. paid $24.9 million to settle FCA allegations that it violated the Anti-Kickback Statute. In particular, the government alleged that Amgen paid kickbacks to long-term care pharmacy providers Omnicare Inc., PharMerica Corporation and Kindred Healthcare Inc. in return for implementing "therapeutic interchange" programs that were designed to switch Medicare and Medicaid beneficiaries from a competitor drug to Aranesp. The government alleged that the kickbacks took the form of performance-based rebates that were tied to market-share or volume thresholds. The government further alleged that, as part of the therapeutic interchange program, Amgen distributed materials to consultant pharmacists and nursing home staff encouraging the use of Aranesp for patients who did not have anemia associated with chronic renal failure.
- In July 2013, a bio-pharmaceutical company based in Ventura County, California paid $14.99 million to settle FCA allegations that it knowingly paid unlawful remuneration to oncology practice groups and doctors in order to induce them to prescribe a cancer- treatment drug to beneficiaries of federally funded health care programs, in violation of the Anti-Kickback Statute. The remuneration included directing data purchase agreements for prescription information to the oncology practice groups.
- In December 2012, Victory Pharma, Inc. (Victory) paid $11.4 million to resolve federal civil and criminal liability arising from its marketing of the pharmaceutical products Naprelan, Xodol, Fexmid, and Dolgic. Under the agreement, Victory entered into a deferred prosecution agreement and paid a criminal forfeiture of $1.4 million to resolve federal Ant-Kickback Statute allegations, and paid $9.9 million to

resolve federal FCA allegations. The settlement resolves allegations that Victory engaged in a scheme to promote its drugs by paying kickbacks to doctors to induce them to write prescriptions for Victory's products, including tickets to sporting events; concerts and plays; spa, golf and ski outings; dinners at expensive restaurants. The settlement also resolves allegations that Victory improperly used paid preceptorships to induce doctors to prescribe Victory's products.

- In July 2013, Mallinckrodt, Inc., a pharmaceutical manufacturer, agreed to pay $3.5 million to settle allegations that it made improper payments to physicians and, as a result, caused the submission of false claims to Medicare and Medicaid for various drugs.

Hospitals

- Fifty-five hospitals located throughout 21 states paid a total of over $34 million to resolve FCA liability related to claims for kyphoplasty, a minimally-invasive procedure used to treat spinal compression fractures. In many cases, kyphoplasty can be performed safely and effectively as an outpatient procedure without any need for a more costly inpatient hospital admission. The settlements resolve allegations that the hospitals knowingly billed Medicare for medically unnecessary admissions for kyphoplasty procedures in order to increase their profits and circumvent lower outpatient reimbursement rates.
- In August 2013, Shands Teaching Hospital & Clinics Inc., Shands Jacksonville Medical Center Inc. and Shands Jacksonville Healthcare Inc. (collectively, Shands Healthcare), paid the government and the state of Florida a total of $26 million to settle FCA allegations that six of its health care facilities submitted false claims to Medicare, Medicaid and other federal health care programs for inpatient procedures that should have been billed as outpatient services.
- In April 2013, Intermountain Health Care Inc. paid $25.5 million to settle claims that it violated the Stark Statute and the FCA by engaging in improper financial relationships with referring physicians. These improper financial relationships included employment agreements under which the physicians received bonuses that improperly took into account the value of some of their patient referrals and office leases and compensation arrangements between Intermountain and referring physicians that violated other requirements of the Stark Statute. These issues were disclosed to the government by Intermountain.
- In December 2012, American Sleep Medicine, LLC (ASM), agreed to pay $15.3 million to resolve allegations that it violated the FCA. ASM operates 19 sleep diagnostic centers throughout the United States. ASM allegedly submitted claims to Medicare and other federal health care programs for sleep diagnostic services that were not eligible for payment because the diagnostic tests were performed by individuals who lacked the required license, certification, or credentials. Between January 2004 and December 2011, ASM submitted nearly 20,000 claims for reimbursement. In addition to the monetary agreement, ASM entered into a CIA with HHS/OIG.
- In July 2013, Sound Inpatient Physicians Inc., a nationwide hospitalist firm, paid $14.5 million to settle allegations that it overbilled Medicare and other federal health care programs. The agreement resolves allegations that the firm upcoded Evaluation

& Management services rendered to inpatients. The parent company bills on behalf of the providers for the professional services, while the physicians are being paid a flat salary.

- In May 2013, Adventist Health System/West, dba Adventist Health, and its affiliated hospital, White Memorial Medical Center, paid $14.1 million to settle FCA allegations that Adventist Health violated the Anti-Kickback Statute and Stark Statute by improperly compensating physicians who referred patients to the White Memorial facility by transferring assets, including medical and non-medical supplies and inventory, at less than fair market value.
- In January 2013, Cooper University Hospital agreed to pay $12.5 million to settle allegations that it created a fraudulent advisory board in an effort to induce referrals to its cardiology department. The hospital recruited local outside primary care physicians and non-invasive cardiologists to serve on a sham advisory board. The physicians were paid approximately $18,000 a year to attend four meetings. However, these meetings were largely marketing affairs and there was little evidence of any services being provided by the physician members. In addition to the monetary settlement, the hospital enacted and agreed to maintain a number of corporate reforms designed to enhance accountability, training, and other aspects of its compliance operations.
- In June 2013, the Chief Financial Officer of a hospital in California was sentenced to 8 months of home confinement and ordered to pay $10.6 million in restitution after pleading guilty to charges of conspiracy to pay kickbacks for patient referrals and other related crimes. According to court documents, the CFO oversaw the issuance of checks to companies owned by co-conspirators for the referral of recruited beneficiaries admitted to the hospital. The hospital executed sham "consultant" contracts with these companies to conceal the kickback payments. The hospital then billed Medicare and Medi-Cal for hospital stays and related services provided to the recruited beneficiaries, including admissions that were medically unnecessary. Medicare and Medicaid paid the hospital more than $10.5 million in reimbursement for these false claims.
- In November 2012, Morton Plant Health Care, Inc. and its affiliated hospitals, all part of the BayCare Health System, paid the United States $10.1 million to settle FCA allegations of improperly billing for certain interventional cardiac and vascular procedures as inpatient care when those services should have been billed as less costly outpatient care or as observational status.
- In November 2012, Freeman Health System paid $9.3 million to resolve FCA allegations that it knowingly provided incentive pay to physicians in a manner that violated the Stark Law. In particular, the government alleged that Freeman provided incentive pay to 70 physicians employed at clinics operated by the health system based on the revenue generated by the physicians' referrals for certain diagnostic testing and other services performed at the clinic.
- In July 2013, Dubuis Health System and Southern Crescent Hospital for Specialty Care, Inc. (Southern Crescent) paid $8 million to settle allegations that they knowingly kept patients hospitalized beyond the time considered to be medically necessary in order to increase their Medicare reimbursement and to maintain Southern Crescent's classification as a long-term acute care facility.

- In July 2013, Beth Israel Deaconess Medical Center (BIDMC) paid $5.3 million to settle civil allegations that it violated the FCA by improperly admitting patients and then billing for inpatient stays with respect to services that should have been provided in an outpatient setting, resulting in overpayment by Medicare for unnecessary hospital stays.
- In February 2013, St. Joseph's Medical Center paid $4.9 million to resolve the hospital's civil liability to the United States under the FCA for admitting patients to the hospital unnecessarily from 2007 to 2009. More specifically, the hospital voluntarily disclosed that it admitted patients for short stays (typically one or two days) that were not warranted by the patient's medical condition, and thereby generated a larger reimbursement than was medically necessary for each patient.
- In April 2013, St. Vincent Healthcare and Holy Rosary Healthcare (collectively, the Hospitals) agreed to pay $3.9 million to resolve allegations under the Stark law. These Montana Hospitals self-disclosed that, between July 2003 and December 2010, they paid certain employed physicians incentive compensation that was based, in part, on the volume or value of referrals made to the Hospitals. More specifically, the physician formula for compensation included inappropriate revenue related to such designated health services as EKG and EMG services at the Hospitals. In addition, the Hospitals identified numerous arrangements or contracts it held with independent physicians or physician groups that the Government contended violated the Stark Law. These arrangements or contracts included violations relative to expired or unsigned contracts, unwritten agreements, untimely payment of rent under lease terms, and potential deviations from fair market value rental charges.
- In January 2013, EMH Regional Medical Center (EMH) paid $3.8 million and North Ohio Heart Center Inc. (NOHC) paid $541,870 to resolve allegations that they submitted false claims for medically unnecessary cardiac procedures. In particular, the government alleged that between 2001 and 2006, EMH and NOHC performed angioplasty and stent placement procedures on patients who had heart disease but whose blood vessels were not sufficiently occluded to require the particular procedures at issue.
- In July 2013, University Medical Center (UMC), doing business as University of Louisville Hospital, paid $2.8 million to settle FCA allegations that it may have violated federal law concerning the relationships it had with certain health care providers. University of Louisville Hospital operates a separate fast track unit within the emergency department to address non-urgent care. This in-house immediate care center, FirstCare, is staffed by UMC-employed physician assistants (PAs) and nurse practitioners (NPs) under the direction of the Department of Emergency Medicine physicians – who in turn operate as University Emergency Medicine Associates (UEMA). From January 1, 2006 through December 31, 2010, the salaries and benefits paid to FirstCare PAs and NPs were claimed on UMC cost reports filed with Medicare. At the same time, UEMA physicians generally treated the FirstCare PAs and NPs as their own employees including, to various degrees, billing and collecting from Medicare for their professional services. The United States contended that UMC provided an improper benefit to UEMA in violation of the FCA and other federal law.

- In October 2012, Wyoming Medical Center (WMC) paid $2.7 million arising from the alleged submission of fraudulent claims to Medicare. More specifically, the settlement resolved allegations that WMC submitted higher-paying inpatient reimbursement claims to Medicare for (a) procedures that had been performed in an outpatient setting, (b) hospital stays where there was no record of a physician ordering inpatient-level care, and (c) services provided to patients who did not meet requirements for inpatient admission. The United States also settled allegations that WMC prolonged inpatient hospital admissions without medical necessity in order to qualify patients for Medicare-covered, long-term care at a skilled nursing facility. In addition to the settlement agreement, WMC agreed to enter into a 5-year CIA with HHS-OIG.

Physicians

- In February 2013, an individual and his two companies (identified as Wasserman), paid $26.1 million to resolve FCA allegations that he and his company violated the Anti- Kickback Statute by accepting free pathology services from Tampa Pathology Lab ("TPL") for biopsy specimens they sent to the lab. The government also alleged that Wasserman billed Medicare for medically unnecessary skin repair procedures and for evaluation and management services that he did not perform. In addition to paying the settlement amount, the individual agreed to a five-year voluntary exclusion from participation in any federal health care programs as part of the resolution.
- In July 2013, the United States District Court for the District of Columbia granted the United States' motion for partial summary judgment against a Doctor and his two companies, Ishtiaq Malik M.D., P.C. and Advanced Nuclear Diagnostics, for submitting false nuclear cardiology claims to federal and state health care programs and awarded over $17 million in damages and penalties. The United States alleged that the doctor and his companies violated the FCA by double-billing multi-day nuclear stress test studies, billed for services that were already included in the payment for these tests, and billing for services not rendered.
- In December 2012, a California physician was sentenced for his role in a hospital fraud scheme to 1 year and 1 day in prison and ordered to pay $11 million in restitution. He previously pleaded guilty to conspiracy to receive kickbacks. According to court documents, Tustin Hospital paid marketers to recruit patients and drive them from "Skid Row" around Los Angeles, past other hospitals, to be admitted to its facility. The physician admitted these patients and then he and the hospital billed Medicare for in- patient services, even if the services were not medically necessary. The physician admitted that many of the recruited patients had been coached to recite false symptoms, and that he falsified medical records to justify the admission of some patients. On average, he admitted approximately 60 patients per month to the hospital, even though some did not require hospitalization.
- In July 2013, Jackson Cardiology Associates (JCA) and its owner paid $4 million to resolve FCA allegations that JCA's owner and certain JCA cardiologists performed medically inappropriate cardiac procedures, including invasive catheterizations at Allegiance Health. Specifically, the government alleged that JCA's owner ordered catheterizations for patients based on findings from nuclear stress tests that he

improperly read as positive. The government found that three-quarters of these patients had no significant heart blockages. These catheterizations involve snaking a hollow tube into the heart through an incision in the patient's groin.

- In August 2013, Imagimed LLC and its former owners and former chief radiologist paid $3.57 million to resolve FCA allegations that they submitted false claims for magnetic resonance imaging (MRI) services. In particular, the government alleged that the defendants submitted claims to Medicare, Medicaid and TRICARE for MRI scans performed with a contrast dye without the direct supervision of a qualified physician. Since a potential adverse side effect of contrast dye is anaphylactic shock, federal regulations require that a physician supervise the administration of contrast dye when it is used for an MRI. The government also alleged that Imagimed submitted claims for services referred to Imagimed by physicians with whom Imagimed had improper financial relationships in violation of the Stark Law and the Anti-Kickback Statute.
- In June, 2013, an oncologist and his wife paid $3.1 million to resolve FCA allegations that they jointly defrauded Medicare, Tricare, and other federal programs by overbilling for medication and services and/or billing for medication and services not provided.
- In December 2012, an Illinois physician was sentenced to 10 years in prison and ordered to pay $2.9 million in restitution after being convicted on charges of health care fraud and fraud of visas, permits, or other documents. The physician was the manager and co-owner of House Call Physicians, LLC, a suburban home health care provider. According to court documents, the physician directed House Call Physicians to bill Medicare for: (a) services that were not medically necessary, including uncomfortable nerve conduction tests; (b) services purportedly provided by physicians when, in fact, they were performed by physician assistants; and (c) services performed by a podiatrist with a suspended license. Two other defendants were sentenced to 6 months and 18 months of incarceration, respectively. The two were also, respectively, fined $20,000 and ordered to pay $791,095 in restitution. After completing his sentence, the physician, a Canadian citizen who was not authorized to work in the United States, will be surrendered to the Department of Homeland Security for a deportability determination.
- In November 2012, a Michigan physician was sentenced to 5 years of incarceration and ordered to pay $2.9 million in restitution after being convicted on charges of health care fraud and conspiracy to commit health care fraud. The physician was an obstetrician/gynecologist who served as a general practitioner for three clinics operating in the same location: Blessed Medical Clinic, Alpha and Omega Medical Clinic, and Manuel Medical Clinic. According to evidence presented at trial, the physician joined a conspiracy to bill Medicare for medically unnecessary neurological tests. Some of the tests involved sending an electrical current through the arms and legs of the patients. Clinic employees, who lacked any meaningful training, administered the diagnostic tests. Patients were recruited with prescriptions for controlled substances, cash payments, and fast food.
- In July 2013, Northwestern University agreed to pay $2.93 million to resolve FCA allegations of grant fraud by one of its cancer center physician researchers. The physician was the principal investigator on several National Institutes of Health

(NIH) grants related to cancer research. Instead of using the funds as the grants required, he allegedly spent the money on family trips, meals, and hotels for himself and friends. He also charged “consulting fees” to the grants which went to unqualified friends and family members, including his brother and cousin. Northwestern additionally allowed the researcher to subcontract work under the grants without following NIH guidelines. A civil suit against the individual doctor is proceeding.

- In April 2013, the owner of Winnetka Medical Group, a cosmetic health care clinic, pled guilty to health care fraud and was sentenced to 42 months in prison and was ordered to make full restitution. The defendant billed Medicare, Anthem Blue Cross, and Blue Shield of California for three unusual and high-paying procedures, even though he lacked the equipment necessary to perform them. The defendant even billed Medicare for 26 patients who were already dead on the date he claimed to have performed the procedures. In total, the defendant submitted approximately $7.5 million in fraudulent claims to Medicare and was paid over $3 million.
- In May 2013, Las Vegas Urology, LLP agreed to pay $1 million to settle allegations that it submitted false claims to federal health care programs. An investigation of the practice’s billing and medical records showed that it had billed for intra-abdominal pressure testing that had never been performed and upcoded its billings for cystourethroscopies, consultations, and ultrasound tests. In addition to the settlement agreement, the practice has entered into a three-year CIA with HHS/OIG.
- In January 2013, a Missouri psychotherapist was sentenced to 36 months’ imprisonment and ordered to pay $1 million in restitution for health care fraud. The defendant also agreed to surrender his psychotherapy license. Between September 17, 2008 and April 5, 2012, the defendant submitted Medicare and Medicaid claims for daily or near daily psychotherapy services to 19 beneficiaries for which he was paid $1.3 million. Although the defendant provided some services for most of the beneficiaries, he admitted that he never saw them more than once a week. The defendant further admitted that he forged, or caused another person to forge, the signatures of five the beneficiaries on patient sign-in sheets in order to obtain payments.

Other Health Care Providers

- In May 2013, U.S. Renal Care, Inc. paid $7.3 million to resolve FCA allegations that Dialysis Corporation of America, which U.S. Renal acquired in June 2010, submitted false claims to Medicare for more Epogen, an intravenous drug commonly given to dialysis patients, than it actually administered.
- In October 2012, Westchester County Health Care Corporation (WCHCC) agreed to pay $7 million to resolve alleged FCA violations. WCHCC operates the freestanding mental health facility Westchester Behavioral Health Center (BHC). WCHCC allegedly submitted false certifications to Medicaid stating that claims for services at BHC complied with applicable regulations. However, WCHCC allegedly knew or should have known that: (1) many of the claims lacked the required supporting documentation, and (2) many of the services either did not meet the minimum duration requirements and/or were provided by staff who lacked proper certification.

BHC also allegedly billed Medicaid for psychiatric services without creating or maintaining treatment plans and progress notes.

- In October 2012, the owner/operator of a halfway house was sentenced to 4 years and 3 months of imprisonment and ordered to pay $2.4 million in restitution after pleading guilty to charges of conspiracy to receive and pay health care kickbacks. According to court documents, the owner/operator accepted kickbacks to send Medicare beneficiaries who resided at the half-way house to American Therapeutic Corporation (ATC) for partial hospitalization services. Investigators believe that these services were not medically necessary and were not provided at ATC. ATC then billed Medicare for these services.
- In October 2012, the owner of Gideon's Gate, a provider of tutoring and day care services, was sentenced to 6 years and 8 months of incarceration and ordered to pay more than $1.9 million in restitution after pleading guilty to health care fraud charges. The owner admitted that she executed a scheme to file more than 2,400 illegitimate reimbursement claims for psychological services that she never performed. The owner conspired with another defendant, who owned the company Primeway. Primeway's owner had a welfare- to-work contract to train Medicaid recipients to become certified nursing assistants. Primeway's owner provided the Medicaid recipients' personal identifiers to the owner of Gideon's Gate, who then back billed these recipients to Medicaid for mental health services that were not rendered. The owner of Primeway previously pleaded guilty to charges of receiving an illegal kickback from a health care program and was sentenced to 5 years of probation and assessed a $2,000 fine.

Pharmacies

- From August, 2011 through July, 2013, twenty-six defendants have been convicted for their roles in a widespread scheme to defraud Medicare and Medicaid of nearly $58 million. According to the indictment, a licensed pharmacist owned or controlled 26 pharmacies in Michigan. The pharmacist concealed his ownership and control over many of his pharmacies through the use of straw owners. He offered and paid kickbacks, bribes, and other inducements to providers in exchange for them writing fraudulent prescriptions for patients with Medicare, Medicaid, and private insurance and directing the patients to fill their prescriptions at one of his pharmacies. In September 2013, the pharmacist was sentenced to 17 years in prison and ordered to pay $18.9 million in restitution, joint and several. His co-conspirators were sentenced between February and May 2013 to a combined 19 years in prison and ordered to pay more than $8.4 million in restitution, joint and several. Nineteen additional defendants are awaiting sentencing.
- In June 2013, Omnicare, Inc. paid $17.2 million to settle FCA allegations that it paid kickbacks to obtain pharmacy contracts in violation of the federal Anti-Kickback statute. The settlement addressed false claims allegedly made to the Medicaid programs of Missouri, Illinois, and Florida.
- In October 2012, RxAmerica LLC., a wholly owned subsidiary of CVS Caremark Corporation, paid $5.25 million to resolve FCA allegations that it made false submissions to CMS regarding prices for certain generic prescription drugs used for Plan Finder, a web-based tool offered by CMS to assist participants to choose a Part

D plan that minimized their out-of-pocket costs by estimating prescription drug prices for each Medicare Part D plan that the beneficiary considered for enrollment. As a result of the false submissions, the government alleged that RxAmerica received Medicare Part D payments for claims for the covered drugs at prices that in some cases were significantly higher than the pricing data RxAmerica submitted to CMS for use on Plan Finder.

- In November 2012, two HHS-OIG Most Wanted Fugitives were captured and later pled guilty to charges related to health care fraud. In April 2013, the first was sentenced to 4 years and 9 months of incarceration and ordered to pay $4.4 million in restitution, joint and several, while the second sentenced to 2 years and 6 months of incarceration and ordered to pay $845,000 in restitution. The two owned and operated pharmacies in Miami. According to court records, the two owners/operators and their co-conspirators were involved in a Medicare scheme in which kickbacks and bribes were paid to patient recruiters and beneficiaries for prescriptions that were then used to submit fraudulent claims to Medicare. An employee, who also participated in the scheme, was sentenced to 3 years and 10 months of incarceration and ordered to pay $4.4 million in restitution, joint and several.
- In August 2013, National Respiratory Services (NRS), a mail-order/closed door pharmacy which supplied compounded inhalation drugs to patients, pled guilty to health care fraud for billing for compounded medications as if they were non-compounded, commercially manufactured FDA-approved drugs. The compounded medications were most often sub- potent, super-potent, and in some cases non-sterile. As a result of the conduct, the government paid NRS over $2 million dollars. The two NRS pharmacists, the minority owner, and the majority owner pled guilty to a FDA misbranding violation and were sentenced to one year probation. The vice-president of operations pled guilty to felony misbranding, felony adulteration, health care fraud, and mail fraud. The defendants must pay restitution jointly and severally in the amount of $2 million.

Clinics

- In May 2013, a captured HHS-OIG Most Wanted Fugitive was sentenced to 9 years and 1 month of incarceration and ordered to pay more than $26 million in restitution, joint and several, after pleading guilty to charges of conspiracy to commit health care fraud and money laundering. According to court documents, as an employee of a provider of physical therapy services, he signed his name on patient files as the provider of such services, including blank treatment data forms, progress notes, and daily physical therapy records. However, he was not licensed, trained, or otherwise qualified to provide physical therapy to patients. This individual was arrested by Nigerian authorities in 2011 and extradited back to the United States in June 2012 to face health care fraud charges.
- In November 2012, a Miami man was sentenced to 12 years and 7 months of incarceration and ordered to pay $11 million in restitution after pleading guilty to charges of conspiracy to commit health care fraud and to pay health care kickbacks, health care fraud, payment of health care kickbacks, and money laundering. The man was the president and co-owner of Research Center of Florida, Inc., a purported medical clinic. He paid more than $2.3 million to fraudulent companies controlled by

outside patient recruiters who paid cash to Medicare beneficiaries to attend Research Center as purported patients. Between October 2003 and November 2004, Research Center submitted claims to Medicare for nearly $21 million, almost exclusively for the purported treatment of HIV-positive Medicare beneficiaries and for the administration of prescription drugs. Co-conspirators were previously sentenced to 6 years and 6 months and 5 years and 10 months of incarceration, respectively, and ordered to pay $14 million in restitution, joint and several, for their roles in the scheme. Two other defendants were sentenced to 3 years and 10 months and 6 years and 6 months of incarceration, respectively, and ordered to pay $10.9 million in joint and several restitution.

- In June 2013, the part-owner and medical biller for the Advanced Clinics was sentenced to serve twelve months and one day in federal prison for her role in a health care fraud scheme. The defendant was also ordered to pay a $1.89 million fine, restitution of $120,689 and a refund of $1 million. The majority of patients of the Advanced Clinics were injured United States Postal Service workers receiving medical benefits under the U.S. Department of Labor, Office of Workers' Compensation Program (DOL-OWCP). The defendant fraudulently billed DOL-OWCP for services not rendered, double billed, and unbundled billing codes to obtain higher reimbursements. The defendant personally received over $4.4 million from the Advanced Clinics.
- In July 2013, Health Guard Inc. and its owner, a unlicensed diagnostic technician, pled guilty to health care fraud, and currently awaits sentencing. Patients went to Health Guard Inc. for medical tests that were not performed or were medically unnecessary. Patients were moved between other commonly owned health care clinics to Health Guard Inc. to repeatedly perform the same unnecessary tests. Five other clinics and their owners have already been sentenced for the same activity. If the patients refused the diagnostic tests at Health Guard Inc., prescriptions for narcotic drugs were withheld. Thereafter, bills for the unnecessary services were submitted to Medicare and Medicaid.
- In March 2013, the medical director of a clinic in Long Beach, California, was sentenced to 42 months' imprisonment and ordered to pay $2.9 million in restitution for issuing bogus prescriptions that led to fraudulent Medicare claims of over $3 million. The doctor and his co-schemers recruited Medicare patients for office visits that typically included unnecessary tests and procedures. The medical director, who was a doctor, also generated fraudulent prescriptions for medical equipment, power wheel chairs and enteral nutritional supplies, prescriptions that were sold to medical supply companies that used the fraudulent documents to bill Medicare for millions of dollars of unnecessary and undelivered medical supplies. Nearly all of the wheelchair prescriptions signed by the doctor were written for people who could walk. As a result of the fraudulent conduct involving the defendant and his co-schemers, $5.6 million in fraudulent claims were submitted to Medicare, which paid approximately $2.97 million. The defendant was convicted following a jury trial in March 2012.
- In July 2013, the owner of two "false front" healthcare clinics operating in Houston, Texas and Euless, Texas was sentenced to 120 months imprisonment and ordered to pay over $2 million in restitution, jointly and severally with four codefendants. Along with the owner, the clinics were operated by the codefendants who were

unlicensed physicians and physician's assistants. These unlicensed employees traveled to Medicare beneficiaries homes to conduct medical examinations. In addition to conducting medical examinations, the unlicensed employees would falsify orders for medical testing in order to make the patient files look legitimate. These tests were never ordered and never administered. The owner of the clinic purchased fake results and subsequently billed Medicare for millions of dollars in phony home visits and fake medical tests.

- In May 2013, a Florida woman was sentenced to 10 years in prison following her conviction for conspiracy to commit health care fraud through several physical and occupational therapy clinics she owned in the Miami area. The owner of the clinics defrauded the Medicare Part A program by falsely billing over $20 million in therapy services that were never rendered. As part of the scheme, patients were recruited and paid kickbacks for allowing their Medicare eligibility to be misused. Clinic employees would rotate the patients, many of whom lived hours away from Miami, through the various clinics in an effort to spread out the fraudulent billing and avoid detection. Eight other employees and therapists at the clinics were convicted and received sentences ranging from two to five years of imprisonment. Collectively, the defendants were ordered to repay almost $14 million in restitution. The owner of the clinics forfeited approximately $200,000 in cash, along with various real properties and personal items seized at the time of her arrest.

Medical Equipment Suppliers

- In November 2012, Orthofix International NV paid $30 million to settle FCA allegations that it paid illegal kickbacks to spinal surgeons to induce them to use the company's products. In particular, the government alleged that Blackstone Medical Inc., a subsidiary of Orthofix, paid kickbacks to spinal surgeons in a number of forms, including sham consulting agreements, sham royalty arrangements, sham research grants, travel and entertainment. As part of the settlement, Orthofix entered into a CIA with HHS/OIG.
- In May 2013, an owner/operator of several durable medical equipment (DME) companies in Nevada was sentenced to 4 years and 3 months of incarceration and ordered to pay over $12 million in restitution after pleading guilty to charges of health care fraud and tax evasion. According to the indictment, the owner/operator paid marketers in Southern California to obtain patients for her various DME companies. The marketers provided patients with money in exchange for their Medicare information, which was used to bill Medicare for items not provided. The owner/operator also forged or caused to be forged prescriptions and falsified or caused to be falsified certificates of medical necessity to make it appear as if a physician had ordered a product for her customers. She then submitted and caused to be submitted false claims to Medicare for DME that was not medically necessary, was not provided to her customers, and was not prescribed by a physician.
- In March 2013, a California DME company owner and operator was sentenced to 156 months imprisonment and ordered to pay $8.2 million in restitution, jointly and severally, after a jury convicted her of multiple counts of health care fraud and anti-kickback violations. At trial, the government presented evidence that the defendant paid marketers to recruit Medicare beneficiaries to seek expensive DME, such as

motorized wheel chairs, that they did not need. The defendant or the marketers she relied on, often paid doctors to write the fraudulent prescriptions. The defendant would then submit the false claims to Medicare. Over the course of the scheme, defendant submitted over $16 million in fraudulent claims to Medicare, of which Medicare paid over $8 million. Other defendants included a marketer, who was sentenced to 41 months imprisonment, as well as a cooperating marketer who received a time served sentence and a cooperating doctor who received a 36-month period of probation.

- In July 2013, TranS1, Inc. (now known as Baxano Surgical, Inc.) paid $6 million to resolve FCA allegations that the company caused health care providers to submit false claims to federal health care programs for surgical procedures involving the company's AxiaLIF System. Specifically, the settlement resolves allegations that TranS1 (1) improperly counseled physicians and hospitals to inflate reimbursement by using incorrect and inaccurate codes intended for more invasive spine fusion surgeries; (2) provided improper remuneration in violation of the Anti-Kickback Statute; and (3) promoted unapproved uses that were not covered by federal health care programs.
- In April 2013, the owner/operator of a DME company in New York was sentenced to 12 years of imprisonment and ordered to pay $4.4 million in restitution for her role in a scheme to defraud Medicare by billing for DME that she did not provide. Through the DME company, the owner/operator and her husband fraudulently billed the accounts of nursing home residents from over 15 New York area nursing homes for DME that was never ordered or provided. According to court documents, the owner/operator entered these nursing homes falsely presenting herself in many roles, including physician, nurse practitioner, and wound care expert. She then stole original medical records, as well as altered and manufactured records, in an effort to justify medical billing. Investigators believe that her husband fled the country and remains a fugitive.
- In June 2013, the owner/operator of a DME company in Louisiana was sentenced to 8 years and 1 month of incarceration and ordered to pay $2.5 million in restitution after being convicted on charges of health care fraud. According to the indictment, the owner/operator submitted approximately $467,000 in claims to Medicare for DME purportedly prescribed by a doctor in Houston, Texas. However, the doctor never prescribed any of the DME for which he billed Medicare. He also submitted more than $6.7 million in claims to Medicare for DME that was not medically necessary, and in some cases, was never provided.
- In June 2013, a DME business owner was sentenced to 70 months of imprisonment and ordered to pay $1.9 million in restitution, after pleading guilty to conspiracy to commit health care fraud and aggravated identity theft. According to court documents, the DME company owner created several different companies and submitted more than 1,500 false and fraudulent claims to Medicare for DME including power wheelchairs, power pressure reducing air mattresses and knee orthosis. The defendant submitted claims using the identities of Medicare beneficiaries for DME that was not medically necessary.
- In October 2012, the co-owner of a Florida DME company was sentenced to 11 years and 3 months of incarceration and ordered to pay $1.7 million in restitution, joint and

several, after pleading guilty to charges of conspiracy to commit health care fraud. The DME company, MA Medical Supply, Inc., paid beneficiaries for allowing them to use their information to create false and fraudulent prescriptions for DME and medical services that were either not rendered or were unnecessary. From January 2006 through July 2011, MA Medical Supply submitted $4 million in false and fraudulent claims to Medicare. In addition, the co-owner and his co-conspirators caused the submission of false and fraudulent claims and prescriptions to Medicare through several pharmacies. From approximately April 2009 through January 2012, Medicare paid more than $16 million to these pharmacies based on claims for medical benefits, primarily prescription drugs, which, in turn, were never actually received by the beneficiaries.

Nursing Homes

- In March 2013, Grace Healthcare LLC and its affiliate Grace Ancillary Services LLC (collectively, "Grace") paid $2.7 million, plus interest, to resolve FCA allegations that they knowingly submitted or caused the submission of false claims to Medicare and Medicaid for medically unreasonable and unnecessary rehabilitation therapy. In particular, the government alleged that in ten nursing home facilities where Grace provided physical, occupational, and speech therapy, Grace pressured therapists to increase the amount of therapy provided to patients in order to meet targets for Medicare revenue that were set without regard to patients' individual therapy needs and could only be achieved by billing for a large amount of therapy per patient.
- In February 2013, Fairfax Nursing Center, Inc. and its owners paid $700,000 to resolve FCA allegations that they provided excessive, medically unnecessary, or otherwise non- reimbursable physical, occupational, and speech therapy services to 37 Medicare beneficiaries.

Home Health Providers

- In April 2013, a Miami man was sentenced to 168 months for his role as one of the owners of a Miami-Dade home health agency which submitted approximately $45 million in false claims to Medicare, causing Medicare to pay the agency approximately $30 million. Almost all of these claims were for providing twice daily insulin injections to purportedly homebound diabetic patients. The investigation revealed that the agency used the services of dozens of patient recruiters who were paid $1,500 per month for each patient that they provided to the agency. Investigation revealed that almost all of these patients were not homebound and many of them were not insulin dependent diabetics. During the course of this investigation, a total of thirty two defendants pled guilty and four were found guilty after trial. These defendants included patient recruiters, office employees, and registered nurses.
- In December 2012, a Miami man was sentenced to 120 months in prison for his role in a home health care fraud scheme in which he submitted and caused the submission of approximately $5.3 million in false claims to Medicare. The defendant recruited individuals so that he could secretly control three separate home health agencies in Miami- Dade County. The defendant would purchase the companies for cash, and within a few weeks of purchasing the companies he used stolen Medicare beneficiary

information to submit claims for services that were never actually rendered to Medicare beneficiaries. The defendant was a former drug trafficker who served nine years in prison from 1999 through 2006.

- Nine defendants were sentenced in April and May of 2013 for their roles in a home health care fraud scheme. According to court records, the president of Safe Home Health Care Agency, Inc., a Miami-based business that purportedly provided home health services to Medicare beneficiaries, and several co-conspirators allegedly offered and paid kickbacks and bribes to patient recruiters in return for referring beneficiaries to Safe Home to serve as patients. Beneficiaries also received kickbacks for agreeing to serve as patients of Safe Home. Safe Home received $9.5 million in reimbursements from these false claims. The nine defendants were sentenced to a combined 16 years and 2 months in prison and ordered to pay more than $5.8 million in restitution, joint and several.
- In February 2013, two owners of a home health company, Alliance Home Health, each received a sentence of 37 months and were ordered to pay over $800,000 in restitution for a conviction on one count of conspiracy to commit health care fraud. They were also permanently excluded from the program. Another owner also received the same sentence in August 2012, and a marketer for the company received a 27 month sentence. The owners of Alliance and the marketer sought out Medicare beneficiaries for home health care, regardless of homebound status and paid the beneficiaries $100 each month to use Alliance services.
- In July 2013, a New Jersey physician and the founder and owner of Visiting Physicians of South Jersey, a provider of home-based physician services for seniors, was sentenced to 24 months in prison and ordered to pay more than $1 million in restitution and forfeiture for charging Medicare for lengthy visits that her elderly patients did not receive. The physician admitted to lying in Medicare billings about the amount of face-to-face time she spent with her elderly and disabled patients, which led to her receiving at least $511,068 in criminal profits. The physician was, for the period January 1, 2008 through October 14, 2011, the highest billing home health care provider of all of the 24,000 doctors in New Jersey.
- In April and June 2013, respectively, a Florida woman and a registered nurse were sentenced after pleading guilty to conspiring to pay and receive illegal health care kickbacks and paying kickbacks in connection with the a home health agency they operated. The woman was sentenced to 70 months imprisonment and ordered to pay more than $5 million in restitution, jointly and severally. The registered nurse was sentenced to 97 months imprisonment and ordered to pay more than $22,000 in restitution, jointly and severally. According to court documents, the defendants paid kickbacks to patient recruiters to obtain Medicare beneficiaries to serve as patients of a home health agency they operated. The defendants also paid bribes to doctors who prescribed the home health services for the beneficiaries. In a little more than two years of operation, Medicare paid the defendant's home health agency more than $11 million dollars, most of which was tied to kickbacks. In addition to these two defendants, seven patient recruiters were convicted in this indictment.
- In August 2013, the owner of a network of Michigan health care companies was sentenced to 4 years in prison, paid a $1 million civil FCA settlement, and agreed to a 20-year exclusion from federal health care programs in connection with pervasive

kickback and upcoding schemes at his physical therapy clinics, medical offices, and home health care agency. This sentence followed the convictions and sentencings of eight other individuals: two physicians, three physician assistants, two practice administrators, and a biller, who participated in these schemes. According to court documents in the criminal case and a parallel civil case against 25 defendants, the defendants paid or received illegal kickbacks in exchange for referring Medicare and Medicaid patients for physical therapy, electrodiagnostic testing, and home health care services. The illegal payments were made in cash and checks disguised as bonuses, mileage reimbursements, and payments for medical director and consulting services that were never performed. At least one of the affiliated health care companies also allegedly engaged in upcoding by fraudulently billing for high-level office visits, among other things. To date, the Government has obtained over 7 years in total prison sentences in these cases, collected $1.1 million in related civil settlements, and OIG has imposed 40 years in total exclusions from federal health care programs.

- In July 2013, the president of a D.C.-based home health care provider was sentenced to 8 months incarceration, to be followed by 4 months home detention, after pleading guilty to one count of falsification of records in connection with an HHS audit. The defendant's company, which provided home healthcare services, was asked by auditors to produce plans of care for 62 patients who had received home health care services from her company. In total, Medicare and D.C. Medicaid had paid nearly $1.9 million in federal funds to the defendant's company for the services these patients had already supposedly been provided. The company lacked the requisite plans of care for these individuals. Rather than admitting that the company lacked the necessary documentation, the defendant and employees of the company devised and implemented a plan to fabricate the plans of care. After creating plans of care for the patients who had already received this nearly $1.9 million in services, the defendant and others had a doctor sign the plans and then the documents were backdated to dates prior to the services. This doctor, who was the medical director, was sentenced to two years of probation after pleading guilty to one count of making a false writing in connection with this audit.

Other Medicare/Medicaid Matters

- In December 2012, Orthofix, Inc. pled guilty to a one count felony information charging obstruction of a health care audit. In addition, the company agreed to a $42 million civil and criminal global resolution in connection with a number of practices, including falsification of certificates of medical necessity and kickbacks. The case also resulted in a number of criminal convictions of Orthofix employees, six of whom were sentenced or charged during FY 2013, including three Territory Managers, a Vice President of Sales, and a Regional Manager. A Virginia physician was also indicted in June 2013 for making false declarations to a grand jury in Boston. Her trial has not yet been scheduled.
- In January 2013, American Sleep Medicine LLC paid $15.3 million to resolve FCA allegations that it billed Medicare, TRICARE, and the Railroad Retirement Medicare Program for sleep diagnostic services that were not eligible for payment. In particular, the government alleged that although federal regulations require that

initial sleep studies must be conducted by technicians who are licensed or certified by a state or national credentialing body as sleep test technicians, American Sleep submitted claims for diagnostic testing services that were performed by technicians who lacked the required credentials or certifications.

- In April 2013, the California Rural Indian Health Board Inc., a nontribal entity and grantee of the HHS Substance Abuse and Mental Health Services Administration, agreed to a settlement worth over $5.1 million to resolve an FCA lawsuit filed by the United States. The lawsuit involved the entity's administration of a grant to provide services to Native American tribes. The United States alleged that the entity eliminated the substance abuse screening and assessment required of certain program applicants, and instructed the service providers to pay for prohibited expenses with the federal grant funds. The entity agreed to pay $532,000 and relinquish federal grant funds valued at over $4.6 million.
- In December 2013, two Regional Vice-Presidents employed with Humana Inc. will be sentenced for their roles in a kickback scheme involving Humana's Medicare Advantage and prescription drug plan. As a result of their conduct, each received a kickback payment of approximately $2 million dollars. The two defendants entered guilty pleas to violation of the Travel Act and the state commercial bribery statute in January and February 2013, respectively. Each defendant has been ordered to pay $100,000 in restitution to Humana and $900,000 in forfeiture.
- In January 2013, a California university paid $925,000 to resolve allegations that its medical center sought Medicare reimbursement for liver transplants and related services when its liver transplant program failed to comply with federal requirements regarding surgeon staffing.

Hospice Providers

- In March 2013, Hospice of Arizona L.C., along with a related entity, American Hospice Management LLC, and their parent corporation, American Hospice Management Holdings LLC, paid $12 million to resolve FCA allegations that they submitted or caused the submission of false claims to the Medicare program for ineligible hospice services. In particular, the government alleged that Hospice of Arizona and its related entities engaged in certain practices that resulted in the admission of ineligible patients or inflated bills, including pressuring staff to find more patients eligible for Medicare, adopting procedures that delayed and discouraged staff from discharging patients from hospice when they were no longer appropriate for such services, and not implementing an adequate compliance program that might have addressed these problems. As part of the settlement, American Hospice Management Holdings has agreed to enter into a CIA with HHS-OIG.

Other Schemes

- In November 2012, a Washington, D.C., woman was sentenced to 6 years and 3 months of incarceration and ordered to pay $3.1 million in restitution after being convicted of charges related to health care fraud. According to the indictment, the woman was part owner and chief executive officer of the Health Advocacy Center, Inc. (HAC), which purportedly was an advocate for improving health care delivery to the community. She was also the owner of Sheridan Rehabilitative and Wellness Centers, Inc., which purportedly provided rehabilitative services to the mentally and physically disabled community. Around October 2002, HAC entered into an agreement with DC Medicaid to provide health care services to District of Columbia Medicaid beneficiaries. The woman's employees transported many of these patients to HAC, where they often slept, watched television, and occasionally received drug and alcohol counseling. From these visits, the woman submitted more than $6 million in claims to DC Medicaid for manual therapy services, despite the fact that: 1) she did not maintain progress notes and related documentation for the purported manual therapy and other services, 2) she frequently billed for services for which HAC lacked the medical equipment to perform, and 3) she frequently billed for more than 24-hours of services for a single patient in a given day.

DEPARTMENT OF HEALTH AND HUMAN SERVICES

Office of Inspector General

A certain portion of the funds appropriated under HIPAA are, by law, set aside for Medicare and Medicaid activities of HHS/OIG.[16] In FY 2013, the Secretary and the Attorney General jointly allotted $197 million to HHS/OIG. Additionally, Congress appropriated $30 million in discretionary funding for HHS/OIG HCFAC activities. Of these amounts, over $11 million was sequestered in FY 2013 and thus unavailable to OIG to fight fraud and abuse in Medicare and Medicaid.

In FY 2013, HHS/OIG investigations resulted in 849 criminal actions against individuals or entities that engaged in crimes related to Medicare and Medicaid; and 458 civil actions, which include false claims and unjust-enrichment lawsuits filed in Federal district court, civil monetary penalties (CMP) settlements, and administrative recoveries related to provider self-disclosure matters. In addition, during FY 2013, HHS/OIG excluded a total of 3,214 individuals and entities, the details of which are below.

In FY 2013, HHS/OIG continued to staff and support Medicare Strike Force operations worked in conjunction with DOJ Criminal Division's Fraud Section, local USAOs, the FBI, and State and local law enforcement agencies. HHS/OIG has assigned agents to Strike Forces in Miami, New York City, Houston, Tampa, Detroit, Los Angeles, South Louisiana, Dallas, and Chicago. HHS/OIG has supported Strike Force operations by providing investigative, analytic, and forensic resources. These Strike Forces have effectively investigated and prosecuted individuals and entities that do not provide legitimate health care services, but exist solely for the purpose of defrauding Medicare and other Government health care programs. The continued support of Medicare Strike Force operations is a top priority for HHS/OIG.

Program Savings

Frequently, investigations, audits, and evaluations reveal vulnerabilities or incentives for questionable or fraudulent practices in agency programs or administrative processes. As required by the Inspector General Act, HHS/OIG makes recommendations to agency managers to address these vulnerabilities. In turn, agency managers recommend legislative proposals or other corrective actions that, when enacted or implemented, close loopholes and reduce improper payments or conduct. The savings from these joint efforts toward program improvements can be substantial. For FY 2013, potential savings from legislative and administrative actions that were supported by HHS/OIG recommendations were estimated by third parties, such as the Congressional Budget Office or actuaries within HHS, to be $19.4 billion – $18.54 billion in Medicare savings and $834 million in savings to the Federal share of Medicaid.

Additional information about savings achieved through such policy and procedural changes may be found in the HHS/OIG fall Semiannual Report to Congress, on-line at http://oig.hhs.gov.

Exclusions

One important mechanism for safeguarding the care provided to program beneficiaries is through exclusion of providers and suppliers who have engaged in the abuse or neglect of patients or fraud from participation in Medicare, Medicaid, and other Federal health care programs. During FY 2013, HHS/OIG excluded a total of 3,214 individuals and entities. Among these were exclusions based on criminal convictions for crimes related to Medicare and Medicaid (1,132) or to other health care programs (311); for patient abuse or neglect (180); or as a result of licensure revocations (1,324). This list of conduct is not meant to be exhaustive, but identifies the most prevalent causes underlying HHS/OIG's exclusions of individuals or entities in FY 2013. Exclusion actions by HHS/OIG included:

- Florida – In February 2013, the owner and operator of a pain clinic, was excluded for a minimum period of 50 years based on his conviction for conspiracy to possess with intent to distribute oxycodone and oxymorphone and conspiracy to commit health care fraud. From November 2007 to about September 2011, he owned and operated the pain clinic for the purpose of obtaining false prescriptions for these drugs for beneficiaries of the Medicare, Medicaid, and private insurance plans and he would offer inducements to beneficiary recruiters so they would bring beneficiaries to his pain clinic. The court sentenced the owner/operator to more than 16 years of incarceration and ordered him to pay $15 million in restitution.
- Pennsylvania – In January 2013, an osteopath was excluded for a minimum period of 20 years based on his drug trafficking conviction. Between September 2000 and March 2010, the osteopath and others distributed controlled substance prescription diet drugs outside of professional practice. This included more than 1.5 million doses of a substance that contained phendimetrazine and more than 2.5 million doses of a substance that contained phentermine. The court sentenced him to 2 years and 10 months of incarceration. The Pennsylvania State Board of Osteopathic Medicine revoked his license to practice.
- Kansas – In December 2012, a licensed practical nurse was excluded for a minimum period of 10 years based on her conviction on charges of consumer product tampering and adulteration of a drug. During the course of her employment, the nurse would steal morphine from a particular patient at the facility where she worked. To conceal her behavior, she added tap water to the patient's medication bottle and then placed the bottle back on the medication cart to dispense to the

patient. The court sentenced her to 3 years of incarceration. In addition, the Kansas State Board of Nursing permanently revoked her license to practice nursing.

- Florida – In August 2013, a chiropractor, was excluded for a minimum period of 40 years based on his convictions for health care fraud, conspiracy to illegally distribute and dispense and cause to be distributed and dispensed schedule III and IV controlled substances, and aiding and abetting transactional money laundering. The chiropractor billed and caused bills to be sent to Medicare, Medicaid, and private insurers for services that were rendered by him or his staff as though they were medical doctors. In actuality, he used the name of a medical doctor to fraudulently bill for services that were never performed or provided by the medical doctor. In addition, he used the names and DEA numbers of medical doctors to illegally prescribe controlled substances to patients with no legitimate doctor-patient relationship. As a result of these crimes, the chiropractor was sentenced to 15 years and 8 months of incarceration and ordered to pay more than $2 million in restitution. The Florida Board of Chiropractic Medicine ordered the voluntary relinquishment of his license to practice.
- Louisiana – In August 2013, an individual who was the owner, manager, and technician of several medical clinics was excluded for a minimum period of 25 years based on his conviction. The owner and his co-conspirators were involved in a scheme to defraud Medicare and Medicaid through fraudulent billing for diagnostic tests that were not medically necessary or not performed. Based on this scheme, he was convicted on charges of conspiracy to commit health care fraud and conspiracy to commit money laundering and was sentenced to 4 years and 1 month of incarceration and ordered to pay more than $6 million in restitution, joint and several. The owner was also excluded from participation in Medicaid by the Louisiana Department of Health and Hospitals.
- Kentucky – In August 2013, a registered nurse was excluded for a minimum period of 20 years based on her reckless homicide conviction. The nurse entered the room of a patient with a cigarette lighter, which started a fire on the patient's bedding. Because he was in a complete vegetative state, the patient was unable to escape and he died as a result. The court sentenced the nurse to 5 years of incarceration. In addition, the Kentucky State Board of Nursing revoked her license to practice.
- Florida – In August 2013, a medical doctor was excluded for a minimum period of 10 years based on his conviction for conspiracy to knowingly and willfully dispense and cause to be dispensed schedule IV controlled substances. From about January 2004 to about February 2008, the doctor conspired with others to dispense controlled substances that involved a mixture and substance containing methadone. Investigators believe that the use of these substances resulted in one or more deaths. The doctor was sentenced to 12 months of incarceration followed by 12 months of home detention.

Other Administrative Enforcement Actions – Civil Monetary Penalties

HHS/OIG has the authority to impose civil monetary penalties (CMPs) against providers and suppliers who knowingly submit false claims to the Federal government, who participate in unlawful patient referral or kickback schemes, who fail to appropriately treat or refer patients at hospital emergency rooms, or who engage in other activities prescribed in statute.

HHS/OIG has continued to pursue its affirmative enforcement actions under these authorities. Examples include:

- South Carolina – In January 2013, Heritage Medical Partners agreed to pay $170,260 to resolve allegations that, from April 2008 through December 2008, Heritage violated the CMP Law by requesting that its 5,474 patients who were Medicare beneficiaries pay a $50 administrative fee. Heritage told these Medicare beneficiaries that "the Federal Government (Medicare) continue[s] to increase the amount of paperwork we're required to fill out to assure you receive the benefits to which you're entitled" and that Heritage instituted the fee as partial compensation for the time the "physician and staff spend assuring [patients] receive prescription renewals quickly [and] maximum benefits from Medicare. . ." HHS/OIG alleged that a portion of the $50 constituted payment for Medicare services that are covered and reimbursed by Medicare and constituted a request for payment other than copayments or coinsurance, which violated Medicare assignment regulations. Heritage agreed to return the money it collected to patients and pay a penalty to HHS/OIG.
- Illinois – In November 2012, ForTec Medical, Inc.; ForTec Litho, LLC; ForTec Litho Florida, LLC; ForTec Litho Central, LLC; and ForTec Litho NY, LLC (collectively, ForTec), agreed to pay $126,249 to resolve their liability under the CMPL for offering remuneration in exchange for referrals. From 2006 through 2011, ForTec allegedly provided customers, including physicians, with an all-expense paid trip to the Masters Golf Tournament in Augusta, Georgia. Invitations to these trips were extended to physicians based on their use of ForTec's products and services and the potential for additional business from those physicians.
- New Mexico – In December 2012, University of New Mexico Hospital (UNMH) agreed to pay $30,000 to resolve its liability under the patient dumping statute. UNMH allegedly failed to provide an adequate medical screening examination and failed to stabilize a suicidal patient when it did not prevent the suicidal patient from hanging himself in the hospital. The patient came to the emergency room experiencing suicidal ideations and was placed in an observation room, but he was not provided a medical screening examination for 7 hours. During this time, the patient used his shoelaces to hang himself from an air vent in the observation room. The patient was found still alive by a security employee. UNMH then treated and admitted the patient. UNMH self-reported the incident to the State.
- Illinois – In October 2012, University of Chicago Medical Center (UCMC) agreed to pay $50,000 to resolve its liability under the patient dumping statute. UCMC allegedly failed to provide appropriate medical screening and stabilizing treatment within its capabilities to a male patient who arrived at their emergency department complaining of severe jaw pain as a result of a physical assault. The results of a CT scan taken by UCMC revealed injuries that he needed corrective surgery. However, UCMC did not provide further treatment and discharged the patient with instructions to go to another hospital for further care.
- Massachusetts – In May 2013, Trustees of Tufts College and Tufts University School of Dental Medicine (TUSDM) agreed to pay $841,120 for allegedly violating the CMP Law. TUSDM submitted claims to Medicare for various services from four of

their clinics. However, HHS/OIG alleged that these claims were improper because the services were provided by dentists who were not credentialed by Medicare or the services were not supported by sufficient medical record documentation.

- Georgia – In May 2013, C.F. Health Management, Inc., d/b/a Gainesville Pain Management (GPM), and its physician agreed to pay $1.5 million for allegedly violating the Civil Monetary Penalties Law. HHS/OIG alleged that GPM submitted false or fraudulent claims by: (1) inappropriately using certain modifiers to submit claims for payment for multiple units when only a single unit may be billed per patient encounter, and (2) inappropriately billing for certain services when less expensive services were actually provided.
- Pennsylvania – In July 2013, Bravo Health Pennsylvania, Inc. (Bravo), agreed to pay $225,000 to resolve its liability under the CMP provisions applicable to a Medicare Advantage organization. HHS/OIG alleged that patient medical records Bravo provided to HHS/OIG were intentionally altered prior to their submission or resubmission. Specifically, Bravo allegedly added apparent diagnoses notations or signatures to the patient medical records.

Audits and Evaluations

Every year, HHS/OIG conducts a substantial number audits and evaluations that disclose questionable or improper conduct in Medicare and Medicaid, and recommends corrective actions that, when implemented, return misspent funds and prevent future wasteful or improper payments. Among those completed in FY 2013 were:

Preventing and Detecting Medicaid Fraud

Medicaid Fraud Control Units (MFCU) are key partners in the fight against fraud, waste, and abuse in State Medicaid programs. HHS/OIG is responsible for overseeing MFCUs' activities. As part of this oversight, HHS/OIG conducts periodic reviews of all Units and prepares public reports based on these reviews.

- HHS/OIG found that from FYs 2009 to 2011, the New Hampshire Unit reported recoveries of $14 million, filed criminal charges against 25 defendants, and obtained 15 convictions. The overall number of cases opened and closed by the Unit decreased. The Unit attributed the overall decrease primarily to staffing limitations; for all 3 years, the Unit's staffing levels were below the number of staff that the Unit requested and HHS/OIG approved. Additionally, although the Unit reported that its best source of fraud referrals was the State's Surveillance and Utilization Review Subsystem (SURS), the Unit noted that the number of referrals from SURS was low. HHS/OIG recommended that the New Hampshire Unit seek to expand staff sizes to reflect the number of staff approved in the Unit's budget, ensure that it maintains an adequate workload through referrals from SURS, ensure that case files contain documented supervisory reviews, and establish annual training plans for each professional discipline.
- HHS/OIG found that from FYs 2009 through 2011, the Louisiana Unit reported recoveries of $95 million, obtained 192 convictions and 86 civil judgments or settlements, and received 1,043 referrals. Provider fraud referrals to the Unit increased, and the Unit received patient abuse and neglect referrals from a variety of

sources. In addition, HHS/OIG found that the Unit had not updated its memorandum of understanding (MOU) with the Louisiana Department of Health and Hospitals (DHH) to reflect current law and practice. HHS/OIG recommended, among other things, that the Louisiana Unit revise its MOU with DHH to reflect current law and practice.

- HHS/OIG's analysis of collected data from FYs 2008 through 2010 shows that the South Carolina Unit's caseload increased by 65 percent and that the amount of funds the Unit recovered nearly doubled, from $15.3 million in FY 2008 to $30.3 million in FY 2010. In addition, HHS/OIG found that the Unit did not report program income properly in FY 2010. HHS/OIG recommended, among other things, that the Unit ensure that program income is reported properly.

Medicaid Payments to Excluded Providers

- HHS/OIG found that California made unallowable Medicaid payments of $1.9 million ($1.2 million Federal share) for items and services furnished, ordered, or prescribed by excluded providers. Although the amount of unallowable payments is small when compared with the $31.5 billion in claims paid by the State agency, no Medicaid payments may be made for items or services furnished, ordered, or prescribed by excluded providers. In addition, HHS/OIG set aside for resolution by CMS $1.1 million ($699,000 Federal share) paid by the State for additional items or services that may have been furnished, ordered, or prescribed by providers whose exclusion status could not be verified. HHS/OIG recommended, among other things, that California refund $1.2 million to the Federal Government for unallowable Medicaid payments and work with CMS to resolve the $699,000 set aside.

Medicaid Data for Program Integrity

- HHS/OIG conducted a review to determine the status of national Transformed Medicaid Statistical Information System (T-MSIS) implementation. T-MSIS is designed to be a detailed national database of Medicaid and Children's Health Insurance Program information to cover a broad range of user needs, including program integrity. HHS/OIG found that overall, as of January 2013, CMS and the 12 volunteer States had made some progress in implementing T- MSIS. However, most other States had not started implementing T-MSIS, and they reported varied timeframes for when they plan to begin. Further, early T-MSIS implementation outcomes raised questions about the completeness and accuracy of T-MSIS data upon national implementation. HHS/OIG recommended that CMS establish a deadline for when national T- MSIS data will be available; ensure that States submit required T-MSIS data; and ensure that T-MSIS data are complete, accurate, and timely upon T-MSIS implementation.

Medicaid Disproportionate Share Hospital Payments

- HHS/OIG found that New Jersey claimed Disproportionate Share Hospital (DSH) payments of about $100 million ($50 million Federal share) for five hospitals that did not meet Federal requirements for DSH payments during our audit period. Specifically, for the five hospitals, New Jersey calculated a Medicaid Inpatient Utilization Rate (MIUR) of less than 1 percent during one or more State fiscal years but claimed DSH payments for the hospitals because it misinterpreted Federal regulations on DSH eligibility. Under the Medicaid DSH program, a State is required to make DSH payments to hospitals that serve a disproportionate share of low-income and/or uninsured patients. For a hospital to receive DSH payments, the State must classify the hospital as a DSH. A State may not define or deem a hospital as a DSH unless the hospital has a MIUR of not less than 1 percent. HHS/OIG recommended that New Jersey refund $50 million to the Federal Government and ensure that all hospitals designated as DSHs meet Federal eligibility requirements for DSH payments.

Medicaid Inpatient Psychiatric Services

- HHS/OIG found that Indiana claimed Federal reimbursement for Medicaid inpatient psychiatric service payments made to Logansport State Hospital (Logansport) that were not in accordance with Federal requirements for inpatient psychiatric hospital services. For States to claim Federal reimbursement for such payments, the hospital's inpatient services must demonstrate compliance with the basic Medicare Conditions of Participation (CoPs) generally applicable to all hospitals and two special Medicare CoPs applicable to psychiatric hospitals. Logansport did not demonstrate compliance with the special Medicare CoPs at any time during the audit period. Therefore, none of the Federal reimbursement for Medicaid inpatient psychiatric service payments made to Logansport for claims with dates of service during the audit period was allowable. HHS/OIG recommended, among other things, that Indiana refund $5.8 million to the Federal Government.

Medicaid Payments for Personal Care Services

- HHS/OIG's first OIG Portfolio synthesized an array of audit and evaluation work addressing improper payments for personal care services (PCS). Eligible beneficiaries can receive PCS under Medicaid State plan options or waivers. PCS must be provided at home or another approved location, must follow a specific plan of care, and are typically performed by care attendants. In the past 6 years, Medicaid costs for such services increased by 35 percent, totaling approximately $12.7 billion in 2011. In the same period, HHS/OIG issued 23 reports on PCS and conducted numerous investigations involving related fraud. Based on this global look at the body of HHS/OIG work on PCS, HHS/OIG recommended, among other things, that CMS issue guidance to States regarding adequate prepayment controls and provide States with the data they need to identify overpayments.

Medicaid Home Health Services

- HHS/OIG found that New York claimed Federal Medicaid reimbursement for home health services claims submitted by Certified Home Health Agencies (CHHAs) in New York City that were not in accordance with Federal and State requirements. Specifically, for 17 claims, the plan of care was not reviewed every 60 days, and for 1 claim, the provider was unable to document that the service was provided. Pursuant to Federal regulations, home health services are provided to a beneficiary at the beneficiary's place of residence and on his or her physician's orders as part of a written plan of care that the physician reviews every 60 days. On the basis of our sample results, HHS/OIG estimated that the State improperly claimed $69.1 million in Federal Medicaid reimbursement during our January 1, 2007, through December 31, 2009, audit period. HHS/OIG recommended that New York should refund $69.1 million to the Federal Government and issue guidance to CHHAs in New York City on Federal and State requirements for physicians' orders and plans of care.

Medicaid Family-Based Treatment Rehabilitation Services

- HHS/OIG found that New York improperly claimed a Federal share of family-based treatment (FBT) rehabilitation services that did not meet Federal and State requirements. FBT rehabilitation services include training and assistance with daily living skills, medication management, socialization, counseling, family support, and health services. Of the 100 claims in our random sample, 84 did not comply and 58 contained more than 1 deficiency. These deficiencies occurred because providers did not fully comply with State regulations, authorizing physicians were not familiar with applicable State regulations and program requirements, and the State did not adequately monitor the program. HHS/OIG recommended, among other things, that New York should refund $27.5 million to the Federal Government.

Medicaid Family Planning Services

The Federal Government pays its share of a State's medical assistance expenditures under Medicaid on the basis of the Federal medical assistance percentage, which varies depending on the State's relative per capita income. Family planning services are reimbursed at an enhanced 90-percent rate. Family planning services are those that prevent or delay pregnancy or otherwise control family size. Following are the results of family planning services reviews in Arkansas and California.

- HHS/OIG found that Arkansas claimed expenditures that did not qualify for the 90-percent rate for family planning. The expenditures exceeded limits specified in the State's infant delivery allocation methodology and resulted from errors in compiling the family planning expenditures and from errors in the computer programming used to identify infant delivery costs. HHS/OIG recommended, among other things, that Arkansas refund to the Federal Government $1.9 million in family planning Federal share and work with CMS to determine the allowable portion of $929,000 in family planning Federal share that it received for allocated sterilization costs.
- HHS/OIG found that California did not always comply with Federal and State requirements when claiming Federal reimbursement at the 90-percent rate for family planning services. The rate was unallowable because the primary purpose of the visits was not family planning, the visits were for follow-up properly reimbursed at the regular rate, or the supporting documentation was insufficient. HHS/OIG also found claims that contained either no procedure code or a procedure code that was not approved by CMS for reimbursement at the 90-percent rate. HHS/OIG recommended, among other things, that California refund $5.7 million to the Federal Government.

Medicaid School-Based Services

- HHS/OIG found that New Hampshire did not always claim Federal Medicaid reimbursement for school-based transportation services submitted by schools in accordance with Federal and State requirements during calendar years 2006 through 2009. Of the 115 items in a random sample, 78 items had 1 or more transportation services that were not reimbursable. The deficiencies occurred because New Hampshire issued incorrect guidance to the school administrative units (SAUs). In addition, the State did not adequately monitor the claims for Medicaid school-based transportation services submitted by SAUs. HHS/OIG recommended, among other things, that the State refund an estimated $2.7 million to the Federal Government.
- HHS/OIG found that Arizona did not always maintain required documentation to support the random moment time study (RMTS) methodology used to allocate school-based administrative costs to Medicaid and the RMTS methodology was not fully consistent with Federal requirements. Federal law provides for States to be reimbursed at a 50 percent matching rate for administrative activities that directly support identifying and enrolling potentially eligible children in Medicaid. HHS/OIG recommended, among other things, that the State refund to the Federal Government $11.7 million for unallowable school-based administrative costs and work with CMS to determine the allowability of $18.8 million that we set aside for further analysis.

Medicaid Overpayments

- HHS/OIG found that as of December 2012, CMS reported collecting $987.5 million of the $1.2 billion in Medicaid overpayments that it had sustained in the 147 audit reports issued by OIG between fiscal years 2000 and 2009. However, CMS had not collected the remaining $225.6 million. The uncollected amount related to overpayments that OIG had identified in 10 audit reports that the States had not agreed to refund. In addition, CMS could not document that $7.2 million that it reported as collected had been collected. HHS/OIG recommended, among other things, that CMS collect the remaining $225.6 million that is due to the Federal government.

Detecting Fraud in Medicare

- HHS/OIG found deficiencies in CMS's and its contractors' ability to identify and respond to potential fraud by home health agencies. The two CMS Medicare Administrative Contractors (MACs) in this review prevented $275 million in HHA improper payments and referred several instances of potential fraud, but the four Zone Program Integrity Contractors (ZPICs) we reviewed did not identify any HHA-specific vulnerabilities and varied substantially in their efforts to detect and deter fraud. Two of the ZPICs recommended administrative actions and referred law enforcement cases for approximately eight times the number of HHAs as the other two. All four ZPICs served fraud-prone geographic areas. In addition, Medicare inappropriately paid five HHAs with suspended or revoked billing privileges. HHS/OIG recommended, among other things, that CMS establish additional contractor performance standards for high-risk providers in fraud-prone areas (including newly enrolled HHAs).

- One of nine MACs reviewed by HHS/OIG performed activities to detect and deter fraud by community mental health centers in 2010, and most of the activities were part of a CMS-led special project. Activities to detect and deter CMHC fraud varied substantially among ZPICs in 2010; one ZPIC performed almost all such activities, most of which were part of the same CMS-led special project. Other MACs and ZPICs performed minimal activities to detect and deter fraudulent CMHC billing, despite having jurisdiction over fraud-prone areas. Also, Medicare paid CMHCs that did not comply with its requirements after their revocations were effective and while their revocations were being approved. HHS/OIG recommended, among other things, that CMS implement additional CMHC fraud mitigation activities in all fraud- prone areas.
- CMS developed a Fraud Prevention System which uses predictive analytics to provide leads to its benefit integrity contractors for investigation. HHS/OIG found that in the first year of implementation, HHS did not fully meet the requirements for reporting actual and projected improper payments recovered and avoided in the Medicare fee-for-service program and reporting HHS's return on investment related to its use of such technologies. HHS did not report some of the amounts required by statute and had inconsistencies in its data; in addition, its methodology for calculating other reported amounts included some invalid assumptions that may have affected the accuracy of those amounts. HHS/OIG's recommendations included that HHS should require contractors to track recoveries that result from Fraud Prevention System leads and that HHS revise its methodologies to calculate projected savings and costs avoided.
- Recovery Audit Contractors (RAC) are designed to protect Medicare by identifying improper payments and referring potential fraud to CMS. HHS/OIG found that in FYs 2010 and 2011, RACs identified half of all claims they reviewed as having resulted in improper payments totaling $1.3 billion. CMS took corrective actions to address the majority of vulnerabilities it identified in FYs 2010 and 2011; however, it did not evaluate the effectiveness of these actions. As a result, high amounts of improper payments may continue. Additionally, CMS did not take action to address the six referrals of potential fraud that it received from RACs. Finally, CMS's performance evaluations did not include metrics to evaluate RACs' performance on all contract requirements. HHS/OIG recommended, among other things, that CMS take action, as appropriate, on vulnerabilities that are pending corrective action and evaluate the effectiveness of implemented corrective actions and ensure that RACs refer all appropriate cases of potential fraud.

Theft of Medicare Identities

- HHS/OIG's review of CMS's response to known breaches of protected health information and to medical identity theft involving Medicare identification numbers revealed opportunities for improvement. Although CMS notified Medicare beneficiaries affected by known breaches, HHS/OIG found that several requirements were not met. CMS has made progress in responding to medical identity theft by developing a compromised number database for contractors, but the database's usefulness could be improved. Further, Medicare's contractors do not consistently develop edits to stop payments on compromised numbers. HHS/OIG recommended, among other things, that CMS ensure that breach notifications meet statutory requirements, and improve the compromised number database.

Part C and Part D Program Integrity Activities

- HHS/OIG's review of the Medicare Drug Integrity Contractor (MEDIC) that has responsibility for preventing fraud, waste, and abuse in both Medicare Part C and Part D revealed that its Part C investigations and case referrals represented only a small percentage of its benefit integrity activities. HHS/OIG identified several problems hindering the MEDIC's ability to identify and investigate fraud and abuse in Part C and Part D. HHS/OIG recommendations included that CMS amend its regulations to require Part C and Part D plan sponsors to refer potential fraud and abuse incidents to the MEDIC and authorize the MEDIC to directly obtain information from entities such as pharmacies, physicians, and pharmacy benefit managers.

Payments for Individuals Ineligible for Medicare

HHS/OIG audited Medicare payments made for patients who were not lawfully present in the United States or were incarcerated. Unlawful presence occurs when a non-U.S. citizen remains in the United States longer than the time authorized by U.S immigration agencies. Incarcerated patients are people who are under arrest, are imprisoned, reside in a halfway house, or are required to live under home detention. Medicare does not make payments for the care of unlawfully present patients and generally does not pay for incarcerated patients.

- HHS/OIG found that CMS's controls were not adequate to ensure that all improper payments for services to unlawfully present beneficiaries were detected and recouped. Also, when CMS received untimely information indicating that the unlawful presence overlapped with the dates of service on previously paid Medicare claims, CMS did not notify Medicare's contractors of this updated information. HHS/OIG recommended, among other things, that CMS ensure that Medicare contractors recoup the $91.6 million in improper payments and that CMS implement administrative policies and procedures to detect and recoup improper payments made for Medicare services when information relating to the unlawful presence is received on previously paid Medicare claims.
- HHS/OIG found that CMS's controls were not adequate to ensure that all improper payments for services to incarcerated beneficiaries were detected and recouped and that CMS does not always receive timely updates regarding incarceration information before Medicare contractors pay providers on behalf of incarcerated beneficiaries. In addition, when CMS's data systems did not indicate until after a claim had been processed that a beneficiary was incarcerated; CMS's controls were not adequate to identify and recoup the improper payments. HHS/OIG recommended that CMS ensure that Medicare contractors recoup the $33.6 million in improper payments and that CMS implement administrative policies and procedures to detect and recoup improper payments when incarceration information is received on previously paid Medicare claims.

Medicare Payment for Cancelled Surgeries

- HHS/OIG estimated that, on the basis of sample results, Medicare made $38.2 million in Part A inpatient hospital payments in calendar years 2009 and 2010 for short-stay, canceled elective surgery admissions that were not reasonable and necessary. For 80 of the 100 claims in the sample, Medicare made payments totaling $346,000 for hospital inpatient claims involving canceled elective surgeries when a clinical condition did not exist on admission or a new condition did not emerge after admission that required inpatient care. Therefore, these inpatient claims did not satisfy Medicare's requirements that the admissions be reasonable and necessary. HHS/OIG's recommendations included that CMS adjust the 80 sampled claims representing overpayments of $346,000 to the extent allowed under the law and strengthen guidance to better explain the Medicare rule that a clinical condition requiring inpatient care must exist for hospitals to bill for Part A prospective payments for elective surgeries that were canceled.

Medicare Medical Equipment and Supplies

- HHS/OIG found that two years after the surety bond requirement for medical equipment suppliers was implemented, CMS did not have accurate surety bond information for all suppliers. Information for thousands of bonded suppliers was missing, and surety bond amounts were not consistently maintained by supplier location. CMS can only collect $50,000 per bonded supplier, so it is unlikely going to be able to reconcile surety bond collections with the tens of millions of dollars in overpayments owed by suppliers. HHS/OIG recommended, among other things, that CMS improve oversight of supplier data to ensure accurate and consistent information and immediately begin using the surety bond requirement to recover outstanding overpayments.

Medicare Payments for Drugs

- Herceptin (Trastuzumab) is a Medicare-covered drug used to treat breast cancer that has spread to other parts of the body. HHS/OIG conducted six reviews of Medicare contractors' payments for Herceptin and identified improper payments. HHS/OIG found that providers reported incorrect units of service on line items with unit counts that represented full multiuse vials, did not provide supporting documentation, billed for unallowable services, and reported a combination of incorrect units of service and incorrectly coded claims. The Medicare contractors made these incorrect payments because neither the Fiscal Intermediary Standard System nor the Common Working File had sufficient edits in place during our audit period to prevent or detect the overpayments. HHS/OIG recommended that the responsible Medicare contractors recover the identified overpayments, implement or update system edits that identify for review multiuse-vial drugs that are billed with units of service equivalent to the dosage on an entire vial(s), and use the results of the audits in provider education activities.

Medicare Skilled Nursing Facilities

Skilled nursing facilities (SNFs) are nursing homes that provide skilled care to Medicare patients. SNFs are required to evaluate each patient's needs and develop a care plan specifically for that patient. Care plans identify problems and set specific treatment goals.

- HHS/OIG found that Medicare paid approximately $5.1 billion for stays in which SNFs did not meet quality-of-care requirements. In addition, HHS/OIG found that for 37 percent of stays, SNFs did not develop care plans that met requirements or did not provide services in accordance with care plans. For 31 percent of stays, SNFs did not meet discharge planning requirements. Additionally, reviewers found examples of poor quality care related to wound care, medication management, and therapy. HHS/OIG recommended, among other things, that CMS strengthen its regulations on care planning and discharge planning.
- HHS/OIG found that SNFs misreported information to Medicare; as a result, inappropriate payments were made. In addition, SNFs billed one-quarter of claims in error in 2009; the incorrect claims resulted in about $1.5 billion in inappropriate Medicare payments. For 47 percent of claims, SNFs misreported information on the Minimum Data Set (MDS), the system used to classify beneficiaries into resource utilization groups (RUGs) for payment. Some SNFs incorrectly reported items such as therapy and activities of daily living, thereby placing beneficiaries into higher paying RUGs. HHS/OIG recommended, among other things, that CMS change the current methodology for determining how much therapy is needed to ensure appropriate payments.

Medicare Incentive Payments for Electronic Health Records

- To qualify for Medicare incentive payments for the use of electronic health records (EHRs), professionals and hospitals must possess certified EHR technology and meaningfully use that certified EHR technology in accordance with requirements defined by CMS. Professionals and hospitals self-report data to demonstrate that they meet program requirements. HHS/OIG found that CMS does not verify the accuracy of professionals' and hospitals' self-reported information prior to payment because data necessary for verifications are not readily available. CMS also does not direct high-risk professionals and hospitals to submit supporting documentation for prepayment review. HHS/OIG recommended, among other things, that CMS obtain and review supporting documentation from selected professionals and hospitals before payment to verify the accuracy of their self-reported information.

Medicare Part C Capitation Payments

Under the Medicare Advantage (MA) program, CMS makes monthly capitated payments to MA organizations for beneficiaries enrolled in the organizations' health care plans. These payments are adjusted on the basis of the health status of each beneficiary. CMS uses a model to calculate these risk-adjusted payments. Under this model, MA organizations collect risk adjustment data, including beneficiary diagnoses, from hospitals and other providers. CMS uses the diagnosis data to calculate a risk score for each beneficiary, which is in turn used to adjust the monthly capitated payments to MA organizations. HHS/OIG conducted two audits to determine the accuracy of MA organizations' calculation of risk scores.

- HHS/OIG found that for CY 2007 Bravo Health Pennsylvania, Inc.'s, submissions of diagnoses did not always comply with Federal requirements. The risk scores calculated using the diagnoses that Bravo submitted for 35 of the 100 beneficiaries in the sample were valid. However, the risk scores for the remaining 65 beneficiaries were invalid because the diagnoses were not supported by adequate documentation. As a result, Bravo received $422,409 in overpayments from CMS. On the basis of these sample results, HHS/OIG estimated that Bravo was overpaid approximately $22.1 million in CY 2007. HHS/OIG recommended, among other things, that Bravo refund to the Federal Government $422,409 in overpayments identified for the sampled beneficiaries and that Bravo work with CMS to determine the correct contract-level adjustment for the projected $22.1 million of projected overpayments.
- HHS/OIG found that for CY 2007 CIGNA Healthcare of Arizona, Inc.'s, submissions of diagnoses did not always comply with Federal requirements. For 60 of the 100 beneficiaries in our sample, the risk scores calculated using the diagnoses that CIGNA submitted were valid. The risk scores for the remaining 40 beneficiaries were invalid because the diagnoses were not supported by adequate documentation. As a result, CIGNA received $151,453 in overpayments from CMS. Based on these sample results, HHS/OIG estimated that CIGNA received approximately $28.4 million in additional overpayments for CY 2007. HHS/OIG recommended, among other things, that CIGNA refund to the Federal Government $151,453 in overpayments identified for the sampled beneficiaries and that Bravo work with CMS to determine the correct contract-level adjustment for the projected $28.4 million of projected overpayments.

Medicare Part D Drugs

- HHS/OIG found that over 1 million individual prescribers ordered drugs paid by Part D in 2009. Prescribing patterns varied widely by specialty. Over 700 general-care physicians had questionable prescribing patterns. Each of these physicians prescribed extremely high amounts for at least one of five measures. For example, many of these physicians prescribed extremely high numbers of prescriptions per beneficiary, which may indicate that these prescriptions are medically unnecessary. Moreover, more than half of the 736 general-care physicians with questionable prescribing patterns ordered extremely high percentages of Schedule II or III drugs, which have potential for addiction and abuse. Although some of this prescribing may be appropriate, such questionable patterns warrant further scrutiny. HHS/OIG recommended that CMS instruct the MEDIC to expand its analysis of prescribers, provide sponsors with additional guidance on monitoring prescribing patterns, provide education and training for prescribers, and follow up on prescribers with questionable prescribing patterns.
- HHS/OIG found that nationwide, Part D inappropriately paid for drugs ordered by individuals who clearly did not have the authority to prescribe, such as massage therapists, athletic trainers, home contractors, interpreters, and transportation companies. This raises concerns about the appropriateness of Part D payments and about patient safety. In 10 States, Part D also inappropriately paid for drugs ordered by other individuals without the authority to prescribe, such as counselors, social workers, and chiropractors. Tens of thousands of these drugs were controlled

substances. These drugs are of particular concern because they have potential for abuse. HHS/OIG recommended that CMS require sponsors to verify that prescribers have the authority to prescribe drugs, increase the MEDICS's monitoring of prescribers, ensure that Medicare does not pay for prescriptions from individuals without prescribing authority, and follow up on the individuals without prescribing authority who ordered prescriptions.

Other Fraud and Abuse Prevention Activities

HHS/OIG's HEAT Provider Compliance Training initiative (HEAT PCT), launched in 2011, provided free, high-quality compliance training for providers, compliance professionals, and attorneys in Strike Force cities and elsewhere, and online. Following six live presentations in FY 2011, HHS/OIG made available online the comprehensive training materials it developed to accompany HEAT PCT, together with sixteen video modules dividing the presentation by subject area. HEAT PCT continues to reach the health care community with HHS/OIG's message of compliance and prevention via these online offerings, which in FY 2012 expanded to include a series of twelve free, downloadable video and audio podcasts that summarize a range of compliance topics.

HCFAC funding also supported HHS/OIG's continued enhancement of data analysis and mining capabilities for detecting health care fraud, including tools that allow for complex data analysis. OIG continues to use data mining, predictive analytics, trend evaluation, and modeling approaches to better analyze and target the oversight of HHS programs. Analysis teams use near- time data to examine Medicare claims for known fraud patterns, identify suspected fraud trends, and to calculate ratios of allowed services as compared with national averages, as well as other assessments. When united with the expertise of OIG agents, auditors, and evaluators, as well as our HEAT partners, HHS/OIG's data analysis fosters a highly effective combination of technologies and traditional skills to the fight against fraud, waste, and abuse.

Industry Outreach and Guidance

Advisory Opinions

Central to the HIPAA guidance initiatives is an advisory opinion process through which parties may obtain binding legal guidance as to whether their existing or proposed health care business transactions run afoul of the AKS, the CMP laws, or the exclusion provisions. During FY 2013, the HHS/OIG, in consultation with DOJ, issued 23 advisory opinions, including two modifications of advisory opinions. A total of 299 advisory opinions have been issued during the 17 years of the HCFAC program.

Corporate and Other Integrity Agreements

Many health care providers that enter agreements with the government to settle potential liabilities for violations of the FCA also agree to adhere to a separate CIA, Integrity Agreement, or other similar agreement. Under these agreements, the provider or supplier commits to establishing a program or taking other specified steps to ensure its future compliance with Medicare and Medicaid rules. At the close of FY 2013, HHS/OIG was monitoring compliance with 201 such agreements.

Centers for Medicare & Medicaid Services

In FY 2013, CMS was allocated approximately $12.5 million by HHS, and appropriated $237.3 million in discretionary funds by Congress to support its comprehensive program integrity strategy for Medicare, Medicaid and the Children's Health Insurance Program (CHIP). With these funds, CMS is working to ensure that public funds are not diverted from their intended purpose: to make accurate payments to legitimate entities for allowable services or activities on behalf of eligible beneficiaries of federal health care programs. CMS also performs many program integrity activities that are beyond the scope of this report because they are not funded directly by the HCFAC Account or discretionary HCFAC funding. Medicare Fee-for-Service error rate measurement and activities, and Recovery Audit activities are discussed in separate reports, and CMS will submit a combined Medicare and Medicaid Integrity Program report to Congress later this year.

Our approach is guided by four major principles that support the strategic goal of improving program integrity:

1. Prevention
2. Detection
3. Transparency and Accountability
4. Recovery

1. Prevention

Moratoria

Building on strong anti-fraud efforts already underway in the home health provider and ambulance supplier arenas, CMS in July 2013 announced the first use of its temporary moratoria authority granted by the Affordable Care Act. The moratoria stops the enrollment of new home health and ambulance enrollments in Medicare, Medicaid and the Children's Health Insurance Program (CHIP) in three fraud "hot spot" areas of the country with demonstrated oversupply of certain types of providers. The temporary enrollment moratoria apply to newly-enrolling home health agencies in the Miami and Chicago metropolitan areas; and newly-enrolling ground ambulance companies in the Houston metropolitan area.

The goal of the temporary moratoria is to fight fraud and safeguard taxpayer dollars, while ensuring patient access to care. Under the moratoria, existing providers and suppliers can continue to deliver and bill for services, but no new provider and supplier applications will be approved in these areas, allowing CMS and its law enforcement partners to remove bad actors from the program while blocking provider entry or re-entry into these already over-supplied markets. CMS is required to re-evaluate the need for such moratoria every six months.

One Program Integrity

In FY 2013, CMS continued making improvements and changes to One Program Integrity (One PI), CMS' centralized portal that provides CMS contractors and law enforcement with a single access point to Medicare data as well as analytic tools to review the data. CMS moved from an integration contractor to a system support contractor while continuing to enhance the existing analytic tools. One PI improves CMS' ability to detect fraud, waste, and abuse with consistent, reliable, and timely analytics.

One PI users have access to the CMS Integrated Data Repository (IDR) to perform data analytics. The IDR contains a comprehensive and accurate set of Medicare provider, beneficiary and claims data from Medicare Parts A, B, and D back to January 2006. The IDR includes claims data at three distinct points in the claim life-cycle: at the time the claims are enumerated, the time claims are adjudicated, and at the time the claims have payment data posted. This access allows users to perform pre-payment analytics on historical data and develop models that can be applied in CMS' predictive analytics system, the Fraud Prevention System. With claims available from 2006, ZPICs will also be able to improve their analytics for post-payment detection of fraud, waste, and abuse.

In order to streamline access for our law enforcement partners, CMS is transitioning STARS, a healthcare fraud, waste, and abuse analytics tool to the One PI suite tools in 2013. The One PI team is also replacing on-site instructor led training with virtual instructor led training to reduce training costs and provide better access to training for law enforcement

Next Generation Desktop

The Next Generation Desktop (NGD) was developed to provide single access point that interacts with all Medicare claims processing systems and multiple other government data sources. NGD has been adapted for law enforcement purposes, providing investigators the ability to examine all claims associated with a specific provider tax ID or a Medicare beneficiary. CMS implemented enhancements to the Next Generation Desktop in September 2012. These enhancements are a result of collaboration between CMS, National Government Services (NGS), the NGD contractor, and Medicare Administrative Contractor (MAC), with specific requests from law enforcement for enhanced views of provider data. CMS and NGS developed tailored training material for law enforcement partners and have conducted several 3-day training sessions in FY 2013. CMS trained 100 individuals in FY 2013.

Compromised Number Checklist

Since January 2010, CMS has maintained a national database of compromised Medicare beneficiary and provider ID numbers called the Compromised Number Checklist (CNC). This database is populated by monthly submissions from CMS program integrity contractors. The purpose of the CNC is to share compromised ID numbers and any associated corrective actions that have been taken among CMS staff and contractors. CMS uses this national CNC database to enhance efforts to detect and prevent fraud and abuse in Medicare.

The compromised numbers list is updated on an ongoing, real-time basis by the PSCs/ZPICs and MEDIC.

The Command Center

CMS opened its state-of-the-art Command Center on July 31, 2012 to facilitate improvements in health care fraud detection and investigation, drive innovation, and help reduce fraud and improper payments in the Medicare and Medicaid programs. The Command Center provides advanced technologies and collaborative environment for a multi-disciplinary team of experts and decision makers to more efficiently coordinate policies and case actions, reduce duplication of efforts, and streamline fraud investigations for more immediate administrative action.

CMS is using the Command Center to collaborate in unprecedented ways with the private sector, law enforcement, and our State partners. The Command Center's advanced technologies and collaborative environment allow multi-disciplinary teams of experts and decision makers to more efficiently coordinate policies and case actions, reduce duplication of efforts, and streamline fraud investigations for more immediate administrative action. These collaborative activities enable CMS to take administrative actions, such as revocations of Medicare billing privileges and payment suspensions, more quickly and efficiently.

In FY 2013, the Command Center conducted 93 missions that included participants from CMS and our partners, including the OIG and FBI, that are designed to lead to improvements in the fraud prevention and detection process. Missions are facilitated collaboration sessions that bring together experts from various disciplines to improve the processes for fraud prevention in Medicare and Medicaid. Approximately 870 experts met since the opening of the Command Center representing policy analysts, investigators, lab modelers, FBI, OIG, ZPICS, field office staff, clinicians, Contracting Officer Representatives (CORs), and other CMS staff. CMS is also working with other Federal agencies in the Command Center to pool resources to tackle cross- cutting issues surrounding fraud prevention.

DME Initiatives

DME suppliers pose a high risk of fraud to the Medicare Program and CMS has undertaken an aggressive strategy to address this risk. Through the DME Stop Gap Project, initiated in 2009, ZPICs/PSCs have increased site visits and interviews of DME suppliers, providers, and beneficiaries receiving DME products in high billing areas for DME supplies and products. In FY 2013, these additional funds supported DME investigations which included site visits to, and interviews of, suppliers, doctors and patients that were identified as potentially suspicious or high risk.

Medicaid and CHIP Business Information Solutions (MACBIS)

The Medicaid and CHIP Business Information Solutions (MACBIS) is a CMS enterprise-wide initiative to modernize and transform the information and data exchanges with States and other key health reform stakeholders in order to ensure we have high performing Medicaid and CHIP programs. This initiative creates a more robust and comprehensive information management strategy for Medicaid and CHIP. We have designed a "transformed data state" that will, for the first time, integrate Medicaid and CHIP program, operational, quality, and performance data. Specifically, the data will be used to support detection of fraudulent patterns in State Medicaid programs as well as comparative analytics across state lines. Implementation of the Transformed- Medicaid Statistical Information System (T-MSIS) by states will be on a rolling basis with a goal of all states submitting data by July 1, 2014. T-MSIS is an expansion of the existing CMS Medicaid Statistical Information System (MSIS) extract process. The new T-MSIS extract format is expected to further CMS and State's goals for improved timeliness, reliability, and more robust data analysis process through monthly updates and an increase in the amount of data provided.

The accomplishments for FY 2013 include:

- MACBIS – Implement change control process for the MACBIS program, of which MACPro and T-MSIS are the two main projects within. The change control process coordinates and manages change across both projects which provide efficiencies and eliminates duplication.

- T-MSIS – Awarded the Baltimore Data Center and Virtual Data Center Contract which will provide the infrastructure to accept, validate and house T-MSIS data from states from a short term and long term perspective. Awarded the Development and Testing contracts that will develop and test the receipt and control of the submitted T-MSIS files, validation routines for ensuring data quality and storage capacity for the T-MSIS data. In addition, provided project management and technical assistance to states during the on-boarding process for migrating from MSIS to T-MSIS.
- MACPro – While MACPro is being designed and developed, we implemented an interim technology solution to support the data collection of Medicaid and CHIP and Alternative Benefit Plan State Plan Amendments for meeting the October 1, 2013 Affordable Care Act mandates.
- Information Technology Support – Integrated MACBIS processes into CMS's enterprise shared services efforts including, master data management, identity management, and portal development.

Outreach & Education Campaign

In FY 2013, CMS developed and implemented a multimedia outreach and education campaign. The campaign included national television, radio, print and outreach to specific ethnic communities where Medicare fraud is more prevalent. The advertising campaign ran from May 27- August 11, 2013, resulted in increased awareness of how to detect and report Medicare fraud.

2. Detection

Strengthened Program Integrity Activities in Medicare Advantage and Medicare Part D

In FY 2013, CMS enhanced its data analysis and improved coordination with law enforcement to get a more comprehensive view of activities in the Medicare Advantage (MA) and Prescription Drug (Part D) programs. All MA and Part D plan sponsors are required to have a comprehensive plan to detect, correct and prevent fraud, waste and abuse. This plan consists of written policies, procedures, and standards that articulate the organization's commitment to comply with all applicable federal and state standards related to fraud and abuse. Sponsors must have a properly trained, effective compliance officer, and provisions for internal monitoring and auditing, as well as other requirements. These requirements help ensure that sponsors track and identify potential beneficiary or provider abuse. CMS issued Compliance Program Guidelines in Chapter 9 of the "Prescription Drug Benefit Manual" (PDBM) and Chapter 21 of the "Medicare Managed Care Manual" Both Chapters are identical, and apply equally to Medicare Advantage Plans and Prescription Drug Plans.

To combat fraud, waste and abuse more effectively, CMS evaluates sponsors operations to ensure that they are compliant with the regulations and guidance. CMS also contracts with a private organization, called the Medicare Drug Integrity Contractor (MEDIC), to assist CMS in managing audit, oversight and anti-fraud efforts. The MEDIC's main functions include identifying and investigating potential fraud, and abuse, developing cases for referral to law enforcement agencies, acting as a liaison to law enforcement and collaborating with sponsors on the identification of potentially fraudulent schemes.

In FY 2013, CMS continued to invest HCFAC discretionary funds to strengthen Medicare Advantage (Part C) and Part D oversight, including:

- Managing all incoming complaints about Part C and Part D fraud, waste, and abuse;
- Utilizing new and innovative techniques to monitor and analyze information to help identify potential fraud;
- Working with law enforcement, MA, and prescription drug plans, consumer groups, and other key partners to protect beneficiaries and enforce Medicare's rules;
- Providing basic tips for beneficiaries on how to protect themselves from potential scams;
- Identifying program vulnerabilities; and
- Performing proactive research utilizing all available data to find trends in order to ferret out fraud, waste, and abuse activities.

As of June 2013, the national benefit integrity MEDIC received on average approximately 532 actionable complaints per month; processed 35 requests for information from law enforcement per month; and referred an average of 34 cases to law enforcement per month. CMS also hosted quarterly workgroup meetings to promote information sharing on the latest fraud schemes. Representatives from sponsoring organizations, Pharmacy Benefit Managers, CMS, law enforcement, and CMS Program Integrity Contractors gather to share information and discuss current fraud trends and anti-fraud efforts.

In FY 2011, CMS established a contract for Medicare Part C and Part D outreach and education. This contractor is responsible for providing support in designing, developing and implementing compliance training, education and outreach for internal and external stakeholders, including plan sponsors. In addition, this contractor supports the development of tools, models and program best practices to share and communicate goals and expectations in order to reinforce CMS' approach to compliance and enforcement. CMS continued efforts to do this by successfully broadcasting the 2013 Medicare Advantage & Prescription Drug Plan Spring Conference using webcast technology. This conference provided guidance and real time information on significant topics such as benefits and formulary updates for 2014; Part C and Part D monitoring, as well as marketing, surveillance and compliance updates.

Since 2011, CMS has been taking steps to ensure that valid prescriber identifiers accompany Part D claims, and that the MEDIC and plan sponsors are monitoring pharmacy billing patterns. In 2011, to enhance then existing practice and in collaboration with the Drug Enforcement Administration (DEA), we directed Part D sponsors to ensure that the prescriber identifier submitted on a Prescription Drug Event (PDE) record was active and valid starting in the 2012 coverage year, whether it was a National Provider Identifier (NPI), DEA number, unique physician identifier number, or state license number. Additionally, we began validating the format of all prescriber identifiers on PDEs that were coded as an NPI and excluded from payment reconciliation PDEs with invalid NPIs. We began assessing each sponsor's performance regarding NPI use and validity and notified them of their performance. We also directed Part D sponsors to check that all prescriptions for controlled substances under Part D were associated with DEA numbers that indicated there was appropriate authority to prescribe the controlled substance.

Through rulemaking finalized in 2012, CMS required Part D sponsors to submit PDEs with active and valid individual prescriber NPIs, beginning January 1, 2013. CMS, through the annual Medicare "Dear Doctor" letter, explained the NPI requirement to prescribers. CMS began to deny any PDE without an active and valid NPI beginning on May 6, 2013. We have continued to assess each sponsor's performance regarding NPI use and validity of submitted NPIs and notified sponsors of their performance in preparation for this deadline. Based on this assessment, we found that 99.6 percent of the 2013 PDEs received during the first quarter of the coverage year reported the prescriber's NPI; all but 0.002 percent of the reported NPIs were valid and currently active, or active within a year of the date of service. We also examined the taxonomy codes, which are self-reported by the providers to identify their specialty. We found 0.5 percent of these codes would be unreasonable for a prescriber. Based on a review of the PDEs reporting these unreasonable taxonomy codes, CMS determined that about 10.6 percent were for controlled substances. We further determined that all but 16.5 percent of these PDEs for controlled substance the prescriber in fact did have a valid DEA number.

These actions ensure improved sponsor compliance with PDE reporting requirements, enhance CMS's ability to review claims data to identify possible fraud and abuse, and help determine whether prescribers of controlled substances are writing prescriptions in accordance with their DEA registration.

Additionally, CMS is working to improve the data available for MA oversight. In January 2012, CMS required MA plan sponsors to begin submitting Part C data to its new Encounter Data System. This new requirement will enable the MEDIC to undertake future Part C projects once the Part C data is located in a central repository.

In addition to the work of the MEDICs, CMS enhanced other Part C and Part D oversight functions in FY 2013 to address new complexities facing law enforcement, contract and plan oversight functions, monitor plan performance assessment and surveillance/secret shopper activities, audit programs, and conduct routine compliance and enforcement tracking. Also in FY 2013, CMS conducted 30 program audits of sponsoring organizations and tested plan policies and procedures for compliance with program requirements in the following areas: Part D formulary and benefit administration, Part C and D organizational/coverage determinations, appeals, and grievances; outbound enrollment verification, special needs plans' models of care, and compliance program effectiveness. The organizations audited provide MA and Part D services to 21 percent of the beneficiaries enrolled in MA and Part D as of April 2013.

Marketing Surveillance Activities

CMS also strengthened program integrity in MA and Part D through marketing surveillance activities and compliance actions based on surveillance activities. In FY 2013, CMS conducted marketing surveillance activities, such as secret shopping and examining newspaper ads for unreported marketing events and content. These activities have improved plan sponsor oversight of marketing and lessened incidents of agent/broker misconduct.

Secret Shopping

Secret shopping provides undercover surveillance of formal MA, MA-PD, and PDP marketing events. Plan sponsors report formal sales/marketing events to CMS from which contractors and CMS identify a sampling of events to secret shop. Shoppers use a CMS developed tool to facilitate and electronically record their evaluations of marketing events' compliance with CMS requirements. The tool is designed to capture various compliance aspects of the representatives' or agents' presentations, actions and provided materials. Additionally, it collects general information about the event, such as the number of people in attendance, the type of venue where the event was held, and the language in which the agent presented the event.

For the 2013 Annual Enrollment Period (AEP), CMS conducted 1,781 secret shopping events Of the events shopped, 1,176 (65.7%) had no validated deficiencies and were considered entirely compliant with Medicare regulations.

Of the 114 parent organizations shopped, 23 (or 20.2%) had no validated deficiencies noted. These 23 parent organizations represented 605 shops or approximately 33% of the total completed shops. Forty-five (2.4%) of the completed shops were presented in a language other than English, including:

- 24 events presented in Spanish;
- 15 events presented in Cantonese or Mandarin;
- 2 events presented in Armenian;
- 1 events presented in Korean;
- 1 event presented in Russian; and,
- 1 event presented in Vietnamese.

Compliance Actions Based on Surveillance Activities

CMS issues the following types of letters to sponsors who have had deficiencies related to our surveillance:

- Technical Assistance Letters (TAL) (not formal compliance notices);
- Notices of Non Compliance (NONC);
- Warning Letters with a Request for Business Plan; and,
- Ad-hoc Corrective Action Plans (CAPs).

To determine the appropriate action for deficiencies identified by secret shopping, CMS developed an objective, data-driven, and performance-based model. This model not only automated the review process, but also accounted for the seriousness of each deficiency to develop proper compliance action for identified deficiencies. Within this model, CMS categorized each deficiency and assigned a weighted value: administrative errors (1 point), errors of omission (2 points), undue beneficiary influence or harm (4 points), and marketing misrepresentations (6 points). To determine a plan sponsor's overall performance score (OPS), CMS added the total number of points for all shops for each plan sponsor and divided by the total number of shops conducted for that plan sponsor.

The following three tables provide additional information on our process and findings. The first table shows how the OPS score is determined, while the second table is CMS' tool to determine what type of compliance action should be issued based on the OPS score. Finally, the Compliance Action table provides a break out, by risk, of the types of compliance actions taken and how many of each action were taken.

The unreported marketing events initiative is an attempt to determine if plan sponsors appropriately reports and represented their sales events activity to CMS. Daily and weekly print publications in U.S. domestic markets nationwide, including advertisements in several non- English languages are reviewed. CMS conducted reviews of 4,846 Medicare advertisements representing 8,699 total advertised events. These advertisements represented events hosted by 36 plan sponsors.

Of those advertisements reviewed, CMS identified 406 marketing events that were unreported, indicating a deficiency for each plan sponsor that had failed to submit a marketing event. Based on the results, CMS issued 18 TALs and 4 NONCs to plan sponsors related to unreported marketing events. NONCs were issued to plan sponsors that incurred deficiency rates of 5% or higher.

$$\frac{\text{Total \# of deficiency points for all shops}}{\text{Total number of shops conducted}} = \text{OPS}$$

OPS Ranges and Corresponding Compliance Actions

Overall Shopping Performance Score Range	Compliance Action Taken
0.01 – 1.49	Technical Assistance Letter
1.50 – 3.49	Notice of Non-Compliance
3.50 – 6.99	Warning Letter with Business Plan
7.00+	Ad–hoc CAP

Compliance Actions Taken by Risk Level for Secret Shopping

Action[b]	High	Medium	Low	Total
Technical Assistance Letter	105	72	13	183
Notice of Non-Compliance	2	1	1	4
Warning Letter	2	0	0	2
Total Letters Issued	109	73	14	189

Medicare Advantage Encounter Data Processing System Contract

The Medicare Advantage (MA) Encounter Data Processing System (EDPS) is currently being maintained and modified out of guidance published in the final FY 2009 inpatient prospective payment system (IPPS) rule. In that rule, CMS revised regulations to clarify that CMS has the authority to require MA organizations to submit encounter data for each item and service provided to MA plan enrollees. Consistent with this authority, CMS is requiring MA organizations to submit encounter data for dates of service January 3, 2012 and later. MA plans are required to submit data for all institutional, professional and DME services provided to MA plan enrollees on or after that date.

What program needs will EDPS be addressing? Over the past several years there has been dramatic growth in the Medicare Advantage program. Today, one-fourth of Medicare beneficiaries are enrolled in Medicare Advantage plans. CMS pays Medicare Advantage organizations approximately $145 billion per year for the care provided to these 15 million beneficiaries. Previously, CMS had not collected encounter data, which will provide CMS with information that is equivalent to the information provided on a FFS claim record. The diagnosis data provided on these claims will be used to risk adjust payments and, as a result, CMS will need complete encounter data records for the MA population being served. Sampling is not an option for processing the approximately 500 million encounter data claims any more than it would be for processing Medicare FFS claims.

To better ensure that CMS is a more prudent purchaser, in January 2012 agency launched an initiative to collect encounter data from Medicare Advantage organizations. The encounter data detail each item and service provided to enrollees of Medicare Advantage organizations. These records are comparable in format and detail to claims submitted to the MACs by FFS providers.

How will CMS use the data collected by EDPS? CMS will use encounter data to determine the risk adjustment factors used to adjust payments, as required under CMS regulations at 42 CFR §422.304, to update risk adjustment models, to calculate Medicare Disproportionate Share Hospital percentages, for Medicare coverage purpose and to conduct quality review and improvement activities. The collection of MA encounter data is expected to provide CMS with a more complete picture of MA member utilization.

Medicaid/CHIP Financial Management Project

Under this project, funding specialists, including accountants and financial analysts, worked to improve CMS's financial oversight of the Medicaid program and CHIP. In FY 2013 through the continued efforts of these specialists, CMS removed an estimated $2.7 billion (with approximately $375 million recovered and $2.4 billion resolved) of approximately $9.7 billion identified in questionable Medicaid costs.

Furthermore, an estimated $188 million in questionable reimbursement was actually averted due to the funding specialists' preventive work with states to promote proper state Medicaid financing. The funding specialists' activities included reviews of proposed Medicaid state plan amendments that related to reimbursement; development of financial management reviews; research regarding state Medicaid financing policy and practices; collaboration with states to resolve the Medicaid and CHIP portions of the A-133 "Single State" audits; and identification of sources of the non-Federal share of Medicaid program payments to ensure proper financing of Medicaid program costs.

HHS-OIG Hotline Database

CMS and its contractor use the OIG Hotline database to perform program integrity activities. Specifically, the contractor currently receives and processes the complaints OIG refers to CMS. OIG receives complaints through its TIPS Hotline and uploads certain complaints to the OIG Hotline database for review by CMS. The complaints from both the OIG Hotline and 1-800- Medicare have been in two separate databases and followed two distinct processes for resolution. These processes will improve as we consolidate and integrate all the complaints received from OIG and 1-800-MEDICARE. The CMS contractor is coordinating this effort with the OIG, ECM and NGD. CMS and the OIG anticipate implementing the new process by September, 2014.

3. Transparency and Accountability

Healthcare Fraud Prevention Partnership

One of the Secretary's key health care fraud prevention initiatives is to establish an ongoing partnership with the private sector to fight fraud across the health care system. Data collected and shared across payers can assist payers in evaluating trends, recognizing patterns consistent with potential fraud, and potentially uncover schemes or bad actors they could not otherwise identify using only their own information. Such collaboration is the purpose of the Healthcare Fraud Prevention Partnership (HFPP) which brings together both public and private, federal and state- level individuals and organizations combatting health care fraud across all payers.

The legal authority for the Partnership is 42 U.S.C. § 1320a-7c. The delegated authority allows for the Partnership to consult with, and arrange for the collection of data from, and sharing of data with representatives of health plans under the HCFAC program.

Several key milestones occurred in FY2013FY 2013 including the signing of the official Healthcare Fraud Prevention Partnership Charter by Secretary Sebelius and US Attorney General Holder and the second Executive Board meeting of the Healthcare Fraud Prevention Partnership which took place on April 1, 2013. The Board Meeting was followed immediately by two days of working sessions with committees at the CMS Program Integrity Command Center. Over 60 participants representing over 20 partnership organizations attended the two days of working sessions. In total, over a dozen meetings were held within the partnership including four in-person meetings which proved highly effective in distilling the critical spirit of collaboration and partnership.

The HFPP has successfully completed a significant pilot information exchange, in which 11 entities, including CMS, contributed fraud related data for aggregation and analysis, realizing in immediate cost savings and additional administrative actions for many of the participants. Future data exchanges, both non-identifiable and identifiable, will significantly expand in complexity and require substantial technologies and infrastructure including relevant contactors and a data exchange partner to serve as a Trusted Third Party. To plan for this function, CMS has invested in a strategic contractor with the objective of defining the requirements for a Trusted Third Party contract, to be procured in FY 2014.

CMS added additional partners to the HFPP and is targeting further expansion of the partnership to include additional willing public and private payers once the technical and legal components of the program are in place. The increase in members providing data will increase the resources necessary for the trusted third party contractor to process and store the increased number of claims data from the new members.

Measured Error Rate – Payment Error Rate Measurement (PERM)

The Improper Payments Information Act (IPIA) of 2002, amended by the Improper Payments Elimination and Recovery Act of 2010 (IPERA), amended by the Improper Payments Elimination and Recovery Improvement Act of 2012 (IPERIA) requires each agency to periodically review programs it administers, identify programs that may be susceptible to significant improper payments, estimate the amount of improper payments, submit those estimates to Congress, and report on actions the Agency is taking to reduce improper payments.

The Medicaid program and CHIP have been identified as at risk for significant improper payments. To comply with the IPIA, IPERA and IPERIA, CMS established the Payment Error Rate Measurement program (PERM) to estimate improper payment error rates in Medicaid and CHIP. The error rates are based on reviews of the fee-for-service (FFS), managed care, and eligibility components of Medicaid and CHIP in the fiscal year under review. CMS measures Medicaid and CHIP error rates using a 17-state rotation so that each state is reviewed once every three years. After several years of development, the PERM error rate was published for the first time in FY 2008.

In FY 2013, after consultation with OMB, CMS made two improper payment rate calculation methodology enhancements to improve the accuracy of the Medicaid improper payment rate estimate. These two enhancements include: (1) replacing the three-year weighted average national Medicaid improper payment rate with a single-year rolling national Medicaid improper payment rate, and (2) incorporating prior year state-level improper payment rate recalculations.

In past AFRs, CMS reported a three-year weighted average national Medicaid improper payment rate representing the percentage of expenditures improperly paid over the past three years. The three-year rate was calculated by utilizing a weighted average of the PERM cycle error rates from the three most recent years. This methodology was implemented to ensure Medicaid improper payment rate reporting included findings from all states.

In response to an OIG report (OIG Report A-06-08-00078, "Oversight and Evaluation of the FY 2007 PERM Measurement Program"), CMS is now reporting a single-year rolling national Medicaid improper payment rate, a more precise estimate that represents the percentage of expenditures improperly paid during one fiscal year. The single-year rolling rate is calculated by multiplying each state's most recently observed error rate by that state's expenditures from the fiscal year being reported and dividing by the expenditures for that fiscal year. The single-year rolling rate treats the three most recent PERM cycles as a contiguous sample (as if all states were observed in the fiscal year being reported) which allows CMS to report on findings from all states with improved precision.

Additionally, past AFRs did not incorporate State-level error rate recalculations that occur after the cycle cut-off date. For the most recent cycle of States measured, these recalculations occur after AFR publication. In response to a Government Accountability Office report (GAO-13-229, Enhancements Needed for Improper Payments Reporting and Related Corrective Action Monitoring), State-level error rate recalculations for the previous two cycles measured are now incorporated into the national Medicaid improper payment rate, and will be incorporated in future calculations.

CMS is reporting in the FY 2013 Agency Financial Report the national Medicaid error rate that is based on measurements that were conducted in fiscal years 2011, 2012, and 2013. The national Medicaid error rate is 5.8 percent or $14.4 billion in estimated improper payments and has decreased from FY 2012 (7.1 percent or $19.2 billion). The national component error rates are as follows: Medicaid FFS – 3.6 percent, Medicaid managed care – 0.3 percent, and Medicaid eligibility – 3.3 percent. The major cause of error in fee-for-service claims is lack of sufficient documentation to support the payment. The vast majority of the eligibility errors were due to beneficiaries found to be ineligible or whose eligibility status could not be determined.

Section 601 of the Children's Health Insurance Program Reauthorization Act of 2009 (CHIPRA) prohibited HHS from calculating or publishing any national or state-specific error rates for CHIP until six months after a new PERM final rule was effective. In addition, Section 205(c) of the Medicare and Medicaid Extenders Act of 2010 exempted HHS from reporting a 2011 CHIP improper payment rate. On August 11, 2010, as part of enhanced efforts to reduce improper payments in federal programs, HHS issued the final regulations that fully implemented improvements to the PERM program. HHS commenced CHIP error rate reporting in FY 2012 and, therefore, only two CHIP cycles of states have been measured for reporting in the FY 2013 Agency Financial Report.

The two Medicaid improper payment rate calculation methodology enhancements described above also apply to the CHIP improper payment rate estimate with one difference since only two cycles of states have been measured. For FY 2013, the 34 measured states will be treated as a contiguous sample and projected to the 17 states that have not yet been measured.

CMS is reporting in the FY 2013 Agency Financial Report the national CHIP error rate that is based on measurements that were conducted in fiscal years 2012 and 2013. The FY 2013 national CHIP error rate is 7.1 percent or $0.6 billion in estimated improper payments. The national component error rates are as follows: CHIP FFS – 5.7 percent, CHIP managed care – 0.2 percent, and CHIP eligibility – 5.1 percent. The main source of error is beneficiaries found to be ineligible for CHIP. Other errors are due to policy violations, payments made for non-covered services, and insufficient documentation.

CMS is currently measuring cycles that will be reported in 2014 and 2015. CMS expects the error rates to decline in future years through program maturation and corrective action initiatives implemented at the state and Federal levels.

As a result of Executive Order 13520—Reducing Improper Payments and Eliminating Waste in Federal Programs, the PERM program also reports error rate information on the Treasury improper payment dashboard at PaymentAccuracy.gov, and annually reports comprehensive improper payment measurement and reduction activities to HHS/OIG.

Error Rate Measurement and Increased Accountability in Medicare Advantage (Part C) and Medicare Prescription Drug Benefit Program (Part D)

In compliance with IPERA, CMS has implemented a systematic plan regarding improper payments for Part C and D programs. Unlike Medicare fee-for-service, CMS makes prospective, monthly per-capita payments to Part C organizations and Part D plan sponsors. Each per-person payment is based on a bid amount, approved by CMS, that reflects the plan's estimate of average costs to provide benefit coverage to enrollees. CMS risk-adjusts these payments to take into account the cost associated with treating individual beneficiaries based on health status. In addition, certain Part D prospective payments are reconciled against actual costs, and risk-sharing rules set in law are applied to further mitigate plan risk.

The Part C payment error estimate reported for FY 2013 (based on calendar year CY 2011) is 9.5 percent, or $11.8 billion. The Part C payment error estimate has decreased from the FY 2012 estimate of 11.4 percent or $13.1 billion. The Part C payment error is driven by errors in risk adjustment data (clinical diagnosis data) submitted by Part C plans to CMS for payment purposes. Specifically, the Part C payment error estimate reflects the extent to which diagnoses that plans report to CMS are not supported by medical record documentation.

In an effort to improve the Part C error rate, CMS has implemented three specific actions described below: contract level audits, Medicare Advantage Organization guidance, and physician outreach.

- Contract-level audits: The contract-specific Risk Adjustment Data Validation (RADV) audits are designed to recover overpayments to Part C plans. CMS will conduct payment recovery based on extrapolated estimated beginning with audits based on calendar year 2011 payments. CMS expects to audit about 30 MA contracts a year. Additionally, the CY 2007 contract-level RADV audits are in the final stages. In FY 2013, CMS recovered a total of$5.0 million from contracts involved in the CY 2007 RADV Targeted audits. CMS plans to conduct further recovery on the CY 2007 audits in FY 2014.
- Medicare Advantage Organization Guidance: CMS has also implemented a process to assist MA plans while they are submitting medical record documentation for review under the Part C error estimate.
- Physician Outreach: CMS has begun a program that enhances physician understanding of the way HHS pays MA organizations and the payment methodology impact on physicians. The focus of this effort is to improve medical record documentation prepared by physicians to support risk adjustment diagnoses.

The Part D payment error estimate reported for FY 2013 (based on CY 201) is 3.7 percent, or $2.1 billion. The FY 2013 Part D error estimate represents the combined impact on Part D payments of four sources of error: Payment error related to low income subsidy status; payment error related to Medicaid status; payment error related to prescription drug event data validation; and payment error related to direct and indirect remuneration.

Probable Fraud Measurement Pilot

There is no reliable estimate of the amount of fraud in the Medicare program. Documenting the baseline amount of fraud in Medicare is of critical importance, as it allows officials to better evaluate the success of ongoing fraud prevention activities. In collaboration with the HHS Office of the Assistant Secretary for Planning and Evaluation (ASPE), CMS developed the methodology for the first nationally representative estimate of the extent of probable fraud in the Medicare fee- for-service program in FY 2011. In FY 2012, CMS developed the measurement tools for the pilot, and collaborated with government partners, including ASPE, on the strategy for implementation. CMS received OMB approval in May 2013.

This project will estimate probable fraud in the Home Health benefit to pilot test the measurement approach and calculate a service-specific estimate. This pilot is measuring "probable fraud" rather than "fraud" because "fraud" is a legal determination that involves establishing intent – a determination that is made through the judicial system. A review panel of experienced health care analysts, clinicians, policy experts, and fraud investigators will review all collected data and determine if there is sufficient evidence to warrant a referral to law enforcement. After the completion of this pilot, CMS will assess the value of expanding the measurement to other areas of Medicare. CMS will begin collecting data on probable fraud and have an estimate of probable fraud within HHAs in 2015.

4. Recovery

Suspension

CMS in FY 2013 continued its use of the new Affordable Care Act authority to suspend payments to providers during an investigation of a credible allegation of fraud. CMS also has authority to suspend payment if reliable information of an overpayment is brought to light. As of September 2013, CMS had 297 providers under active payment suspension, with 105 of those suspensions having been approved in FY 2013.

Field Offices

CMS has designated program integrity field offices located in or near the HEAT cities of Miami, Los Angeles, and Brooklyn that provide a CMS presence in high risk fraud areas of the country. All three field offices have staff that are designated CMS Strike Force Liaisons, who coordinate with law enforcement, facilitate data analysis, and expedite suspension requests. The field offices also work with CMS central office and the ZPICs to conduct data analysis to proactively identify targets and to coordinate efforts among various contractors and agencies to identify local issues and vulnerabilities with national or regional impact.

The field office staff performs outreach and education to partners in their areas, including law enforcement, Senior Medicare Patrol and state Medicaid agencies. The field offices train US Attorneys, OIG and FBI agents, analysts and forensic accountants on Medicare policy and coding clarification, as well as provide data and billing analysis for specific cases. These staff also provides significant support during the prosecution of health care fraud cases through testimony, depositions and victim impact statements.

The field offices develop solutions to the most challenging program integrity issues in their region. In Miami, for example, the field office has boots on the ground working to root out fraud in home health by performing provider and beneficiary interviews. The Los Angeles staff is working with county Emergency Medical Service licensing authorities, CMS contractors and local law enforcement to address emerging schemes in ambulance providers. These efforts have resulted in nearly 100 revocations of Medicare billing privileges in FY 2013. Additionally, the trial support provided by the Brooklyn field office has helped result in three convictions in FY 2013.

In FY 2013, the field offices also expanded their collaboration with Medicaid program integrity staff, including the CMS Medicaid Integrity Contractor (MIC) and the state Medicaid agency. The Los Angeles field office began two projects around the hospice benefit which is anticipated to result in administrative actions against providers.

Enrollment Special Study

The Enrollment Special Study is a project designed to stop fraudulent providers from obtaining new Medicare provider numbers, reduce the number of habitual "bad providers" from re-entering the Medicare system after they have been kicked out, and shift from the pay and chase approach that has existed in years past. In this project, site visits are conducted prior to enrollment, and providers are targeted for a closer review. The project is limited to Community Mental Health Centers (CMHCs), Comprehensive Outpatient Rehabilitation Facilities, and Independent Diagnostic Testing Facilities in South Florida. Once the MAC conducts a site visit, it assesses the provider's individual risk. If the provider appears to be suspect or pose an elevated risk of fraud, the provider is referred to the ZPIC for investigation and administrative action, as appropriate. This project began as a one year project in July 2009 and has been extended due to its success.

As of June 30, 2013, First Coast Service Operations, Inc. (FCSO), the MAC conducted 5,492 site verifications to verify providers and suppliers' operational status, deactivated 77 practice locations, and revoked or denied 486 providers. FCSO saved $10,834,126 from prepayment review. Safeguard Services, Services (SGS), the ZPIC conducted over 296 on-site investigations resulting in 102 requests for provider revocation or deactivation. SGS placed 48 providers on prepayment review saving $3,766,349.36 and requested $133,232,024 in overpayments.

South Florida Fraud Hot Line

CMS also continued a successful initiative aimed at increasing fraud reporting in South Florida. As part of a two-year infusion therapy demonstration, CMS established a special fraud hotline in 2007 to protect Medicare beneficiaries in South Florida from fraudulent providers of infusion therapy. As a result of the hotline's success in FY 2009, CMS expanded the scope of this infusion therapy fraud hotline to handle all Medicare fraud-related calls in South Florida. The fraud hotline number is included on monthly Medicare Summary Notices (MSNs) sent to beneficiaries in Miami-Dade, Broward and Palm Beach counties.

Trained, bilingual, or trilingual staff fielded and routed calls, and acknowledged receipt of complaints in writing. A rapid response team at the ZPIC investigated the highest priority leads received from the fraud hotline within 48 hours of receipt of the call and then collaborated with CMS and law enforcement to pursue appropriate follow up action(s). CMS worked with its partners to conduct beneficiary outreach and education to ensure beneficiaries understood the types of fraud that may occur and how to read their MSNs to detect potential fraudulent billings.

As of August 31, 2013, the hotline has received more than 107,938 calls leading to 1,057 new fraud investigations. In addition, the ZPIC has placed 223 providers on prepayment review saving over $16 million, revoked or deactivated 192 provider numbers, referred 52 cases to law enforcement, and sent 160 Immediate Advisements to the HHS-OIG. Additionally, law enforcement has seized $3 million in provider bank accounts.

Administration for Community Living

The mission of the Senior Medicare Patrol (SMP) program is to empower and assist Medicare beneficiaries, their families, and caregivers to prevent, detect, and report health care fraud, errors, and abuse through outreach, counseling, and education. In FY 2013, the Administration for Community Living (ACL) was allocated $3.378 million in HCFAC funding by HHS to support infrastructure, technical assistance, and other SMP program support. In addition to this funding, ACL was initially allocated $7.331 million for capacity-building activities designed to enhance the effectiveness of state-wide SMP programs. This funding was reduced to $7.170 million later due to the funds requested by the SMP grantees. During FY 2010 and FY 2011, CMS had provided this capacity funding to ACL for the SMP projects. In FY 2012 and FY 2013 the funding came directly to ACL. The base SMP project grant is funded from a separate Congressional appropriation.

SMP Project Activities and Outcomes

ACL funds 54 SMP statewide projects (each state, Guam, Puerto Rico, US Virgin Islands and D.C.) with funds authorized in the Older American Act and the HCFAC Wedge. In addition to the projects' base grants, funded from the Older American Act, the SMP program offers HCFAC funds to each grantee so that they can expand their program. Prior to FY 2013, the additional funding was based largely on the known fraud prevalence within each state. However, in FY 2013, the program moved to a formula-driven allocation taking into account the number of Medicare beneficiaries living in each state and the ruralness of the state. The new formula is intended to provide a more equitable allocation of funds and reflects the reality that the prevalence of fraud is much broader than a few selected states.

According to the most recent annual performance report from HHS-OIG's Deputy Inspector General for Evaluation and Inspections, issued July 2013, 5,137 active volunteers served SMP projects during 2012. These volunteers performed an essential function of this program, contributing 120,953 hours and conducting over 113,000 one-on-one counseling sessions in efforts to educate beneficiaries about how to prevent and detect Medicare fraud within local communities.

Outreach to Medicare beneficiaries is a key element of the SMP program. During 2012, SMP projects held 10,032 community outreach education events reaching more than 996,000 people, and were responsible for over 188,199 media airings to increase beneficiary awareness about issues related to Medicare fraud. In addition, over 449,500 beneficiaries were educated through 14,748 group educational sessions conducted by SMP programs in local communities.

SMP projects nationwide received 86,331 inquiries for information or assistance in 2012 from or on behalf of beneficiaries. This included receipt of 2,270 complex issues—i.e., beneficiary complaints requiring further research, assistance, case development, and/or referral. SMP projects reported that 1,748 complex issues were resolved for beneficiaries during 2012, while 908 complex issues with an estimated dollar value of over $27.5 million, were referred to law enforcement, CMS integrity contractors, state Medicaid Fraud Control Units, or other entities for further action. During this period, HHS-OIG documented that $133,971 in health care expenditures were avoided and nearly $6.2 million in Medicare, Medicaid and other savings resulted from actions taken by the SMP program.

Since the program's inception, the program has educated over 5.2 million beneficiaries in group or one-on-one counseling sessions and has reached nearly 28 million people through community education outreach events. While SMPs make numerous referrals of potential fraud to investigators, it is still difficult to measure the outcome of these cases without a tracking mechanism. Therefore, we have no measure of these outcomes, though we anticipate that they would demonstrate an additional benefit of the SMP program's ability to detect and prevent fraud and abuse in the Medicare program. In addition, the impact of the SMP program's primary activities—education of beneficiaries to prevent health care fraud—is difficult to measure and impossible to quantify in dollars and cents. As HHS-OIG indicated in the July 2013 report:

> "We continue to emphasize that it is not always possible to track referrals to Medicare contractors or law enforcement from beneficiaries who have learned to detect fraud, waste, and abuse from the projects. Therefore, the projects may not be receiving full credit for savings attributable to their work. In addition, the projects are unable to

track the substantial savings derived from a sentinel effect whereby fraud and errors are reduced by Medicare beneficiaries' scrutiny of their bills."

ACL recognizes the importance of measuring the value of the SMP program impact to the fullest degree possible. Toward that end, in 2012, ACL contracted for the first-ever SMP program evaluation that will assess the national design and implementation of the SMP program, the adequacy of current SMP performance measures, and seek to determine the most appropriate measures of SMP program value (benefits, results and impact). The contract will conclude in December 2013. In addition, in FY 2013, the SMP program issued a research grant designed to measure the value of prevention activities. As the SMP program is focused on education and prevention, the true value of the program comes from beneficiaries avoiding fraud in the first place. This new grant is intended help the program identify a way to measure that effect.

Despite the factors that have limited ACL's ability to quantify the value of the SMP program in preventing, identifying, and reporting health care fraud, the OIG has documented over $112 million in savings attributable to the program as a result of beneficiary complaints since its inception in 1997.

SMP Infrastructure and Program Support

National Consumer Protection Technical Resource Center

The Center, established October 1, 2003, provides technical assistance, support and training to the SMP projects, ensuring a fully consolidated national approach to reaching Medicare and Medicaid beneficiaries. The goal of the Center is to provide professional expertise and technical support, serve as an accessible and responsive central source of information, and maximize the effectiveness of the SMP projects in healthcare integrity outreach and education. The Center has been instrumental in supporting ACL efforts to forge national visibility for the SMP program.

National Hispanic SMP Project Grant

In September 2008, AoA awarded an initial three-year grant to the National Hispanic Council on Aging for the development and implementation of a National Hispanic SMP (NHSMP) Program. The problem of health care fraud and abuse becomes even more challenging to address with hard- to-reach populations, particularly those with cultural and language barriers. The NHSMP project also promotes collaborations among key community players in order to promote the prevention, detection and reporting of fraud within the Hispanic community. The NHSMP program is working to create a model to provide technical assistance to SMP projects who work with Hispanic populations so that they can expand their reach to Hispanic older adults.

Integration Project Grant

The goal of the SMP program is to provide education to all Medicare beneficiaries. However, there are specific populations that are historically hard-to-reach. Three of these populations: Medicare beneficiaries under age 65; Lesbian, Gay, Bisexual and Transgender (LGBT) Medicare beneficiaries; and American Indian/Alaska Native (AI/AN) Medicare beneficiaries, were specifically identified as target populations. In FY 2013, ACL awarded five grants to organizations who have initiated 17 month projects which seek to increase awareness, empowerment, and actions to prevent healthcare fraud amongst these generally underserved populations. The goal of these grants will be to develop new, efficient, and sustainable approaches for ensuring high quality and culturally competent service delivery and help educate consumers to prevent health care fraud.

Prevention Research Grant

As mentioned above, in FY 2013, the SMP program has issued a three-year research grant to identify a way to measure the overall impact of the SMP program. Specifically, the grantee will develop and test an evaluation method to determine how to best measure the effects of the SMP program's community education techniques on health care fraud prevention.

Office of the General Counsel

In FY 2013, the Office of the General Counsel (OGC) was allocated approximately $8.88 million in HCFAC funding by HHS to supplement OGC's efforts to support program integrity activities. OGC's efforts in FY 2013 focused heavily on program integrity review, in which OGC reviews CMS' programs and HCFAC activities in order to strengthen them against potential fraud, waste, and abuse. OGC also continued its active litigation role in order to assist in the recovery of program funds. During FY 2013, OGC was involved in a wide range of HCFAC efforts that resulted in Government recoveries of over $1.57 billion in judgments, settlements, or other types of recoveries, savings, or receivables as described elsewhere in this report.

The Affordable Care Act

The ACA significantly amended existing anti-fraud statutes. These provisions established fundamental expectations for compliance, disclosure, transparency, and quality of care, and are matched by corresponding enforcement provisions. Some specific provisions of the ACA that particularly support HCFAC priorities include amending Medicare and Medicaid provider/supplier enrollment requirements, overpayment provisions to specifically invoke the FCA, strengthening the anti-kickback statute, and creating a statutory disclosure protocol for violations of the physician self-referral prohibition known as the "Stark law." During FY 2013, as new ACA programs were implemented, OGC spent significant time and resources working with the relevant agencies to ensure that program integrity issues were reviewed and resolved, and assisted the agencies in addressing program integrity and compliance problems as they occurred.

HEAT

During FY 2013, OGC was involved in HEAT initiatives and worked closely with other HEAT members to combat fraud, waste, and abuse in the Medicare and Medicaid programs by providing advice on the myriad legal issues presented as the government works to initiate innovative anti- fraud programs in various hotspots throughout the country. OGC continued to assist DOJ in pursuing both criminal and civil cases involving individuals and entities seeking to defraud the Medicare and Medicaid programs and to defend any Federal court challenges that are brought as a result of HEAT initiatives. OGC's involvement in HEAT also included advising CMS on provider and supplier revocations, payment suspensions, recoupments, and defending the administrative appeals that resulted.

FCA and Qui Tam Actions

OGC assisted DOJ in assessing *qui tam* actions filed under the FCA by interpreting complex Medicare and Medicaid rules and policies in order to assist DOJ in discerning which allegations were program violations and should be pursued and to help DOJ focus on those matters which were most likely to result in a recovery of money for the government. When DOJ filed or intervened in a FCA matter, OGC provided litigation support, including interviewing and preparing witnesses and responding to requests for documents and information. In FY 2013, OGC participated in FCA and related matters that recovered over $1 billion for the government. The types of FCA cases that OGC participated included: drug pricing manipulation; illegal marketing activity by pharmaceutical manufacturers that resulted in Medicare and Medicaid paying for drugs for indications not covered; underpayment of rebates to state Medicaid programs; physician self- referral violations; and provider up coding cases.

Provider/Supplier Suspensions and Enrollment Revocations or Denials

Suspensions play a critical role in protecting against the abuse of program funds. OGC advised CMS on whether to suspend payments to Medicare providers and suppliers and defended the suspensions when challenged. In FY 2013, OGC attorneys were involved in a myriad of suspension and recoupment actions, which involved fraudulent billings and different segments of the health care industry: DME suppliers, ambulance companies, physicians, infusion clinics, therapists, home health agencies, and diagnostic testing facilities. OGC also represented CMS when a provider or supplier appealed a denial of enrollment or revocation. In FY 2013, OGC represented CMS in appeals before the Departmental Appeals Board (DAB) and often resolved these cases without formal hearings. OGC also continued to advise CMS on the interpretation of enrollment regulations and reviewed proposed enrollment rules and manual changes.

Medicare Prescription Drug Program (Part D) & Medicare Advantage (Part C) Compliance

During FY 2013, OGC continued to provide extensive advice to CMS on a variety of Part D and Medicare Advantage (MA)-related contract compliance issues, including identifying enforcement options against sponsors that are noncompliant or violate program rules, such as the Marketing Guidelines. OGC reviewed compliance-related correspondence that CMS issued to Part D sponsors and MA plans in the form of warning letters, corrective action plan letters, intermediate sanctions, CMP notices, and non-renewal or termination notices.

Civil Monetary Penalties

CMS has the responsibility for administering numerous CMP provisions enacted by Congress to combat fraud, waste, and abuse by enforcing program compliance and payment integrity. In FY 2013, OGC provided legal advice to CMS regarding the development and imposition of CMPs and defended CMS in many administrative appeals and judicial litigation resulting from these cases.

Petitions for Remission

OGC collaborated with Federal law enforcement, including the FBI, the USAOs, the Secret Service, U.S. Postal Service, and the U.S. Marshal's Service in filing petitions for remission directed to recover assets subject either to administrative forfeiture by Federal law enforcement or civil judicial forfeiture by DOJ. Each petition set forth the background of the fraudulent scheme, the history of Medicare's payments, and how the fraudulently induced payments could be traced to the seized assets. During FY 2013, OGC petitioned these agencies to recover funds in both criminal and civil litigation matters in which Medicare was a victim of fraud.

Regulatory Review and Programmatic Advice

In FY 2013, OGC advised CMS on a variety of regulatory and program issues, all to assist CMS in strengthening its programs and activities against fraud and to prevent the wrongful disbursement of program funds in the first instance. Some highlights of OGC efforts include its work to develop and implement the Physician Payment Sunshine Rule, the Durable Medical Equipment (DME) Face-to-Face Rule, and the Provider Enrollment and Incentive Reward Program Proposed Rule. Further, OGC provided extensive counsel regarding the CMS final rule on new survey procedures and alternative sanctions available for Home Health Agencies (HHAs) that are not meeting program participation requirements.

Medicaid Integrity

Continuing recent trends, OGC saw continued increasing involvement in FY 2013 in Medicaid integrity issues as CMS devoted more resources to financial reviews and oversight and as states continued to present innovative proposals to reconfigure their programs.

Physician Self-Referral

OGC provided valuable assistance to CMS in navigating the complexities of the Stark physician self-referral law. In FY 2013, OGC reviewed and offered extensive comments on participation agreements or amendments to such agreements governing various initiatives of the Center for Medicare & Medicaid Innovation, including the Pioneer Accountable Care Organization Model, Bundled Payment for Care Improvement ("BPCI") Models 2-4, and the Comprehensive ESRD Care Initiative. In addition, OGC worked closely with OIG and CMS in devising new waivers of the fraud and abuse laws for the BPCI models. OGC also advised CMS regarding matters disclosed under the new Stark self-disclosure protocol, now numbering over 200.

Medicare Secondary Payer (MSP) Workload

OGC's efforts to recover conditional payments by Medicare that are the primary responsibility of other payers directly supports the HCFAC statutory goal of facilitating the enforcement of all applicable legal remedies for program fraud and abuse. During FY 2013, OGC has been successful in establishing the right to recover over $7.7 million for Medicare under the MSP program. Recent statutory changes implementing mandatory insurance reporting requirements to the MSP law have strengthened and expanded OGC's efforts in this area – to the benefit of the Medicare Trust Funds – including substantial CMPs for failure to report.

Bankruptcy Litigation

OGC protects Medicare funds from waste in bankruptcy cases by asserting CMS's recoupment rights to collect overpayments, arguing to continue suspension or termination actions against debtors, seeking adequate assurances from the bankruptcy court that CMS interests in the debtor's estate will be protected, arguing for the assumption of the Medicare provider agreement as an executory contract, and petitioning for administrative costs where appropriate. In FY 2013, OGC asserted CMS' interests in numerous bankruptcy and receivership actions involving physicians, hospitals, independent diagnostic test facilities, DME suppliers, nursing homes, and nursing home chains, collecting or establishing the right to collect over $2.4 million in recoveries involving bankrupt providers.

Denial of Claims and Payments

CMS and its contractors engaged in various activities and initiatives to detect and prevent abusive and fraudulent billing practices. These measures included provider and beneficiary education, use of claim sampling techniques, and a more rigorous scrutiny of claims with increased medical review. In FY 2013, OGC played a major role in advising CMS regarding the development and implementation of these types of program integrity measures and defended CMS in litigation brought by providers and suppliers who challenged these efforts. OGC continued to aggressively defend CMS and its contractors in cases seeking damages for the alleged wrongful denial of claims, for being placed on payment suspension, and for not being granted extended repayment plans.

Food and Drug Administration Pharmaceutical Fraud Program

In FY 2013, FDA was allocated $3.37 million in HCFAC funding by HHS for the FDA Pharmaceutical Fraud Program (PFP). The PFP was instituted to enhance the health care fraud- related activities of FDA's Office of Criminal Investigations (OCI) and the Office of the General Counsel (OGC) Food and Drug Division. OCI, with the support of OGC, investigates criminal violations of the Federal Food, Drug, and Cosmetic Act (FFDCA), the Prescription Drug Marketing Act, the Federal Anti-Tampering Act, and related Federal statutes.

The PFP is designed to detect, prosecute, and prevent pharmaceutical, biologic, and medical device fraud. The PFP gathers information from sources inside and outside FDA and focuses on fraudulent marketing schemes, application fraud, clinical trial fraud, and flagrant manufacturing- related violations concerning biologics, drugs, and medical devices. The goal of the program is the early detection and prosecution of such fraudulent conduct and furthers FDA's public health mission by helping to reduce health care costs, in most cases before they are incurred, and deter future violators. As described below, the PFP has identified multiple alleged medical product fraud schemes through various avenues.

Since the inception of the PFP, OCI has opened a total of sixty-four criminal investigations. In FY 2013, FDA's third full fiscal year of HCFAC Program activity, OCI, through its PFP, opened twenty-three criminal investigations, described below:

- One investigation involving misbranding allegations, including minimization of risk and marketing two drugs by a single manufacturer for unapproved uses. The investigation involves marketing of the drugs for conditions not indicated in the approved labeling and for deceptive marketing practices regarding the safety of the drug products.

- Three investigations involving allegations of misbranding by medical device manufacturers for selling and/or distributing devices for conditions which are not FDA cleared and/or for making misleading representations about the device benefits and efficacy.
- Seven investigations involving allegations of flagrant manufacturing practices concerning both drugs and devices causing those products to be misbranded and/or adulterated and resulting in a safety risk to the public.
- Twelve investigations involving allegations of clinical trial and/or application fraud. These investigations consist in part of individuals suspected of improperly commencing and conducting clinical trials, falsifying clinical trial data, forging signatures of clinical investigators, and enrolling ineligible or non-existent subjects in clinical trials, as well as falsifying approval and/or clearance applications made to the FDA.

In regards to judicial action, the types of criminal investigations conducted through the PFP tend to be complex in nature requiring extensive document review and coordination with the affected FDA Center. It is not unusual for these complex fraud investigations to last five years or more from initiation to conclusion. Nevertheless in March 2013, an application fraud investigation, opened in FY 2011, obtained an individual guilty plea for submitting a report to the FDA which was materially false or misleading during the device approval process. The individual has agreed to assist in the prosecution of additional subjects related to this investigation and will be sentenced after this cooperation obligation is completed. Additionally in August 2013, an indictment was secured against the main target in a clinical trial fraud case, also opened in FY 2011, charging false statements in a matter within the jurisdiction of the FDA.

Furthermore, FDA believes that various investigations already initiated under the PFP show promise of future judicial action that may include criminal prosecution and monetary recoveries. These cases include an investigation of a large drug manufacturer for serious and pervasive manufacturing violations, as well as several investigations of clinical trial principal investigators who have allegedly fabricated study subjects, omitted exclusion/inclusion criteria and provided false data to drug and device sponsors representing these investigational products as safe and effective when, in fact, they are not.

In addition to these investigative activities, FDA conducted a three day training session in late June 2013 for criminal investigators and supervisors covering PFP related topics. The instruction consisted of legal training provided by OGC on the FFDCA in areas relevant to PFP cases, investigative scenario training on clinical trial fraud investigations and case presentations on successful prosecutions involving misbranding and other fraud schemes encompassing both drugs and medical devices. The training also provided background on FDA's participation in the HCFAC Program and resources available to assist in investigations being conducted under the PFP.

THE DEPARTMENT OF JUSTICE

United States Attorneys

In FY 2013, the United States Attorney's Offices (USAOs) were allocated approximately $42.0 million in FY 2013 HCFAC funding to support civil and criminal health care fraud and abuse litigation, as exemplified in the Program Accomplishments section. The USAOs dedicated substantial district resources to combating health care fraud and abuse in 2012, and HCFAC allocations have supplemented those resources by providing funding for attorneys, paralegals, auditors and investigators, as well as funds for litigation of resource-intensive health care fraud cases.

The 93 United States Attorneys and their assistants, or AUSAs, are the nation's principal prosecutors of Federal crimes, including health care fraud. Each district has a designated Criminal Health Care Fraud Coordinator and a Civil Health Care Fraud Coordinator. Civil and criminal health care fraud referrals are often made to USAOs through the law enforcement network described herein, and these cases are usually handled primarily by the USAOs, although the civil referrals are sometimes handled jointly with the Civil Division's Commercial Litigation Branch (Fraud Section). The other principal source of referrals of civil cases for USAOs is through the filing of *qui tam* (or whistleblower) complaints. These cases are often handled jointly with trial attorneys in the Frauds Section. USAOs also handle most criminal and civil appeals at the Federal appellate level.

USAOs play a major role in health care fraud enforcement by bringing criminal and affirmative civil cases to recover funds wrongfully taken from the Medicare Trust Funds and other taxpayer- funded health care systems as a result of fraud, waste, and abuse. Civil and criminal AUSAs litigate a wide variety of health care fraud matters, including false billings by physicians and other providers of medical services, overcharges by hospitals, Medicaid fraud, kickbacks to induce referrals of Medicare or Medicaid patients, fraud by pharmaceutical and medical device companies, home health and hospice fraud, and failure of care allegations against nursing home owners. Working closely with their partners in the Civil Division, several civil health care fraud AUSAs have focused their efforts on pharmaceutical fraud, resulting in significant recoveries including: $1.5 billion from Abbott Laboratories and $500 million from Ranbaxy Laboratories Limited and its subsidiary, Ranbaxy USA, Inc.. Most of the civil settlements, including these settlements were part of a global resolution, which also addressed the criminal liabilities, resulting in criminal pleas, as well as significant fines and forfeitures. The criminal portion of these investigations and resolutions was handled by criminal health care fraud AUSAs, often working with their counterparts at the Consumer Protection Branch of the Civil Division. These global settlements resolved allegations including, reporting of false and inflated drug prices, manufacturing and distributing adulterated drugs, off-label marketing and kick-backs. These cases are detailed earlier in this report.

Several of the USAOs have dedicated significant resources to investigate fraud perpetrated on our most vulnerable citizens. To this end, the USAOs have partnered with Civil Frauds in the Elder Justice and Nursing Home Initiative to address elder abuse and neglect. As a result of USAO efforts, the owner and operator of three nursing homes was sentenced to serve 20 years in Federal prison on charges of conspiring with his wife to defraud the Medicare and Georgia Medicaid programs by billing them for "worthless services" in the operation of three nursing homes. This is the first time that a defendant has been convicted after a trial in Federal court for submitting claims for payment for worthless services. The defendant was also ordered to pay $6.7 million in restitution to Medicaid and Medicare

The USAOs partner with the Criminal Division in the Strike Forces, which are currently operating in nine USAOs across the country. Each USAO has dedicated several AUSAs and support personnel to work with Criminal Division attorneys in this important initiative. The Strike Forces use data analysis to identify high-billing levels in health care hot spots so that emerging or migrating schemes can be targeted. The significant successes of the Strike Forces have been detailed earlier in this report.

Special Focus Teams, consisting of criminal and civil AUSAs, paralegals, and auditors, are operational in three districts and focus on pharmaceutical, biologics, and medical device fraud. The teams have contributed significantly to the success of the pharmaceutical investigations and recoveries this year. To increase the capacity of other districts to successfully litigate these complex health care fraud cases, the Special Focus Teams have organized monthly training Webinars and serve as advisors for the USAO community in the various complex areas of health care fraud.

Criminal Prosecutions

In FY 2013, the USAOs received 1,013 new criminal matters involving 1,910 defendants, and had 2,041 health care fraud criminal matters pending,[17] involving 3,535 defendants. The USAOs filed criminal charges in 480 cases involving 843 defendants, and obtained 718 Federal health care fraud related convictions.

Civil Matters and Cases

In FY 2012, the USAOs had opened 1,083 new civil health care fraud investigations. At the end of FY 2012, the USAOs had 1,079 civil health care fraud investigations pending.[18]

Civil Division

In FY 2013, the Civil Division received approximately $28.0 million in FY 2013 HCFAC funding to support the health care fraud activities of the Commercial Litigation Branch's Fraud Section and the Consumer Protection Branch. This amount also included funding to support the Department of Justice's Elder Justice and Nursing Home Initiative.

The Commercial Litigation Branch's Fraud Section

The Civil Division's Commercial Litigation Branch (Fraud Section) investigates complex health care fraud allegations and files suit under the FCA to recover money on behalf of defrauded federal health care programs including Medicare, Medicaid, TRICARE, and the FEHBP. The Fraud Section works closely with the Consumer Protection Branch, United States Attorneys' Offices, HHS-OIG, state Medicaid Fraud Control Units and other law enforcement agencies. As a result of these efforts, the Fraud Section has obtained settlements and judgments in health care cases of over $1 billion almost every year since 2000 and over $2.3 billion in FY 2013 alone.

The Fraud Section investigates and resolves matters against a wide array of health care providers and suppliers. Matters involving pharmaceutical and device manufacturers continue to constitute some of the most complex and resource intensive cases handled by the Fraud Section. These matters commonly involve nationwide conduct, raise legally and factually complicated issues, and demand significant resources to investigate, resolve, and litigate, if necessary. Many of these cases-- including the Abbott, Amgen, AstraZeneca and Wyeth matters discussed above-- involved allegations that the pharmaceutical manufacturer improperly promoted its drug for uses not approved by the FDA. Other cases, like the Ranbaxy matter, involved allegations relating to the manufacture and distribution of adulterated drugs. Lastly, many pharmaceutical fraud cases involve allegations that the drug or device manufacturer paid kickbacks to physicians to prescribe its products. These cases are significant not only because of the significant dollars involved, but because they protect Medicare and Medicaid beneficiaries by preserving the integrity of the FDA's approval process as well as the doctor-patient relationship.

In addition to pharmaceutical fraud, the Fraud Section also investigated and resolved several matters involving hospitals and physicians. For example, the Fraud Section resolved several hospital matters involving allegations that the hospitals overbilled Medicare by treating patients on an inpatient basis when they should have been treated as observation patients or treated on an outpatient basis. Likewise, the Fraud Section successfully resolved its investigation against a Florida doctor for violating the Anti-Kickback Statute by accepting free pathology services and billing Medicare as if he had personally performed those services. As a result of its investigation, the government recovered over $26 million, and the doctor agreed to be voluntarily excluded for five years from participating in any federal health care program.

Because the Fraud Section receives every FCA complaint filed across the country by whistleblowers (otherwise known as "relators"), it has a unique vantage point over health care fraud trends and developments nationwide and therefore regularly takes the lead on coordinating national investigations with its law enforcement partners. Likewise, given the diversity of health care fraud cases pursued by the Fraud Section, it frequently provides training and guidance to AUSAs and agents on the FCA and health care fraud issues. The Section works closely with HHS-OIG, Office of General Counsel, in all settlements of health care fraud allegations in order to ensure that the administrative remedies possessed by HHS are appropriately considered and to enable the negotiation of compliance terms that diminish the risk that the offending conduct will be repeated. The Section also collaborates with and counsels CMS and HHS-OIG on interagency initiatives and proposed rules and regulations.

The Elder Justice and Nursing Home Initiative, which is housed in the Civil Division, coordinates and supports law enforcement efforts to combat elder abuse, neglect, and financial exploitation. The Initiative supports law enforcement efforts by maintaining an information bank of Elder Justice related materials (including briefs, opinions, indictments, plea agreements, subpoenas templates); funding medical reviewers, auditors, and other consultants to assist DOJ attorneys and AUSAs in their nursing home and/or long term care facility cases; hosting quarterly teleconferences with DOJ attorneys and AUSAs across the country to discuss issues or developments in connection with our nursing home and failure of care cases; and coordinating nationwide investigations of skilled nursing facilities. In addition to supporting law enforcement efforts, the Initiative continues to fund research projects awarded by the Office of Justice Programs, National Institute of Justice, to study the abuse, neglect, and exploitation of elderly individuals and residents of residential care facilities.

The Consumer Protection Branch

The Consumer Protection Branch (CPB) investigates and prosecutes manufacturers and individuals who are illegally promoting and distributing unapproved, misbranded, and adulterated drugs and devices in violation of the Food, Drug, and Cosmetic Act (FDCA). CPB works closely with the Commercial Litigation Branch's Fraud Section, the USAOs, and the FDA on a wide variety of health care fraud matters. In recent years, CPB has convicted dozens of companies and individuals. The prosecutions resulted in significant jail terms and fines, penalties, and forfeitures; since 2009, these fines, penalties, and forfeitures have totaled more than $6 billion.

In the area of pharmaceutical and medical device fraud, CPB coordinates complex investigations with districts nationwide, staffing the cases directly as well as providing assistance to USAOs. Because these investigations are complicated, both legally and factually, they demand significant resources. These cases, such as the Amgen, Ranbaxy, and Wyeth cases mentioned above, which involve allegations of misbranding or adulteration of pharmaceuticals, often require in-depth analyses of pharmaceutical and medical device manufacturers' clinical studies, manufacturing practices, or commercial activities. Typically, they involve the review of hundreds of thousands or even millions of company and third party documents, as well as dozens of witness interviews or testimony. These cases are significant not only because of the monetary fines and non- monetary remedies that are imposed for criminal violations of the FDCA, but because of the public health and safety issues that they implicate. In the Abbott case discussed above, for instance, not only did the company misbrand Depakote through its unlawful promotion and targeting of vulnerable elderly dementia patients, but it downplayed safety risks apparent from its own clinical studies and encouraged nursing homes to use Depakote to avoid reporting requirements designed to prevent the use of unnecessary drugs.

In addition to prosecuting major pharmaceutical and medical device companies for health care offenses, CPB prosecutes smaller-scale, yet equally dangerous schemes involving online sale of pharmaceuticals and drug diversion. For example, in FY 2013, together with the U.S. Attorney's Office in the Southern District of Florida, CPB prosecuted a Canadian citizen, Andrew J. Strempler, for his role in a scheme to defraud consumers purchasing pharmaceuticals online. Strempler pled guilty to conspiracy to commit mail fraud in connection with his role as owner and president of Mediplan Health Consulting Inc., a Canadian company that also operated under the name RxNorth.com. RxNorth was an Internet, mail, and telephone order pharmacy, through which Strempler and others marketed and sold prescription drugs to residents of the United States. Strempler and his co-conspirators falsely represented that RxNorth was selling safe prescription drugs in compliance with regulations in Canada, the United Kingdom and the United States, when in fact, Strempler obtained the prescription drugs from various other source countries without properly ensuring the safety or authenticity of the drugs. In fact, some of the drugs sold by Strempler included counterfeit drugs. In January 2013, Strempler was sentenced to 48 months in prison, and was ordered to pay a fine of $25,000 and restitution in the amount of $300,000.

In yet another example, in FY 2013, CPB prosecuted Lina Ada Mendoza, a/k/a Nicole Rodriguez and Michael Jackson in the Southern District of Florida for their role in a conspiracy involving the operation of an Internet pharmacy business that illegally shipped over $1.5 million of pharmaceuticals to U.S. and overseas purchasers. Rodriguez owned an Internet-pharmacy business used to advertise, sell and distribute a wide variety of controlled substances and prescription drugs in the United States and abroad. Rodriguez and Jackson conspired to sell the prescription drug known as Adderall, which contains amphetamine, a Schedule II controlled substance. Rodriquez was sentenced to 72 months' imprisonment, and ordered to forfeit $36,112. Jackson was also sentenced to 72 months' imprisonment and ordered to forfeit $18,862.

Criminal Division

In FY 2013, the Criminal Division was allocated $8.1 million in FY 2013 HCFAC funding to support criminal health care fraud litigation and interagency coordination, which is carried out primarily by the Fraud Section and, to a lesser extent, the Organized Crime and Gang Section (OCGS).

The Fraud Section

The Fraud Section initiates and coordinates complex health care fraud prosecutions and supports the USAOs with legal and investigative guidance and training and trial attorneys to prosecute health care fraud cases. Beginning in March 2007, the Fraud Section, working with the local USAOs, the FBI and law enforcement partners in HHS-OIG, and state and local law enforcement agencies, launched the Medicare Fraud Strike Force in Miami-Dade County, Florida, to prosecute individuals and entities that do not provide legitimate health care services but exist solely for the purpose of defrauding Medicare and other government health care programs. Since 2007, DOJ and HHS have expanded the Strike Force to nine cities. In FY 2013, the Fraud Section continued to provide attorney staffing, litigation support, and leadership and management oversight for numerous Strike Force prosecutions in eight of the nine cities. A summary of the Fraud Section's key litigation accomplishments in FY 2013 follows:

- Filed 60 new health care fraud cases involving charges against 159 defendants who collectively billed the Medicare and Medicaid programs more than $1 billion;
- Obtained 93 guilty pleas and litigated 18 jury trials, winning guilty verdicts against 29 defendants;[196]
- Secured prison sentences in health care fraud cases averaging more than 62 months; and
- Secured court-ordered restitution, forfeiture and fines exceeding $1.1 billion.

Fraud Section attorneys staffed and coordinated the Division's health care fraud litigation through the existing Medicare Fraud Strike Force teams in Miami, Los Angeles, Detroit, Houston, Brooklyn, South Louisiana, Tampa, Dallas, and Chicago.

Section attorneys coordinated two major multi-district Strike Force arrest takedowns during the fiscal year and handled many of the investigations and indictments that were filed in these operations.

On May 14, 2013, Fraud Section and USAO Strike Force prosecutors in eight cities executed a nationwide operation that resulted in charges against 89 individuals, including doctors, nurses, and other medical professionals, for their alleged participation in Medicare fraud schemes involving approximately $223 million in false billing. Earlier in the fiscal year, on October 4, 2012, Fraud Section and USAO Strike Force prosecutors in seven cities executed a nationwide operation that resulted in charges against 91 individuals, including doctors, nurses, and other medical professionals, for their alleged participation in Medicare fraud schemes involving approximately $492.2 million in false billing.

Of particular note during the FY2013, the Fraud Section charged a Michigan oncologist/hematologist in August 2013 with health care fraud in wide-ranging and dangerous fraudulent billing scheme. According to the original complaint and subsequent indictment, the doctor allegedly provided chemotherapy and other medical treatments to patients who did not need the treatments, including patients who were in remission and did not need chemotherapy; the defendant also supposedly directed his staff to falsify medical documents to justify the treatments. The allegations against the defendant raised serious health concerns, particularly given the physical effect of chemotherapy and some of the other treatments administered to patients. At the time of arrest, the defendant was treating 1200 patients. The Fraud Section, working with the U.S. Attorney's Office for the Eastern District of Michigan, undertook a massive and aggressive effort to make insure that victim witnesses received all necessary support in finding new medical care. Between August 2010 and August 2013, the defendant's business, Michigan Hematology Oncology, Inc. (MHO), billed Medicare $150 million and was paid $62 million. In addition, private insurer Blue Cross/Blue Shield also paid the doctor $78 million on claims submitted by MHO.

In addition to Medicare Fraud Strike Force cases, the Fraud Section handles other types of complex criminal health care fraud litigation. Often, such cases are handled in a parallel manner by Fraud Section prosecutors along with DOJ Civil Division attorneys and/or AUSAs from the USAOs.

In addition to health care fraud litigation, the Fraud Section also provided legal guidance to FBI and HHS-OIG agents, health program agency staff, AUSAs, and other Criminal Division attorneys on criminal, civil, and administrative tools to combat health care fraud. Throughout FY2013, Fraud Section prosecutors met with federal prosecutors and agents across the United States to provide training, investigative leads based on data analysis, and related support. The Fraud Section also provided advice and written materials on patient medical record confidentiality and disclosure issues, and coordinated referrals of possible criminal HIPAA privacy violations from the HHS Office for Civil Rights; monitored and coordinated DOJ responses to legislative proposals, major regulatory initiatives, and enforcement policy matters; reviewed and commented on health care provider requests to the HHS-OIG for advisory opinions, and consulted with the HHS-OIG on draft advisory opinions; worked with CMS to improve Medicare contractors= fraud detection, referrals to law enforcement for investigation, and case development work; and prepared and distributed to all USAOs and FBI field offices periodic summaries of recent and significant health care fraud cases.

The Organized Crime and Gang Section (OCGS)

The Criminal Division's Organized Crime and Gang Section (OCGS) supports investigations and prosecutions of fraud and abuse targeting the 2.5 million private sector health plans sponsored by employers and/or unions, as well as investigations and prosecutions of health care frauds perpetrated by domestic and international organized crime groups. OCGS is also working to improve strategic coordination in the identification and prosecution of domestic and international organized crime groups engaged in sophisticated frauds posing a threat to the health care industry.

In FY 2013, four OCGS attorneys and one paralegal were assigned to health care fraud prosecutions, although the section has remained under severe budget restrictions. Three OCGS attorneys worked with AUSAs in the Organized Crime Strike Force in Philadelphia on prosecutions involving Medicare fraud in the operation of hospice facilities and ambulance companies. A fourth OCGS attorney worked on an investigation of health care fraud involving a private sector employment based health care plan.

In Philadelphia, an OCGS attorney partnered with an AUSA in the prosecution of four cases involving seven defendants for criminal charges in connection with the operation of a hospice facility. In June 2013, a doctor who served as the medical director of the hospice was convicted after trial of receiving more than $300,000 in illegal payments for regularly referring Medicare and Medicaid patients to the hospice. Sentencing was pending at the end of the fiscal year. The conviction will result in the doctor's mandatory exclusion from participation in any federal health care program and the possible loss of his medical license. A second doctor remains under indictment for receiving illegal referral payments from the hospice. In September 2013, the trial of a hospice co-owner commenced on charges of conspiring to defraud Medicare by submitting $14.3 million in fraudulent medical claims for hospice services provided to patients who did not receive services or were ineligible for the benefits claimed. His trial was ongoing at the close of the fiscal year. Four nurses who worked at the hospice are scheduled for trial in late 2013 and early 2014 on charges that they fabricated and falsified documents in support of hospice care for patients who were not eligible for hospice care, or for a higher, more costly level of care than was actually provided to the patients. The nurse defendants are alleged to have submitted approximately $9,328,000 in fraudulent claims to Medicare and created fraudulent nursing notes for approximately 150 patients indicating that services were being provided, when, in reality, they were not.

Two additional OCGS attorneys worked with Philadelphia AUSAs on prosecutions of the 5 defendants involved in the operation of three different ambulance service companies. In May 2013, the operator of one ambulance company was sentenced to 92 months' imprisonment for defrauding Medicare of approximately $5.4 million by billing for ambulance services which were not medically necessary. The operator, who was an émigré from Ukraine, recruited a straw owner, with the payment of $60,000, to apply for a license to operate after he was denied a license under his own name due to a prior criminal conviction. Once licensed, the operator recruited patients who were capable of walking and submitted claim forms to Medicare falsely claiming that patients were unable to transport themselves. The straw purchaser and wife of the ambulance company operator have pleaded guilty to charges in connection with the operation of this ambulance company and await sentencing. Owners of two additional ambulance companies were indicted in May 2013 for health care fraud and conspiracy to pay kickbacks to patients in an alleged scheme to recruit ambulatory dialysis patients for whom they billed Medicare for medically unnecessary ambulance services.

In addition to conducting health care fraud investigations and prosecutions, OCGS attorneys routinely provide litigation support and advice to AUSAs and criminal investigative agencies in the investigation and prosecution of corruption and abuse of private employment-based group health plans covered by the Employee Retirement Income Security Act (ERISA). Such private sector employment-based group health plans are the leading source of health care coverage for individuals not covered by Medicare or Medicaid. OCGS attorneys also provide support to investigations of fraud schemes by corrupt entities that sell unlicensed health insurance products as well as fraud schemes by corrupt employers that cheat workers out of health benefits required by the prevailing wage laws and regulations.

OCGS attorneys regularly provide health care fraud and abuse training and legal guidance to AUSAs and to criminal investigators and agents of the Department of Labor's Employee Benefits Security Administration and Office of Inspector General. Such guidance and training covers prosecutions involving abuse of private sector employee health plans subject to ERISA and health plans sponsored by labor organizations as well as fraud and abuse committed in connection with the operation of multiple employer welfare arrangements. OCGS also drafts and reviews criminal legislative proposals affecting employee health benefit plans. In addition, OCGS provides legal guidance to prosecutors and required approvals in the use of the Racketeer Influenced and Corrupt Organizations (RICO) statute in prosecutions of Medicare or Medicaid fraud and private sector health care frauds.

Civil Rights Division

In FY 2013, the Civil Rights Division was allocated approximately $4.1 million in FY 2013 HCFAC funding to support Civil Rights Division litigation activities related to health care fraud and abuse. The Civil Rights Division pursues relief affecting public, residential health care facilities and service systems. The Division conducts investigations to eliminate abuse and grossly substandard care in public, Medicare and Medicaid funded long-term care facilities. Consistent with the Supreme Court's decision in *Olmstead v. L.C.*, 527 U.S. 581 (1999), the Division has also undertaken initiatives to eliminate the needless institutionalization of individuals who require health care supports and services.

The Division plays a critical role in the HCFAC Program. The Special Litigation Section of the Civil Rights Division is the sole DOJ component responsible for the Civil Rights of Institutionalized Persons Act, 42 U.S.C. ' 1997 (CRIPA). CRIPA authorizes the investigation of conditions of confinement at state and local residential institutions (including facilities for persons with developmental disabilities or mental illness, and nursing homes) and initiation of civil action for injunctive relief to remedy a pattern or practice of violations of the Constitution or Federal statutory rights. The review of conditions in facilities for persons who have mental illness, facilities for persons with developmental disabilities, and nursing homes comprises a significant portion of the program.

The Disability Rights Section of the Civil Rights Division has primary enforcement authority for the Americans with Disabilities Act (ADA). Title II of the ADA authorizes investigation of allegations of discrimination by public entities against individuals with disabilities, including discrimination in the form of needless institutionalization of persons who require health care supports and services. *See Olmstead*, 527 U.S. 581. Title II also authorizes the initiation of civil action to remedy discrimination in violation of the ADA. Both the Special Litigation Section and the Disability Rights Section have undertaken initiatives to combat the unjustified institutionalization of persons with disabilities.

The Special Litigation and Disability Rights Sections work collaboratively with the USAOs and HHS.

Fiscal Year 2013 Accomplishments

Special Litigation Section staff conducted preliminary reviews of conditions and services at 16 health care facilities in 13 states during Fiscal Year 2013. The task in preliminary inquiries is to determine whether there is sufficient information supporting allegations of unlawful conditions and needless institutionalization to warrant formal investigation under CRIPA and/or the ADA. The Section reviews information pertaining to areas such as abuse and neglect, medical and mental health care, use of restraints, fire and environmental safety, and placement in the most integrated setting appropriate to individual needs. Separately, in Fiscal Year 2013, the Section opened or continued formal investigations, entered remedial agreements, or monitored existing remedial agreements regarding 64 health care facilities in 15 states, the District of Columbia, and the Commonwealth of Puerto Rico.

The Section found that conditions and practices at 12 state facilities for persons with intellectual and developmental disabilities and/or mental illness violate the residents' statutory rights. Those facilities are: Boswell Regional Center, in Magee, Mississippi; Ellisville State School, in Ellisville, Mississippi; Hudspeth Regional Center, in Pearl, Mississippi; Southern Mississippi Regional Center, in Long Beach, Mississippi; Mississippi Adolescent Center, in Brookhaven, Mississippi; North Mississippi Regional Center, in Oxford, Mississippi; Mississippi State Hospital, in Whitfield, Mississippi; South Mississippi State Hospital, in Purvis, Mississippi; Central Mississippi Residential Center, in Newton, Mississippi; East Mississippi State Hospital, in Meridian, Mississippi; North Mississippi State Hospital, in Tupelo, Mississippi; and the Specialized Treatment Center, in Gulfport, Mississippi.

In Fiscal Year 2013, the Section entered into a letter agreement to resolve its investigation of Oregon State Hospital and the State of Oregon's state-wide system for serving individuals with mental illness. The Agreement will be effective for four years. Pursuant to the Agreement, Oregon will collect and furnish state-wide system data to the Section. Throughout the Agreement period, Oregon and the Section will continue discussions on identifying gaps in the community service system, development of outcome measures, and whether positive outcomes are being achieved in the process.

The Section entered into a settlement agreement to resolve its investigation of Maple Lawn Nursing Home in Palmyra, Missouri. Pursuant to the Agreement, the facility will implement pre- admission measures to ensure that individuals who are inappropriate for admission to this facility are not housed there. The Agreement also requires discharge and transition planning, provision of adequate care and protections from harm for individuals, and quality outcome measures.

The Section filed a memorandum in support of class certification in *Amanda D. v. Hassan*, (D. N.H.), a proposed class action involving claims under the ADA that the State of New Hampshire failed to provide adequate community-based services to persons with mental illness, unnecessarily segregating them in institutions and placing them at risk of unnecessary and more costly institutionalization. The case is scheduled to go to trial in 2014.

The Section entered into an interim settlement agreement in *Steward v. Perry*, (W.D. TX.), to resolve a suit against the State of Texas for its failure to provide adequate community-based services to persons with intellectual disabilities residing in nursing homes. Negotiations are continuing to resolve all issues pursuant to a comprehensive agreement.

The Section filed four statements of interest in ongoing litigation: *ILADD v. Quinn*, (N.D. Ill.); *Hunter v. Cooke*, (N.D. Ga.); *J.B. v. Bryant*, (S.D. Miss.); and *Sciarrillo v. Christie*, (D.N.J). The Section filed the statements of interest to clarify and articulate the views of the United States pertaining to the Title II of the ADA and Olmstead and remedies therein, in matters where the United States is not a formal party.

The Section continued its investigations of 12 residential facilities for persons with intellectual and developmental disabilities, including: Northwest Habilitation Center, in St. Louis, Missouri; Bellefontaine Habilitation Center, in St. Louis, Missouri; Sonoma Developmental Center, in Eldridge, California; Lanterman Developmental Center, in Pomona, California; Utah State Hospital, in Provo, Utah; Clyde L. Choate Developmental Center, in Anna, Illinois; and, five Arkansas facilities, including: Arkadelphia Human Development Center, in Arkadelphia, Arkansas; Alexander Human Development Center, in Alexander, Arkansas; Booneville Human Development Center, in Booneville, Arkansas; Jonesboro Human Development Center, in Jonesboro, Arkansas; and Southeast Arkansas Human Development Center, in Warren, Arkansas.

The Section also continued its investigations of three facilities for persons with mental illness, including: Ancora Psychiatric Hospital, in Hammonton, New Jersey; Oregon State Hospital, in Salem and Portland, Oregon; and Kingsboro Psychiatric Center, in Brooklyn, New York.

The Section also continued its investigations of two nursing facilities: Maple Lawn Nursing Home, in Palmyra, Missouri; and Casa del Veteranos, in Juana Diaz, Puerto Rico.

The Section monitored the implementation of remedial agreements for 22 facilities for persons with intellectual and developmental disabilities: Beatrice State Developmental Center, in Beatrice, Nebraska; Woodbridge Developmental Center, in Woodbridge, New Jersey; Clover Bottom Developmental Center in Nashville, Tennessee; Greene Valley Developmental Center in Greeneville, Tennessee; Lubbock State Supported Living Center, in Lubbock, Texas; Denton State Supported Living Center, in Denton, Texas; Abilene State Supported Living Center, in Abilene, Texas; Austin State Supported Living Center, in Austin, Texas; Brenham State Supported Living Center, in Brenham, Texas; Corpus Christi State Supported Living Center, in Corpus Christi, Texas; El Paso State Supported Living Center, in El Paso, Texas; Lufkin State Supported Living Center, in Lufkin, Texas; Mexia State Supported Living Center, in Mexia, Texas; Richmond State Supported Living Center, in Richmond, Texas; Rio Grande State Supported Living Center, in Harlingen, Texas; San Angelo State Supported Living Center, in Carlsbad, Texas; San Antonio State Supported Living Center, in San Antonio, Texas; Central Virginia Training Center, in Lynchburg, Virginia; Northern Virginia Training Center, in Fairfax, Virginia; Southeastern Virginia Training Center, in Chesapeake, Virginia; Southside Virginia Training Center, in Portsmouth, Virginia; Southwestern Virginia Training Center, in Hillsville, Virginia. These remedial agreements include the provision of adequate community supports and services. The Section also litigated the issue of whether the closure of Arlington Developmental Center in Memphis, Tennessee should result in the dismissal of its case involving the facility and community services for individuals with intellectual and developmental disabilities in West Tennessee.

The Section also monitored the implementation of remedial agreements regarding 13 state- operated residential facilities for persons with mental illness: Napa State Hospital, in Napa, California; Metropolitan State Hospital, in Norwalk, California; Kings County Hospital

Center, in Brooklyn, New York; Delaware State Psychiatric Center, in New Castle, Delaware; Georgia Regional Hospital, in Atlanta, Georgia; Georgia Regional Hospital, in Savannah, Georgia; Central State Hospital, in Milledgeville, Georgia; Southwest State Hospital, in Thomasville, Georgia; West Central Georgia Hospital, in Columbus, Georgia; East Central Georgia Regional Hospital, in Augusta, Georgia; St. Elizabeth's Hospital, in Washington, D.C.; Connecticut Valley Hospital, in Middletown, Connecticut; and Oregon State Hospital, in Portland, Oregon. These remedial agreements include the provision of adequate support and services to enable individuals to live successfully in the community.

In addition, the Section monitored remedial agreements at two nursing facilities: William F. Green State Veterans' Nursing Home, in Bay Minette, Alabama; and Maple Lawn Nursing Home, in Palmyra, Missouri.

In Fiscal Year 2013, the Disability Rights Section monitored the implementation of its eight-year settlement agreement with the State of North Carolina resolving the Section's *Olmstead* investigation of North Carolina's mental health service system, which currently serves thousands of individuals with mental illness in large, costly institutional settings known as adult care homes. Under the agreement, North Carolina is providing opportunities to individuals with mental illness in adult care homes to transition to less costly, supported housing settings – integrated housing that promotes inclusion and independence and enables individuals with mental illness to participate fully in community life.

The Section intervened in *Lane v. Kitzhaber* (D. OR.), a class action brought on behalf of persons with intellectual and developmental disabilities alleging that Oregon is in violation of Title II of the ADA and *Olmstead* by unnecessarily segregating individuals with disabilities in sheltered workshops when such individuals can and want to work in more integrated supported employment settings. The litigation is ongoing.

The Section also filed suit against the State of Florida, in *United States v. Florida*, (S.D. Fla. 2013) alleging that it administers its service system for children with significant medical needs in violation of the ADA and *Olmstead* by unnecessarily segregating children in nursing facilities, when they could, and want to, be served at home or in other community-based settings. The Section's complaint further alleges that the State violates the ADA by administering its system of care in a manner that places many other children with complex medical conditions at risk of unnecessary institutionalization in nursing facilities.

The Section entered into an interim settlement agreement with the State of Rhode Island and the City of Providence, in *United States v. Rhode Island and City of Providence*, (D.R.I. 2013), resolving the Section's findings that the State and City unnecessarily segregated persons with intellectual and developmental disabilities (I/DD) in a sheltered workshop and segregated day activity service program, and placed public school students with I/DD at risk of unnecessary segregation in that same program. Under the agreement, the State and City will provide supported employment services to individuals with intellectual and developmental disabilities and provide integrated day services to enable such individuals to participate in integrated activities when they are not working.

The Section also entered into a settlement agreement with the State of New York and private plaintiffs regarding New York's mental health service system, in *United States v. New York* (E.D.N.Y. 2013). The agreement remedies discrimination by the State in the administration of its mental health service system and ensures that individuals with mental illness who reside in 23 large adult homes in New York City receive services in the most integrated setting appropriate to their needs consistent with the ADA and *Olmstead*. Under the agreement, such individuals will have the opportunity to live and receive services in the community such that they are able to live, work, and participate fully in community life. The Section also continued its ongoing investigation of the State of New York regarding the placement of children with disabilities at certain restrictive out-of-state facilities.

The Division filed six statements of interest or *amicus* briefs in litigation raising issues of needless segregation in Illinois, the District of Columbia, Florida, Mississippi, Georgia, and New Jersey. These briefs have addressed a wide range of issues, including unnecessary institutionalization of individuals in state-run and private institutions and cuts to community services placing individuals at risk of unnecessary, and more costly, institutionalization.

Federal Bureau of Investigation

In FY 2013, the FBI was allocated $128.1 million in funding from HIPAA to support the facilitation, coordination and accomplishment of the goals of the HCFAC Program. This yearly appropriation was used to support 801 positions (480 Agent, 321 Support). In FY 2013, the FBI initiated 674 new health care fraud investigations and had 2,868 pending investigations. Investigative efforts produced 794 criminal health care fraud convictions and 1,023 indictments and informations. In addition, investigative efforts resulted in over 425 operational disruptions of criminal fraud organizations and the dismantlement of the criminal hierarchy of more than 115 HCF criminal enterprises.

The FBI is the primary investigative agency involved in the fight against health care fraud that has jurisdiction over both the Federal and private insurance programs. Each of the 56 FBI field offices has personnel assigned specifically to investigate health care fraud matters. With national health care expenditures projected to exceed $2.9 trillion dollars in FY 2013, it is especially important to coordinate all investigative efforts to combat the significant fraud and abuse within the health care system.

The FBI leverages its resources in both the private and public arenas through investigative partnerships with agencies such as HHS-OIG, the FDA, the DEA, the Defense Criminal Investigative Service, the Office of Personnel Management-OIG, the Internal Revenue Service- CI, state Medicaid Fraud Control Units, and other state and local agencies. On the private side, the FBI is actively involved in the Healthcare Fraud Prevention Partnership, an effort to exchange facts and information between the public and private sectors in order to reduce the prevalence of health care fraud. These efforts will enable members to share successful anti-fraud practices and effective methodologies and strategies for detecting and preventing health care fraud. In addition, the FBI maintains significant liaison with private insurance national groups, such as the National Health Care Anti-Fraud Association, the National Insurance Crime Bureau, other professional associations, and private insurance investigative units.

Health care fraud investigations are considered a high priority within the FBI White Collar Crime Program. In addition to being a partner in the majority of investigations listed in the body of this report, FBI field offices throughout the U.S. have pro-actively addressed significant health care fraud threats through coordinated initiatives, task forces, working groups, and undercover operations. These activities seek to identify and pursue investigations against the most egregious offenders involved in health care fraud and abuse, including criminal enterprises and other crime groups; corporations; companies; and providers whose schemes affect public safety.

In an effort to ensure sufficient FBI HCF resources are dedicated to address priority threats within the health care system for which the FBI has responsibility, the FBI provides oversight and guidance to field offices. The guidance has included three initiatives to combat the crime problem, including the Health Care Fraud Prevention & Enforcement Action Team (HEAT), Large Scale Conspiracies, and Major Provider Fraud.

A description of, and examples of results obtained by, the HEAT Initiative are contained in the body of this report. Contained within the HEAT section of the report is a description of, and examples of results obtained by, the Medicare Fraud Strike Forces (MFSFs), a key component of HEAT. The FBI coordinates with the DOJ and HHS-OIG on all HEAT aspects including funding, resource allocation, MFSF expansion, target identification, training, and operations. The FBI has 62 agents assigned to the nine Strike Forces in Miami, New York City, Houston, Tampa, Detroit, Los Angeles, South Louisiana, Dallas, and Chicago. In addition to funding agent resources, the FBI funded undercover operations expenses, financial and investigative analysis support, offsite and evidence storage locations, and other investigative costs. These Strike Forces have effectively investigated and prosecuted individuals and entities that do not provide legitimate health care services, but exist solely for the purpose of defrauding Medicare and other Federal government health care programs. The continued support of Medicare Strike Force operations is a top priority for the FBI.

The Large Scale Conspiracies Initiative seeks to identify and target criminal enterprises and other groups whose schemes result in significant losses, or potential losses, to health care benefit programs. Large Scale Conspiracies include criminal enterprises and other crime groups collaborating in fraud schemes. Intelligence efforts for this initiative include information sharing and analysis of billing data with DOJ components, CMS, and HHS-OIG. Additional review of suspect/abnormal providers is conducted by the FBI's HCF Fusion Cell. Investigative assistance provided to field offices as part of the initiative can include support for undercover operations, source identification and support, and funding of investigative costs. An example of these types of cases was the Biscayne Milieu Health Center, Inc., investigation involving the submission of over $50 million in false or fraudulent claims for partial hospitalization program services. Instead of providing these services, the clinic owners paid recruiters kickbacks to obtain Medicare beneficiary information and billed Medicare for services which were not rendered or necessary. Over 35 defendants have been charged and over 30 have either pled guilty or have been convicted at trial as part of the investigation.

The Major Provider Fraud Initiative seeks to identify and target corporations, companies, and other groups involved in fraud schemes with significant billing to government and private healthcare benefit programs. The related schemes are frequently complex, challenging to identify, and can involve conduct that is nationwide in scope. Extensive resources and coordination are frequently required due to the complexity and scope of the schemes. Qui Tams are a significant intelligence source for these types of cases. In addition to the work completed at the field office level, and in response to this substantial threat, the FBI has established a centralized support team to provide investigative assistance on these types of cases nationwide. Examples of significant major provider investigations have included Amgen Inc. and Wyeth Pharmaceuticals which agreed to pay $762 million and $491 million respectively, to resolve criminal and civil liability. The FBI coordinates efforts against the crime problem with our law enforcement partners, such as DOJ components, HHS/OIG, and FDA.

In addition to the FBI's involvement in the above initiatives, each field office is involved in a HCF Task Force and/or working group. The groups include US Attorney Office and HHS-OIG personnel, and in many cases also include state, local, and private insurance personnel. Based on information sharing, including billing analysis by the group partners, additional cases are vetted and identified for investigation.

The FBI actively provides training and guidance on health care matters. The FBI has teamed with the DOJ, HHS, and private insurance organizations to provide training in the priority threat areas of health care fraud. Funded training has included innovative methods of employing advanced investigative techniques, basic HCF training for FBI special agent and professional staff newly assigned to HCF, and sessions on new and current HCF trends and issues. FBI personnel training opportunities included sessions offered by other government agencies and the private sector. In FY 2013, more than 160 FBI health care fraud investigators and analysts received training. FBI personnel also conducted a wide range of training for external audiences, including personnel involved in the investigation of health care fraud matters and industry representatives.

Funding received by the FBI is used to pay direct and indirect personnel-related costs associated with the 801 funded positions. Funds not used directly for personnel matters, are used to provide operational support for major health care fraud investigations, national initiatives, training, specialized equipment, expert witness testimony, and Strike Force operations.

Return-on-Investment Calculation

- The Return-on-Investment (ROI) for the HCFAC program is calculated by dividing the total monetary results to the Federal government (not including relator payments) by the annual appropriation for the HCFAC Account in a given year (not including portions of CMS funding dedicated to the Medicare Integrity Program, listed in the table on page 103).
- The monetary results include deposits and transfers to the Medicare Part A Trust Fund and the Treasury, as well as restitution and compensatory damages to Federal agencies.
- The HCFAC Account is made up of three funding sources: mandatory funding for HHS and DOJ, including HHS-OIG, appropriated through Section 1817(k)(3)(A) of the Social Security Act; mandatory funding for FBI activities appropriated through Section 1817(k)(3)(B) of the Social Security Act; and discretionary funding for the HCFAC Account appropriated through the annual Labor-HHS-Education appropriation. FBI mandatory HIPAA funding is included in ROI calculations given the important role the FBI plays in achieving the monetary results reflected in the HCFAC annual report and because that statute states that the funds are for the same purposes as the funds provided for HHS and DOJ under the Social Security Act, even though FBI spending and monetary results are not required to be reported, per the statute.

- While all mandatory HCFAC Account funding is included in the ROI calculation of this report, only certain portions of discretionary HCFAC funding is included. All discretionary HCFAC funding for HHS-OIG and DOJ are included in the HCFAC report ROI since they spend their discretionary funding on the same types of activities that they support with mandatory funding. Only the portion of CMS Medicare discretionary HCFAC funding that supports law enforcement is included in the HCFAC report ROI. The remainder of CMS's HCFAC Medicare discretionary funding supports activities in the Medicare Integrity Program (MIP) that are included in the MIP ROI, which is calculated separately and outside of the HCFAC report. All discretionary CMS Medicaid Integrity program funding is included in a separate Medicaid Integrity program ROI published in a separate report.

Total Health Care Fraud and Abuse Control Resources

The table below sets forth HCFAC funding, by agency, for health care fraud and abuse control activities in FY 2013, including sequester reductions. The FBI also receives a stipulated amount of HIPAA funding for use in support of the Fraud and Abuse Control Program, which is shown below. Separately, CMS receives additional Mandatory Resources under the Medicare Integrity Program (section 1817(k)(4) of the Social Security Act). The inclusion of the activities supported with these funds is not required in this report, and this information is included for informational purposes.

Since 2009, Congress has also appropriated annual amounts to help carry out health care fraud and abuse control activities within DOJ and HHS. Those amounts are set forth as Discretionary Resources in the table below and the results of the efforts supported with these funds are contained within this report.

Mandatory Resources	**Fiscal Year 2013**
Office of Inspector General	$187,097,926
Health and Human Services Wedge[1]	$34,819,122
Medicare Integrity Program[2]	$851,509,634
MIP/Medicare (non-add)	*$797,581,005*
Medi-Medi (non-add)	*$53,928,629*
Department of Justice Wedge[1]	$58,164,042
Federal Bureau of Investigation[3]	$128,149,615
Subtotal, Mandatory HCFAC	**$1,259,740,339**
Discretionary Resources	
Office of Inspector General	$28,121,691
CMS Program Integrity	$237,343,109
Medicare Program Integrity (Non-Add)	*$207,984,175*
Medicaid Program Integrity (Non-Add)[4]	*$29,358,934*
Department of Justice	$28,121,691
Subtotal, Discretionary HCFAC	**$293,586,491**
Grand Total, HCFAC	**$1,553,326,830**

[1] The HHS and DOJ Wedge funds are divided among multiple agencies within HHS and DOJ. Page 7 of this report includes the allocations of the HHS and DOJ Wedge by agency or activity.

[2] Medicare Integrity Program (MIP) and Medi-Medi fund fraud prevention and detection activities within Medicare and Medicaid, which are not included in this report to Congress. There is another mandatory report due to Congress in April regarding MIP activities.

[3] The FBI receives funding annually to conduct anti-fraud activities authorized by HIPAA. This funding is included in the HCFAC ROI calculation for this report.

[4] This is not to be confused with the Medicaid Integrity Program authorized in the Deficit Reduction Act of 2005, which receives funding separately from the HCFAC account.

GLOSSARY OF TERMS

The Account – The Health Care Fraud and Abuse Control Account

ACA – Affordable Care Act

AoA – Department of Health and Human Services, Administration on Aging

ACL – Department of Health and Human Services, Administration for Community Living

ASPA – Assistant Secretary for Public Affairs (HHS)

AUSA – Assistant United States Attorney

CHIP – Children's Health Insurance Program

CIA – Corporate Integrity Agreement

CMP – Civil Monetary Penalty

CMS – Department of Health and Human Services, Centers for Medicare & Medicaid Services

CNC – Compromised Number Contractors

CPI – Center Program Integrity

CRIPA – Civil Rights of Institutionalized Persons Act

CY – Calendar Year

DME – Durable Medical Equipment

DMEPOS – Durable Medical Equipment Prosthetics, Orthotics, and Supplies

DOJ – The Department of Justice

FEHBP – Federal Employee Health Benefits Program

FBI – Federal Bureau of Investigation

FCA – False Claims Act

FDA – Food and Drug Administration

FDCA – Food, Drug, and Cosmetic Act

FY – Fiscal Year

HCFAC – Health Care Fraud and Abuse Control Program or the Program

HEAT – Health Care Fraud Prevention & Enforcement Action Team

HHA – Home Health Agency

HHS – The Department of Health and Human Services

HHS-OIG – The Department of Health and Human Services - Office of the Inspector General

HI – Hospital Insurance Trust Fund

HIPAA – The Health Insurance Portability and Accountability Act of 1996, P.L.104-191

HIV – Human Immunodeficiency Virus

MEDIC – Medicare Drug Integrity Contractors

MFCU – Medicaid Fraud Control Unit
OCGS – Organized Crime and Gang Section
OGC – Office of the General Counsel, Department of Health and Human Services
PERM – Program Error Rate Measurement
PFP – Pharmaceutical Fraud Pilot Program
The Program – The Health Care Fraud and Abuse Control Program
Secretary – The Secretary of the Department of Health and Human Services
SMP – Senior Medicare Patrol
USAO – United States Attorney's Office
ZPIC – Zone Program Integrity Contractor

End Notes

[1] Hereafter, referred to as the Secretary.

[2] The amount reported as won or negotiated only reflects Federal recoveries and therefore does not reflect state Medicaid monies recovered as part of any global, Federal-State settlements.

[3] Also known as the Medicare Hospital Insurance (Part A) Trust Fund and the Supplemental Medical Insurance Part B) Trust Fund.

[4] The CPI-U adjustment in TRHCA did not apply to the Medicare Integrity Program (MIP). Section 6402 of the ACA indexed Medicare Integrity Program funding to inflation starting in FY 2010.

[5] In FY 2007, mandatory funds became available until expended. Discretionary funding is two-year funding.

[6] Total includes $0.8 million in FY 2013 HCFAC mandatory funding. In addition, HHS-OIG obligated $17.3 million in funds received as "reimbursement for the costs of conducting investigations and audits and for monitoring compliance plans" as authorized by section 1128C(b) of the Social Security Act, 42 U.S.C. § 1320a-7c(b).

[7] Amounts only represent those that are provided by statute, and do not include other mandatory sources or discretionary appropriated sources provided through Departments' annual appropriations.

[8] Note that some of the judgments, settlements, and administrative actions that occurred in FY 2013 will result in transfers in future years, just as some of the transfers in FY 2013 are attributable to actions from prior years.

[9] While the Strike Force in southern Louisiana started in Baton Rouge, LA, it now operates in New Orleans as well.

[10] The accomplishments figures presented in the bullets include all reported Strike Force cases handled by DOJ Criminal Division attorneys and AUSAs in the respective USAOs during FY 2013.

[11] These statistics are for the period of May 7, 2007, through September 30, 2013.

[12] These are national statistics. Miami-specific statistics are not presently available.

[13] The charts included in this section were prepared by HHS-OIG's Consolidated Data Analysis Center (CDAC), which has data available starting in the first quarter of 2006 through the first-quarter of 2013. Core-Based Statistical Areas (CBSAs) are defined by the U.S. Census Bureau. The OIG's CBSA definitions use the smaller metropolitan division if it exists; the CBSA metro division or CBSA is identified on each chart. The OIG Miami-Miami Beach- Kendall, FL CBSA includes Miami-Dade County.

[14] In December 2009, the Inspector General for HHS issued a report entitled "Aberrant Medicare Home Health Outlier Payment Patterns in Miami-Dade County and Other Geographic Areas in 2008." (OEI-04-08-00570). Among other findings, the report concluded that Miami-Dade County accounted for more home health outlier payments in 2008 than the rest of the United States combined.

[15] The OIG CBSA for Detroit includes only Wayne County.

[16] In addition to the funds made available to OIG from the HCFAC account under HIPAA, Congress has provided funds to OIG specifically for oversight of the Medicaid program. The Deficit Reduction Act of 2005 (DRA, P.L. 109-171), and the Supplemental Appropriations Act of 2008 (Pub. L. 110-252) at § 7001(b) each appropriated funding for Medicaid-related oversight efforts. Therefore, OIG's Medicaid activities cited throughout this report may have drawn from these funding sources, in addition to HCFAC.

[17] When a USAO accepts a criminal referral for consideration, the office opens it as a matter pending in the district. A referral remains a pending matter until an indictment or information is filed or it is declined for prosecution.

[18] The accomplishments figures presented in this paragraph include all reported Strike Force cases handled by DOJ Criminal Division attorneys and AUSAs in the respective USAOs during FY 2013.

[19] Fraud Section attorneys were responsible for many of the cases summarized in the "Medicare Fraud Strike Force" section of this report.

INDEX

A

B

C

D

E

F

N

O

P

Q

R

S